Brian Redman
DARING DRIVERS, DEADLY TRACKS

Published in March 2016
Reprinted twice in 2016 and once in 2017, 2018 and 2021

ISBN 978-1-910505-10-6

Published by Evro Publishing
Westrow House, Holwell, Sherborne, Dorset DT9 5LF

Edited by Mark Hughes
Designed by Richard Parsons

Printed and bound in Bosnia and Herzegovina by GPS Group

www.evropublishing.com

Editorial contributor
Jim Mullen was a Mazda factory driver in IMSU GTU from 1980 to 1982, co-drove the GTO championship Porsche 934 in 1983 (winning Sebring overall), ran a Group C Rondeau at Le Mans in 1984, joined Bob Akin and Hans Stuck in a Porsche 962 in 1985, and continued with independent GTP teams through 1986. He was the founder and original CEO of what is now Mullen/Lowe, an international communications company.

Photograph credits
Front: Porsche 908/03, Targa Florio, 1970 (Porsche-Werkfoto).
Back (from top left): Ford GT40, Nürburgring 1,000Kms, 1968 (LAT); Porsche 917K, Spa 1,000Kms, 1970 (Porsche-Werkfoto); Ferrari 312PB, Nürburgring 1,000Kms, 1973 (Getty Images/Rainer Schlegelmilch); Lola T330, Road Atlanta, 1973 (Bill Oursler).
Frontispiece: Brian Redman, 1970 (Hal Crocker).

Brian Redman
DARING DRIVERS, DEADLY TRACKS

BRIAN REDMAN WITH JIM MULLEN

FOREWORD
MARIO ANDRETTI

CONTENTS

FOREWORD
Mario Andretti

Brian Redman has been both my teammate and my competitor. Surprisingly, over 30 years of racing, our careers overlapped just twice, leaving us more peers than pals. Still, I know a lot about Brian. When you're part of a factory team, you learn if drivers can work together to make everyone faster. And when you're late braking at 170 for a one-car corner in a tight championship, you find out about the other guy's car control, and his grit.

In 1972, Brian and I were paired with Jacky Ickx in Ferrari 312PBs, not bad yardsticks for measuring quickness. Neither Ferrari nor Jacky suffered slow teammates gracefully. That year, Jacky and I took four wins with Brian and Jacky notching another two. Essentially, we three drivers ensured that Ferrari won the World Sports Car Championship.

When I raced against Brian in Formula 5000, I discovered something else about him. He fought hard but he fought fair. I felt safe around Brian, knowing his will to win was never more important than his life, or mine. I think we brought out the best in each other, and that made our racing sharper and more fun. We each won a lot of races, and championships; his were in Formula 5000 and sports racers, mine in Formula 1 and Indy cars. No driver can do everything but, as an Italian, I sure wish I had a Targa Florio trophy and I bet Brian wouldn't mind having his name on one in Indianapolis.

Now it turns out that Brian writes like he drove, right to the point and always with passion. He has managed to cap a pretty terrific racing career with a pretty terrific racing memoir. Buckle up, readers, you're in for a great ride.

CHAPTER 1
The original Spa-Francorchamps

Between 1965 and 1975, one in three top-level drivers of world championship sports prototypes were killed in their cars or as a result of on-track crashes. The odds were worse for those of us who also drove in Formula 1. To understand how and why, no circuit is more illustrative than Spa-Francorchamps.

On the opening lap of the 1966 Belgian Formula 1 Grand Prix, the tightly packed field streamed into an unexpected rainstorm at the fastest part of the Spa* circuit, spraying cars across the countryside. Jackie Stewart's BRM aquaplaned at the feared *Masta* kink, scythed through a woodcutter's hut and plunged into the basement of a nearby farmhouse. Stewart was trapped upside-down in the car with broken ribs and a damaged shoulder while the electric fuel pump discharged a full tank of petrol over his body. Providentially, BRM teammates Graham Hill and Bob Bondurant had crashed less violently nearby and were able to release Jackie with tools borrowed from a spectator.

Not only were racing cars of that era built without driver protection or even equipped

The original name for the track, first used in 1921, was the Circuit de Francorchamps, which morphed into Spa-Francorchamps and then just Spa, associating it with that nearby town's curative waters in which pilgrims have soaked since the 16th century.

with radios, circuits such as Spa were romantic constructs from 40 years earlier. There was very little in the way of protection for competitors and spectators, track marshal support was inadequate, there were no on-site medical capabilities, and organisers were oblivious to the ever-increasing speeds. Stewart's horrifying experience at Spa turned him into racing's most tireless and resolute safety evangelist, frequently unloved but ultimately successful. Unfortunately for me, Jackie's influence on safety didn't begin to take root until 1976, but then it became a movement. By the end of the decade, the modern age of racing safety was firmly established and it has improved each year since. I think that every driver who has survived a racing collision over the past four decades would do well to kneel down tonight and offer an appreciative little prayer for the life-saving contributions of three-time Formula 1 World Champion Sir John Young 'Jackie' Stewart OBE.

Current racers who know the 4.5-mile Belgian track rhapsodise about the way in which its quick corners curl on to high-speed straights, long and short, uphill and down. Sooner or later the stories get around to the challenging *Eau Rouge/Raidillon* complex, giving drivers the opportunity to glaze their tales with hints of diffident valour. It's doubtful that any will mention today's wide asphalt run-off areas, or

OPPOSITE My final Spa 1,000Kms win (of four) came in 1972 in a Ferrari 312PB I shared with Arturo Merzario.
LAT

the comprehensive rim of steel barriers, or the ubiquity of the marshalling points, or the chicane that brings cars nearly to a crawl. Nor should they. Modern Spa is a fine circuit that produces excellent racing in enviable safety, and all sane drivers should be grateful for that.

But this isn't the Spa I drove in the 1960s and 1970s. It isn't the Spa that nearly broke my spirit and did break my body. Nor is it the Spa on which I won five momentous races in five fragile racing cars.

The original course was an 8.7-mile triangle of rustic byways anchored at each corner by the villages of Francorchamps, Malmedy and Stavelot. The circuit had been conceived in the early 1920s for cars with as little as 50bhp capable of less than 100mph, and continued as a magnificent folly onto which we threw 620bhp machines at over 200mph with ill-advised eagerness. By the time of my début, Spa already had earned a reputation for being an unforgiving circuit, even in an era when safety concerned very few drivers and absolutely no team managers.

Apart from a single hairpin corner, the original Spa was a ribbon of long straights punctuated by blazingly fast curves, all to be negotiated as aggressively as cross-ply tyres would allow. If, at full throttle, a driver exited the *Malmedy* corner 3mph faster than his competitors, he carried that additional speed down the full 1½-mile length of the *Masta* straight, and did so again on the equally long *Hollowell*. Consider the arithmetic: at 214mph a Porsche 917 covered the length of a football pitch (105 yards) in a single second and did so for about 26 long seconds on each of these two straights. If the speeds of two competitive cars were exactly the same at all other parts of the track, the driver who was 3mph faster on the *Masta* and *Hollowell* straights would pull out an advantage of 14½ car lengths each and every lap of his 15-lap stint, and would be nearly 1,150 yards ahead when his co-driver took over – total domination.

Conversely, a driver's tiniest miscue through the *Masta* kink – a quick left/right in the middle of the *Masta* straight – or the slightest lift at the *Burnenville*, *Stavelot* or *Blanchimont* corners

OPPOSITE My first race at Spa, the 1,000Kms of 1966, was only my second trip abroad. Peter Sutcliffe, a privateer from northern England, invited me to co-drive his Ford GT40 and we finished a very pleasing fourth.
LAT

increased his lap time not by just a few tenths of a second but by two or even three full seconds, costing as much as 1¼ miles during his turn at the wheel. Such a performance was unthinkable and would have led swiftly to unemployment.

More sobering was the harsh punishment for even the smallest mistake or the slightest error in judgement. A racing car with sticky tyres spinning on grainy asphalt will scrub off speed, but the tyres of one that departs the circuit onto slippery grass sacrifice most of their grip and the car loses little momentum. Unimpeded, it could travel a great distance at a disturbingly rapid rate. At Spa, however, no car could slide very far before encountering a house, a tree, a telegraph pole, a wall, an embankment, a ditch or a wire fence garrotte. These hazards were compounded by the provincial nature of the countryside and the region's unpredictable weather. One part of the track might bask in sunshine while another was awash in rain. Without radios, drivers had no warning about deteriorating conditions and often would rush

into a veil of water that hadn't been there on the previous lap. It was accepted that crashes on the original Spa circuit often meant serious injury, or worse.

The first test – 1966

My initial engagement with Spa occurred in May 1966 when Charles Bridges put up £60 for me to co-drive Peter Sutcliffe's Ford GT40 Mk1 in the 1,000Kms. The hubris of my successful campaigns with Charles's Lightweight Jaguar E-type and Can-Am Lola T70, overlaid with the universal fearlessness of inexperience, left me unprepared for Spa's stretches of full-bore straights, the breakneck corners, and the narrow country roads with stone houses and stout trees pressing against the circuit.

By the end of Saturday practice, I was sufficiently intimidated by Spa's speeds and perils that the night before my international début was sleepless. Calling my wife Marion and discussing my fears with her wasn't an option. She remained silent to me about her feelings on

BELOW My GT40 slides through *La Source*, ready for the plunge down to *Eau Rouge*. *Ford*

racing's realities, as I did with her and everyone else. In truth, I was ready to retire, immediately.

That I didn't quit owed much to my ambition of making racing a career and even more to my trust in the superb vehicle I was to drive. With its massively strong steel monocoque, the early Ford GT40 was more robust and safer than any other sports prototype I ever raced. Peter and I drove conservatively without any dramas, finishing an excellent fourth in our maiden year behind the third-placed Ferrari 330P of Michael Parkes and Ludovico Scarfiotti. I was now racing with the big boys and, for the first time, put my fears behind me and carried on with my exciting new career.

The incipient pro – 1967

Once again I was invited to join Peter Sutcliffe in his GT40 for the 1,000Kms of 1967. Even after a full year of serious racing, the circuit's pace was no less disquieting but time and practice were moulding me into a true professional. I had learned the trick of burying reason under layers of confidence and pretence.

Spa is in the lush forests of the Ardennes, where in May – the driest month – it rains more days than not. Denny Hulme, New Zealand's only Formula 1 World Champion and a racer known for his unflinching bravery, shared this advice about the original circuit.

'Spa? In the rain? Shit. Park it.' Kiwi wisdom.

I was aware of the likelihood of rain so I wasn't surprised when threatening clouds gathered soon after I began my first stint. Approaching *Stavelot*, the 150mph right-hander taken in fifth gear in a GT40, I could see rain in the distance and slowed to about 100mph by the time the curtain fell. Incredibly, a glance in my mirrors revealed the fast-approaching headlights of a driver much braver than me. Worrying more about survival than position, I pressed my car as close to the apex as possible, practically scraping its right side against the corner of a house.

'Wild' Willy Mairesse in the yellow *Equipe Nationale Belge* Ferrari 412P came blasting past on the outside – and immediately lost it. The telegraph pole that took the first hit deflected

him back onto the asphalt where he bounced off the side of a building and continued down the track in the balletic contortions of a monster shunt. I missed a shift while attempting to avoid Willy's gyrating car and began sliding sideways, now in danger of an accident of my own making. With the windscreen misting and my vision obscured, I steered with one hand and fumbled for a gear with the other. Miraculously, the car ended up pointing in the right direction, with me considerably shaken. Just as I began to recover my resolve to return to serious motoring, Racing Team Holland's Porsche 906 flew past, went off the road, flipped and rejoined the track, spinning upside-down like a top. After 1,000 kilometres of such dramas, our sixth place felt sufficient.

Mairesse returned to racing until he sustained a career-ending crash in the 1968 Le Mans 24 Hours. Physically and mentally damaged, and knowing no other means of earning a livelihood, this brave Belgian took his life in an Ostend hotel in 1969.

Willy Mairesse was 40 years old.

ABOVE Our 1966 race went so well that Peter Sutcliffe repeated the invitation for the following year. Once again we finished in his reliable old GT40, this time in sixth place.
LAT

A win, at last – 1968

By now my professional racing career was a
reality, gracefully accepted by Marion and
energetically embraced by me. As a result of my
1967 win in the Kyalami Nine Hours in South
Africa with Jacky Ickx in the JW Automotive
Mirage M1, John Wyer signed us to continue
our partnership the following year. Wyer's 1968
entries were Ford GT40s, splendidly liveried in
what became the most iconic team colours ever,
Gulf Oil cerulean blue with a broad orange stripe.
Less providentially, John Cooper also hired me
(for £500) to drive in selected Grands Prix.

While I was grateful to Cooper for the Formula
1 opportunity, I was less enthusiastic about his
car. The rear-engine Cooper T81B was powered
by a heavy, thirsty Maserati V12 engine that had
been first used 12 years earlier in the Maserati
250F. While the Wyer relationship led to glory,
my Cooper experience ended in tears.

The 1968 Spa 1,000Kms pitched Wyer's GT40
against Alan Mann's fast – though unstable and
temperamental – Ford P68 sports prototype,

driven by Frank Gardner and Hubert Hahne.
Frank had handily outqualified us by four full
seconds on Saturday but on race day Spa's great
leveller materialised – hard, implacable rain. This
was perfect Jacky Ickx weather.

Jacky loved Spa and he especially loved Spa
in the wet. Over my 22 years of professional racing,
I never witnessed a lap as brilliant as Jacky's
opener that day. When he stormed past the pits
to begin lap two, everyone in the paddock was
convinced that the rest of the field had been halted
by a horrendous accident. Thirty-nine seconds
passed before the second-placed car, a Porsche
908 coupé driven by Vic Elford, finally sloshed
into sight. By then Jacky had rounded *Eau Rouge*,
crested *Raidillon* and disappeared up the *Kemmel*
straight – this despite Vic's skill in the rain and
the known superiority of the lightweight 908
on a slippery track.

The 908's wet-weather efficiency didn't
necessarily empower all Porsche drivers. When
I attempted to pass Vic's co-driver, Jochen
Neerpasch, at *Malmedy*, he suddenly spun directly

in front of me, skating about wildly before leaving
the track and crashing violently. The car was
destroyed and Jochen was knocked out by a steel
tube from the bus shelter he demolished. A month
later, his racing enthusiasm much diminished,
Jochen said, '*Brian, you can only play Russian Roulette
so long.*' True to his sentiments, he redirected his
skills towards race management, building a series
of successful touring car teams, first around the
Ford RS Capri (as competition director for Ford in
Germany) and then the BMW CSL.

The race continued, as did the rain. Although
I had qualified in the dry with the same lap time
as Jacky, Wyer now instructed me, to my great
relief, to '*maintain the gap*' and not attempt to equal
the wet-weather pace of the otherworldly Mr Ickx.
In the end we won by more than a lap, ahead of
the Gerhard Mitter/Jo Schlesser Porsche 907. Being
damned with faint praise usually rankles, but it
was with satisfaction that I read Wyer's post-race
comment: '*Redman drove extremely well and did all
that was required of him.*' Job secured, at least
for now.

ABOVE Note the broken front suspension on my Cooper in Peter Burn's photo, taken just before my crash and proving it was not driver error.
LAT

OPPOSITE After vaulting the barrier and breaking my arm, the Cooper caught fire. The marshals were woefully equipped; the one wielding the fire extinguisher and smoking reignited the blaze. Once the fire was out, they dragged me from the wreckage, dumped me on the ground and returned to their injured compatriot.
Sutton Images

Formula 1 – 1968

I returned to Spa again in June as part of my Formula 1 commitment, burdened to drive the troublesome Cooper. Despite an engine transplant (a BRM V12 for a Maserati V12) and a chassis redesign (to Type 86B), the car remained the same old affliction. By this time Cooper was on an irreversible downhill slide and the team's technical expertise was antediluvian. I complained that the car wanted to spin entering each corner, pushed towards the outside of the track at the apex, and displayed so much instability at the exit that it lifted the inside rear wheel. The Cooper engineer's solution was to lower my rear tyre pressures by five pounds, a change that did nothing for the handling. Of course, a professional driver is paid to carry on regardless, a questionable practice as events later confirmed.

Ludovico Scarfiotti, my usual Cooper teammate, was excused from Spa so that he could fulfil a Porsche commitment at Germany's Rossfeldstrasse hillclimb. On the Saturday of our Grand Prix weekend, just after qualifying, I learned that Ludovico's Porsche 910 left the rain-soaked road and crashed into a tree, throwing him out of the car and killing him instantly.

Ludovico Scarfiotti was 35 years old.

Sunday came. I put Scarfiotti's accident out of my mind and went racing. Even the faint-hearted Cooper-BRM took the *Eau Rouge/Raidillon* complex at 130mph, cresting the hill flat out and gaining speed on the *Kemmel* straight to arrive at *Les Combes* at about 160mph. As I approached this fast left-hander, I felt something fail in my suspension and attempted to spin so I could crash backwards – the safer way to self-destruct. Unhelpfully, the steering had locked and I careened sideways into the barrier. The car's rolling momentum carried it up and over the guardrail with my right arm caught between the unyielding steel and the car's chassis. Once on the other side, the Cooper continued to slide, demolishing a marshals' post and slamming into a parked Vauxhall Velox. The big Vauxhall may have completed the Cooper's ruin, but at least it

prevented my car, and me, from disappearing into the forest. Three wheels came off the Cooper – one severely injuring a track marshal – before it burst into flames. Had I not been strapped inside, I might have cheered.

Accidents seem to unravel slowly for racing drivers and, short of being concussed (something we didn't understand in that era), memories record surprising detail. I distinctly recall feeling the two bones in my lower arm snap as I rolled over the barrier and then holding my breath when marshals applied a spray of fire extinguishant. Even damaged and shaken, I was concerned as much about inhaling that toxic cloud as being burned. A Belgian marshal's face appeared through the mist and, without removing the cigarette from his mouth, he started to undo my belts, igniting spilled fuel and causing the car once again to burst into flames.

The marshals finally put out the fire, dragged me out of the wreck and deposited me on the ground. With the driver who created this mayhem temporarily dispatched, they went back to tending their comrade, who not only suffered a ruptured spleen but also a heart attack. From my prone position, the horizon filled with the pensive face of journalist David Phipps as I repeatedly shouted, '*The bloody steering broke!*'

Eventually the corner marshals remembered to cart me off on a stretcher and I was taken by helicopter to Hôpital de Bavière, the teaching facility at Université de Liège. There I was placed under the care of *Professeur* F. Orban, who had been an aide to Winston Churchill during the Second World War. *Professeur* Orban had volunteered for duty that day knowing it was likely that his skills would be needed.

As I lay on the operating table, the masked-and-gowned physician looked hard at me and cautioned, '*Monsieur Redman, it may not be possible to save your arm.*' I smiled and thanked him. Perplexed, he asked how I could be so pleased, to which I truthfully replied, '*Because I am here.*' Somehow, this brilliant surgeon dragged the broken ulna and radius bones back into alignment and managed to insert two stainless-steel Rush pins down the medullary canals, one from the wrist to the elbow and the other in the reverse direction.

This was the first time Marion had to learn from a television broadcast about the downside of her husband's profession. After flying to Belgium, she was collected and watched over by Lucien Bianchi, who replaced Scarfiotti as my new Cooper teammate. Marion provided her usual competent management; Lucien and his wife Marianne offered their unsparing tenderness. It was a blow to us both when, in testing at Le Mans the following year, Lucien was killed in an accident that ended with his Alfa Romeo T33 stopped by a telegraph pole.

Lucien Bianchi was 34 years old.

John Cooper visited me the day after the race and politely inquired as to what caused the crash that destroyed his valuable racing car. *'Something broke in the suspension,'* I told him. John didn't respond well to this assessment but gave a shrug and delivered this rather unsympathetic comment: *'You'll heal, my boy.'* By the next day, I understood. Beneath John Cooper's studied indifference rested his determination to protect the Cooper Car Company's reputation, at the expense of mine, if necessary. On Thursday, *Motoring News* ran a story in which I was quoted as saying the suspension failed, inciting John to call editor Michael Tee and demand a retraction. *'The car didn't fail,'* insisted John, *'it was driver error.'* Serendipitously, the next day's *Autosport* published a photo by Peter Burn, the magazine's chief photographer, that clearly showed the front suspension adrift.

In his 'On The Scene' column in *Autosport*, journalist Patrick McNally wrote:

'The responsibility of those actively involved in motor racing, particularly journalists and photographers, is a heavy one when they record the reasons behind accidents, which they may or may not witness. It is so easy to rush into print with hearsay information that is not based on concrete facts.

'The stories that surrounded Brian Redman's nasty incident last Sunday was a typical example; the personal accounts of apparent eye witnesses varied to the point where they sounded like four separate accidents. On a lighter note, Brian Redman was sitting up in hospital on Monday, his usual cheerful self, and his injuries are confirmed as a broken arm and a burned hand.'

Thank you, *Professeur* Orban, for saving my arm; your two pins remain on duty to this day. Thank you also to Peter Burn for rescuing my career.

The second win – 1969

Life took a swift and positive upturn. I was named a Porsche factory driver, paired in a long-tail 908 coupé for the Spa 1,000Kms with Jo 'Seppi' Siffert, the brilliant Swiss driver who came up through the hard-knocks school of motorcycle racing. Seppi and I (as well as every other Porsche factory driver) spent much of the 1969 season doing our best to avoid testing the new, unsorted 917. It was inevitable that, in the close confines of the Porsche team at Spa, there would be no escape. I was trapped like a rabbit in its hole by a ferret of a team manager.

BELOW By 1969 I was a factory Porsche driver. Jo Siffert and I insisted on racing this tried-and tested long-tail 908 instead of the troublesome – and dangerous – new 917. *Porsche-Werkfoto*

ABOVE Our first pit-stop in the 1969 1,000Kms with me about to climb into the 908 to take over from 'Seppi' Siffert: Porsche engineer Peter Falk looks on from the left whilst Seppi confers with Helmut Bott.
Grand Prix Library

OPPOSITE Our decision to race the Porsche 908 in the 1969 1,000Kms proved to be wise. We won after a tough battle with the Pedro Rodriguez/David Piper Ferrari 312P.
LAT

'*Herr Redman,*' queried engineer Helmut Bott, '*you vud like to drive the 917? Now is güt?*'

'*But it's raining, Herr Bott,*' I explained, hoping that Spa's monsoons might provide an excuse.

'*Zen go slow,*' he patiently instructed.

Reluctantly I levered myself into the seat, cramming my knees behind the steering column with my head pressed against the roof. As I started the car, the windscreen wiper blade made one sweep to the right before hurling itself gloriously into the pits. Feeling saved, I undid my belts and climbed out.

'*Yah, vas iss da matter, Herr Redman?*'

'*Well, Herr Bott, you see the windscreen wiper has gone missing, and it's raining.*'

'*Yah, yah, yah. You go slow. Is not raining so much.*'

In the description of a flying lap of Spa that accompanies this chapter, I explain the furious potential of a fully developed 12-cylinder Porsche 917K, which had become a most formidable car by 1970. That day in 1969, however, I carefully explored the lowest possible limits of Herr Bott's unsorted car.

For the race, Seppi and I agreed that we would be far more competitive in a tried-and-tested long-tail Porsche 908 coupé, and how right we were. Gerhard Mitter blew up the lone 917 almost immediately, no doubt by inadvertently selecting third gear instead of fifth, allowing his partner Udo Schütz to go home with a clean uniform. That left Jo and me to fight a hard battle with the Ferrari 312P of Pedro Rodriguez and David Piper and, by the end, we had managed to gain nearly a full lap on them to take the win. While fulfilling my role as 'rear gunner' for Seppi, I did manage to sneak in a lap at 3 minutes 37 seconds, the fastest of the race.

During Porsche's annual Christmas party at the company's Weissach proving ground, engineer Helmut Flegel asked if I wanted to see the new 908/03 and, of course, I said '*yes*'. When he whipped the cover off the car, I began to perspire. Without bodywork, it looked like a go-kart on steroids, but that's not what caused my alarm. In order to position the gearbox ahead of the rear axle, the eight-cylinder engine had

been moved forward, pushing the driver even further into the nose. Not only would his feet stick out beyond the front wheels, but there was only an aluminium oil cooler and some delicate bodywork between the soles of his shoes and whatever solid object the car might hit. With the body off, a driver could actually touch the right front tyre from his seat. Gallows humour followed when I suggested that the car was perfect for Douglas Bader, the legless Second World War aviator.

Group Captain Sir Douglas Bader actually deserved more respect. Despite an aerobatics crash in the early 1930s that cost him his lower limbs, he persuaded an undermanned RAF to accept him as a fighter pilot during the 1940 Battle of Britain, ultimately achieving 20 confirmed kills with four more shared and six probable, plus 11 enemy aircraft damaged. It was theorised that Bader actually had a fighting advantage. Legless, more of his blood could be retained in his torso and he was less likely to pass out when executing high-speed turns.

Win number three – 1970

John Wyer took over the testing of the Porsche 917 in 1969 and his organisation, JW Automotive Engineering, was named the official Porsche race team for 1970. By the time we returned to Spa in 1970, the 917K had already proven itself with wins in the 24 Hours of Daytona, the Brands Hatch 1,000Kms and the Monza 1,000Kms. For the Spa 1,000Kms we had new rear bodywork with a tunnel down the middle of a slightly modified tail section that swept up at its trailing edge. This aggressive configuration was designed to give us added speed on the long straights, not that any of the drivers had lobbied for this particular favour. It turned out that the car's tyres shared our misgivings.

During the opening lap of practice, Seppi had a terrifying high-speed incident when a front tyre parted from its rim on the *Masta* straight at about 180mph. After all four wheels and tyres were replaced, it appeared that I was not to be left out of the fun. '*Herr Redman, now iss your turn.*' When I offered my opinion that something might be seriously wrong, Herr Bott gave me the same counsel he had imparted the previous year – go slowly.

I followed this advice impeccably for three laps as I built my speed and confidence. On the fourth lap I felt obliged to take an aggressive run down the *Masta* straight at about 215mph, and then around *Stavelot* at 170mph. So far, so good. But as I approached the flat-out *Les Carrières* at 175mph, my left rear tyre detached itself from the rim, flinging the 917 sideways and causing the car to slew from one edge of the road to the other. In desperation I took both hands off the steering wheel, having once read that the caster (forward tilt) of the front wheels would automatically straighten the car. It worked and eventually the car stopped, undamaged. The same could not be said for my confidence. When I returned to the pits, Seppi fell on the ground laughing, pointing out that my face matched the colour of my white driver's suit.

Incredibly, neither of the tyres that failed on our cars had actually blown. Rather, the centres

ABOVE With Jo Siffert in the pits in 1970, minutes before the left front tyre of our 917 came off the rim at 180mph on his first practice lap – the same thing as later happened to me. *LAT*

BELOW Siffert in our Gulf Porsche (24) begins his duel with Rodriguez (25) at the start of the 1970 1,000Kms. Four more 917s lie behind: Jürgen Neuhaus/Helmut Kelleners (30), Hans Laine/ Gijs van Lennep (43), Richard Attwood/Hans Herrmann (29) and Vic Elford/Kurt Ahrens (28). *LAT*

of the tyres had expanded so much from spinning at such high speeds that their inside beads were pulled away from the rims. Safety pins and studs had yet to be devised but, clearly, a solution had to be found. The night before the race, all of the team's magnesium-alloy wheels were taken to the nearby city of Liège and roughly sandblasted, the better to grip the tyres. No one knew if this would work, although we drivers would be the first to find out.

It rained heavily during the night and, as was normally the case, I slept in fits and starts, often waking in a cold sweat. My thoughts were of Spa's dangers, of course, but I also found myself dwelling, as a child of the Second World War, on how local families suffered when the region was savaged during the Battle of the Bulge*. Somehow, the spectre of senseless losses during the war dovetailed with my fear of Spa's random uncertainties. Even now, I don't know if this grim combination made things worse or better.

The next day was race day. Pedro Rodriguez had put one of the JW Automotive Porsche 917Ks on pole with my teammate Jo Siffert alongside in ours. Two factory Ferrari 512s were our main competition, one driven by Jacky Ickx – on his favourite track – and John Surtees, the 1964 Formula 1 World Champion. We had our work cut out. The track was still wet when the race began, so Pedro and Seppi started on intermediate tyres.

*The last German attack of the war was spearheaded by the armoured column of Hitler's crack fighting force, the First SS Panzer Division, just returned from Russia and led by a young, fanatical Nazi named Joachim Peiper. These battle-hardened soldiers were privileged to wear the Death's Head skull on their collars and had the Führer's name sewn onto their sleeves. The SS, notorious for its atrocities, butchered 130 Stavelot townspeople and continued murdering civilians beyond. At Malmedy the Germans surprised about 100 American GIs at lunch who yielded when they found themselves facing tanks with rifles. After guards herded their prisoners into the centre of a field, a sudden pistol shot revealed the SS's intentions and gunners from the passing tanks and half-tracks joined in, spraying the unarmed Americans with heavy, automatic weapons. Just two soldiers survived by playing dead beneath piles of their comrades.

LEFT Teammates Siffert and Rodriguez attack *Eau Rouge* and each other, swapping paint with little concern for the four hours of racing ahead.
LAT

A lap of Spa-Francorchamps

Allow me to take you back to 1970 and share a lap of the original 8.7-mile track – what historians now like to call 'l'ancien circuit' – in my Porsche 917K.

I'll begin at *La Source*, the final hairpin corner where I progressively squeezed the accelerator until my car was nearly straight, and then mashed the pedal to the floor to begin the downhill dive. As I hurtled past the pits and start/finish line, I slipped from second gear into third as my speed built to about 160mph. A tap on the brakes at the bottom allowed me to swivel through the *Eau Rouge* S-bend, charge uphill at about 140mph and tiptoe through the right/left *Raidillon* sequence. Snatching fourth gear (top in a 917K), I blasted up the gradually rising *Kemmel* straight with speed continuing

to increase. In every gear, I revved to a maximum of 8,000rpm; one missed shift and delicate valves would have confronted flailing pistons, resulting in a thoroughly broken engine.

As the sweeping *Les Combes* left-hander rushed into view at 170mph, I braked hard, grabbed third gear and, using every inch of the road, opened the throttle to surge down another steep hill towards the flat-out right called *Burnenville*. Still in top gear, I hammered through the connecting chute into *Malmedy* and onto the *Masta* straight, that narrow 1½-mile country road where I pushed the car to its top speed – 214mph. I tried not to think about this as I neared the *Masta* kink, possibly the most intimidating turn in all of

Spa-Francorchamps 1970

La Source
Clubhouse
Eau Rouge
Raidillon
Blanchimont
Kemmel
Les Combes
Les Carrières
Burnenville
Malmedy
Masta kink
Stavelot
Masta straight
Hollowell straight

N

motor racing. At that velocity, I couldn't indulge even the briefest of unnecessary lifts without losing precious seconds (and my drive). Left/right through there at 180mph and onto the *Hollowell* straight, flat out again at top speed for another 1½ miles.

Stavelot, a long right-hander, was taken in top gear at about 170mph and followed by a fast left that promptly shifted to a 160mph right with its apex at the corner of a stone building. Straight uphill now towards the blind, flat-out *Les Carrières*, still gaining speed into an equally blind 170mph left called *Blanchimont*, where a narrow patch of grass was all that separated the track from a steel barrier. A final uphill straight returned me to *La Source*, the first-gear corner where this lap began. Ploughing around this slow turn allowed a few seconds to breathe, flex and relax before it was time to repeat the exercise – 14 more times.

At the drop of the flag, the two of them contested
the narrow road side by side, banging their
917s' flanks through *Eau Rouge*, then up the hill
and out of sight. I'm sure the hairs on the back of
John Wyer's neck stood on end; they did on mine.
This spirited Rodriguez/Siffert rivalry turned out
to have serious consequences for me at the Targa
Florio a year later, to the detriment of my career
and the devastation of my body.

The JW Automotive Porsche 917 duos of
Rodriguez/Kinnunen and Siffert/Redman soon
put distance on the field, leapfrogging each other
back and forth as the race unfolded. Ultimately
Seppi and I extended our lead, to take the win
over the Ickx/Surtees Ferrari at an average speed
of 149.42mph, including pitstops. It was the
fastest road race ever run. I was able to match
Siffert's best time, but Pedro Rodriguez blitzed
us all by setting a single lap record of 3 minutes
16.5 seconds at an astonishing average speed
of 160.513mph.

At 10 o'clock in the evening, after the
interminable prize-giving, Siffert said, '*Come on,*

ABOVE Seppi and I are both in view, with mechanics hard at work, including Peter Davies (refuelling). The four main figures on the pit counter are (from left) Grady Davis (Gulf boss), John and Tottie Wyer (both seated) and John Horsman (chief engineer).
LAT

RIGHT In our 1970 win, Jo Siffert and I averaged 149.42mph – the fastest road race ever run.
Porsche-Werkfoto

let's have a drink with the mechanics.' Marion, who was there with our young son James, asked when I expected to return. 'About midnight' seemed a reasonable enough estimate, although I was unaware that the mechanics were lodging 20 miles away. In sweet, celebratory relief, we partied and sang until four in the morning: 'Prost, Prost Kamerad; Prost, Prost Kamerad.' Back at the hotel, Seppi demonstrated 360-degree spins with his Porsche 911 in the car park, showering the windows with gravel. The management – both the hotel's and mine – were not amused, but neither Seppi nor I much cared. We had won and remained whole – and the Spa 1,000Kms was behind us for another year.

No Spa – 1971

I missed the Spa 1,000Kms in 1971. This was the year I attempted retirement in South Africa and returned to racing, only to endure a fiery accident in the Targa Florio, as recounted in Chapter 5.

LEFT Porsche's poster listing the top six finishers in the 1970 race demonstrated the company's supremacy over Ferrari.
Porsche-Werkfoto

LEFT Celebrating with Seppi after our second successive victory together, and my hat-trick.
Getty Images/ Rainer Schlegelmilch

ABOVE After my Targa
Florio accident, I missed
the 1971 Spa 1,000Kms,
returning in 1972 as
a works Ferrari driver.
Here I talk things over
with my teammate
Ronnie Peterson.
Getty Images/
Rainer Schlegelmilch

Win number four – 1972

Rain was a constant of my racing at Spa and once
again played a pivotal role in the 1972 1,000Kms.
I had been hired by Ferrari to share a 312PB with
Arturo Merzario, a very good but temperamental
driver. In the race, with only one hour left to run,
the Jacky Ickx/Clay Regazzoni 312PB was leading
when Clay picked up a puncture and hit the
barrier, damaging the bodywork and oil tank.

Suddenly I was in the lead, but with Ronnie
Peterson in the team's third 312PB closing quickly.
As we approached the fast *Les Combes* left-hander,
I took my usual prudent line to give myself a
touch more room in case of trouble – a legacy of
my 1968 accident. At that moment there was a
wave of movement among the fans clustered by
the corner as if something had abruptly startled
them *en masse*. It spooked me sufficiently that
I lifted and touched the brakes. The spectators,
as a group, were closing their umbrellas after a
shower that had made the road surface wet but
without any obvious puddles. My conservative
line and early braking allowed me to make it

RIGHT My Ferrari
312PB rounding the La
Source hairpin during the
1972 1,000Kms, made
dramatic by 'speed-blur'
photography.
Getty Images/
Rainer Schlegelmilch

through the corner while hard-charging Ronnie ended up riding along the top of the guardrail like a slot car.

There are moments of wisdom like this that contribute to every win, but I've noticed that the more experienced a driver becomes, the more often they occur.

No joy – 1973

For the 1973 Spa 1,000Kms I was again paired in the Ferrari 312PB with the formidable Jacky Ickx, who set the fastest-ever lap during qualifying at a speed of 163.679mph.

Alas, in the race our gearbox oil cooler failed at about half distance, leaving the race to Derek Bell and Mike Hailwood in their Gulf Mirage M6 – and a new 163.086mph lap record to Henri Pescarolo in his Matra MS670B.

The new Spa-Francorchamps

My move to Formula 5000 and the American Can-Am series ended my string of 1,000Kms races at Spa. Six years later, in 1979, the track management sensibly pruned the circuit's length from 8.7 miles to 4.5, connecting *Les Combes* and *Blanchimont* by a new sector and ceding the 4.4 miles between *Malmedy* and *Stavelot* to full-time public use. I returned to Spa in 1989 to drive Peter Livanos' Aston Martin AMR1 and found the new layout to be fast and fun, the killer kinks and corners now mercifully absent. You can drive much of the original circuit in a road car today, but carefully. It remains largely unchanged.

I won at Spa on five occasions: four in 1,000Kms races – one each in a Ford GT40, Porsche 908, Porsche 917 and Ferrari 312PB – and once with a Chevron B16S in the 1970 500Kms. These successes weren't often pleasurable but they were always rewarding. I recall that each time I stepped from the car at the end, the grass was greener, the sky bluer and the air purer. Now, from the gauzy perspective of over 45 years, I can report that I'm glad to have had the opportunity to engage and conquer the original circuit.

Time does that, even to racing drivers.

OPPOSITE The Ferrari 312PB I shared with Arturo Merzario in 1972 is seen at *Stavelot*, before I took the lead in the final hour for my fourth win in the Spa 1,000Kms. *LAT*

BELOW In 1973, when I drove with Jacky Ickx, my Ferrari 312PB turns into *Les Combes* at the end of the rising *Kemmel* straight, in rare Spa sunshine. A broken gearbox oil cooler ended our effort. *LAT*

CHAPTER 2
Lancashire's fastest mop deliveries

None of my early careers ever lasted long, possibly because I wasn't very good at them. Still, it's tempting to wonder how life might have turned out had I resigned myself to a position in the family grocery chain, or worked harder in the mop business, or even taken a flyer at catering. Instead, I made a career out of racing.

Had I pursued any of the normal options, life would have been different: more stable but less fun; less dangerous but more mundane. With years of diligent effort, I might even have provided a legacy for my heirs and funded a wholesome retirement for my wife and me. Sorry about the inheritance, James and Charlotte, and sorry about our sparse retirement, dear, faithful Marion. I fear your father and your husband chose racing instead of prosperity. More accurately, racing chose him – though it took a while.

In the small industrial town of Burnley, Lancashire, where I appeared in 1937, sport meant football and motor racing was as remote to most inhabitants as the prospect of peaceful labour relations. First the region's coal mines petered out, triggering one era of union foment, and then falling demand for expensive British cloth precipitated another. In Burnley we were sufficiently disconnected from the broad sweep of industry and culture that the region's most celebrated public monument, in nearby Colne, was a statue of Wallace Hartley, the luckless

bandleader on the *Titanic*. Colne has a better reason to be proud; it was Marion's birthplace.

By definition, youth in Burnley centred on family and, since mine owned a chain of 25 grocery stores, our home life simmered in the pleasures of upper-middle-class living. Little drama upset the domestic Redman tranquillity until 1939, when the threat of a German invasion mobilised all of Britain. Just as Hitler was launching his pre-invasion aerial bombardments, the remnants of Britain's battered troops returned from Dunkirk in no condition to fend off an attack. Inspired by Prime Minister Churchill's never-give-up spirit, the public coalesced around a general with the fitting name of Ironside who organised able-bodied men and women into a Home Guard. It is conventionally believed that England would have been unable to resist a Nazi invasion, but I disagree. Unlike the hapless characters of TV's *Dad's Army*, the Home Guard progressed in rapid steps from thinly armed patriots to a sophisticated militia. Potential enemy landing areas were well protected by barriers and a mobile fighting unit was held in reserve, trained to confront an invading force. Our country was ready. Thankfully, the assault never came.

By 1941, my brother Christopher was born, my father was posted to the Royal Artillery in India, and the Blitz turned Lancashire's industrial centres – indeed all of England's – into a war

OPPOSITE At the wheel of my father's car at the time the Second World War broke out: am I projecting a later aptitude?
Brian Redman collection

ANOTHER OF REDMAN'S MODERN SHOPS.

REDMAN'S ORIGINAL BACON STALL, MARKET HALL, OPENED 1909.

211, Padiham Road.
Bacon Stall, Market Hall.
Dried Fruit Stall, ,,   ,,
Duke Bar.

—NOTE—
ADDRESSES

Coal Clough Lane.
6-8, Oxford Road.
Rosegrove Lane.
9, Burnley Road, Padiham.

ABOVE My father Tom and his brother Walter jointly owned and ran a grocery business that my grandfather had founded. When I was a child they had 25 shops in northern England.
Brian Redman collection

zone. Manchester and Liverpool, our nearby port cities, were the targets of relentless German bombing and both sustained heavy damage. In April 1941 Liverpool suffered six consecutive nights of *Luftwaffe* raids, which battered or destroyed half of the commercial docks. The bombing greatly impaired the unloading of incoming supply ships from America, each carrying desperately needed essentials. In Burnley we could only listen to the muffled barrage and imagine the hell that people were enduring.

Yet despite my memories of the Second World

War, many childhood recollections are much more personal and a whole lot less noble. I fear that my rebellious nature emerged early, revealing itself with misdemeanours such as breaking greenhouse windows and purposely getting tar on my clothes. For each of these and myriad similar offences, I was remanded for long hours in a dark cupboard beneath the stairs. These periods of incarceration did little to improve my behaviour, but they did give me a lifelong aptitude for stubborn endurance.

My difficulties with discipline may also explain my tenuous relationship with the rigours of formal education. At eight, my parents sent me off to a classically regimented boys' boarding school, 200 miles away in Wales, near Aberystwyth. By 16, they concluded that it was pointless to spend good money educating a son who wasn't learning anything, and I quite agreed. Three years at Courtfield Catering College in Blackpool ended without graduation, thus confirming the wisdom of my parents' earlier judgement. Still, that modicum of culinary

RIGHT With my mother, Pearl, on the beach at Blackpool, where I later went to catering college.
Brian Redman collection

RIGHT On my tricycle, the first of my high-performance vehicles, at our comfortable home in Burnley.
Brian Redman collection

expertise was enough to qualify me to serve
the Queen and the Duke of Edinburgh when
they graced demure Burnley. I'm sure it was the
highlight of their visit.

I did like cars, an interest piqued by my
grandfather's serial purchases of high-end
sporting machines: a BMW 328, two Bristols (400
and 401), an Aston Martin DB2/4, a Triumph TR2
and an MGA coupé. My parents' transport was
more family-oriented but equally distinguished:
a Wolseley 18/85 followed by Mark V and Mark
VII Jaguars.

I vividly recall accompanying my father and
grandfather to the 1955 British Grand Prix at
Aintree where I watched Juan Manuel Fangio
chase Stirling Moss all afternoon, nose to tail.
There was some speculation that the Argentinian
allowed Moss to win his home Grand Prix. If so, it
was a gesture of racing gentility never repeated in

my experience. I simply loved everything about
that day: the engine noises, the beautiful cars,
the heroic drivers and, especially, the concept
of going fast. That innocent outing seeded the
direction of my life.

Perhaps the tipping point came when, after
passing my driving test at 17, I went on a hunting
trip with my grandfather in his Triumph TR2,
which he invited me to drive. With a twinkle in
his eye, he said, '*Send it on, boy, send it on*', and so
I did until we reached 100mph. '*That's by far the
fastest I've ever been on this road,*' he shouted. Little
did he suspect that it was by far the fastest I'd ever
been on any road.

My automotive portfolio expanded in 1956
when I did my National Service with Her
Majesty's East Lancashire Regiment, otherwise
known as the PBI (Poor Bloody Infantry). I spent
my first year at the Fulwood Barracks in Preston

RIGHT Aged seven, preparing to launch my model aeroplane, a good one that had a little petrol engine. After numerous crashes it ceased to be airworthy.
Brian Redman collection

BELOW I played the soldier early in the Second World War while the men were fighting. One bomb landed in Burnley and I remember air-raid warnings.
Brian Redman collection

ABOVE Chris, Jennifer and me – the oldest – with our father in 1950.
Brian Redman collection

ABOVE With my mother, Grandpa Simpson and his TR2, the car that provided my early experience of 100mph motoring. The Singer tourer was mine, my second car, following on from a 1932 Morris Minor tourer.
Brian Redman collection

BELOW Just before my National Service in the army, I acquired this formidable beast, powered by a flathead Ford V8. The Grenfell Special was my regular road car despite the absence of weather protection.
Brian Redman collection

manoeuvring three-ton Bedford trucks, which some officer deemed to be sufficient 'training' for a new role chauffeuring the commanding officer in his government-issue Land Rover.

For personal transport I graduated from a Zundapp Bella scooter to a 1948 Grenfell Special, a fearsome two-seater with a Ford V8 flathead designed primarily for hill-climbs. After my discharge in 1958 I settled into a mop business that I inherited from my maternal grandfather, and concluded that selling these products required deliveries. To make deliveries I needed a suitable vehicle and one soon appeared in the form of a Morris 1000 Traveller 'Woody'. In this I took to challenging every vehicle I met – and overtaking became such an obsession that I sometimes found myself 20 miles beyond a delivery destination.

My earliest motorsport

Not surprisingly, the little Traveller began to sprout performance tweaks: a Shorrock supercharger, anti-roll bars, harder brake linings. It was inevitable that, one day, my bread-and-

butter delivery van would find itself on the grid with its completely novice driver. As the green flag dropped on Easter Monday, 1959, at Rufforth, a now-defunct airfield circuit near York, my legs were shaking so badly that I could barely operate the accelerator. I recall that two cars passed me before the first corner, Rodney Bloor in a Riley 1.5 on one side and Harry Ratcliffe in his fast Morris Minor on the other. Even more streamed by as the race progressed. I don't remember where I finished – a good thing, that – but the inauspicious results of my début set the pattern for equally humbling drubbings throughout the year.

While success remained elusive, I did absorb a basic competition lesson: racing had as much to do with thinking ahead as it did with fast reflexes, and thinking ahead was something I seemed to do well. It also became apparent that competing in a mundane little estate car was not the short road to Formula 1. I wanted (in my mind, needed) something racier and settled on the preferred track option of our local winners – an 848cc Morris Mini Minor.

Like the Traveller, the Mini also developed a habit of acquiring performance mods: 2½-inch SU carburettors, hot Alexander racing cam, Downton cylinder head with big Peco inlet manifold, and Peco exhaust system. These go-faster tweaks made the car virtually undriveable below 4,000rpm but quite strong at higher revs. In my second racing season, decent outcomes became usual with podium finishes occasional. As I soon learned, success has a practical side; it spawns overtures for better drives in better cars owned by other people. My first invitation came from Downton Engineering, tuner of Minis, fabricator of my cylinder head and entrant in the 750 Motor Club's six-hour relay race at Silverstone.

Peering over my shoulder, Daniel Richmond, Downton's owner and resident Mini tuner, asked, *'Whose exhaust manifold is that?'*

'Peco,' I replied.

'Whose camshaft?'

'Alexander.'

'You do know, old boy, that these things have to be matched to work?'

LEFT This Morris 1000 Traveller was originally acquired to carry my mops before its transition into a racing car, with many bolt-on tweaks.
Brian Redman collection

LEFT In 1959, aged 22, I competed all over northern England in my hotted-up and stripped-down Traveller, driving it to and from events. For racing, I taped the headlamps and applied competition numbers in white shoe polish.
Brian Redman collection

Actually, I didn't but, correctly matched or not, I still set a fast time in practice. At the end of the day, Daniel approached me with a Formula Junior cylinder head – a form of engineered speed – saying, *'Do you think you could fit this?'*

I made the change overnight but in the following day's race our team effort came to naught when Minis began pulling the centres out of their wheels. After a wheel was launched into a grandstand, all Minis were banned from the rest of the event. The experience taught me another lesson. Winning takes more than driving skill; it takes proper equipment. Now, when young racers consult me about how they might jumpstart their careers, I give them my most practical advice: *'Buy a fast car.'*

Alas, my infatuation with racing did little to enhance the charm of hustling mops, leading to the sale of my grandfather's business. I found a job building Lotus Elite performance kits and selling Morris parts for a local dealer where my partner was Mike Wood, navigator to 1955 British rally champion John Waddington. Mike and

ABOVE I had a big accident in my Austin-Healey Sprite when its single-piece aftermarket fibreglass front bodywork came loose, blocking my vision at over 100mph. The dog is Louis, my mother's Manchester Terrier.
Brian Redman collection

BELOW A front-drive Mini was much more suitable for racing than a half-timbered estate car and mine served me well through the 1960 season. Here I am taking to the grass at Aintree.
John Holroyd

ABOVE After the 1960 season I changed from my Mini to a handsome 10-year-old Jaguar XK120, not yet appreciating how costly maintenance could be.
Brian Redman collection

BELOW After two races in the XK120 I decided that I couldn't afford to keep buying new tyres and took up hill-climbing and sprinting instead. This photo was taken at Burton's Sprint, Leeds.
Brian Redman collection

John fanned the flames of my racing ambitions. In an ill-advised acquisitive burst, I came into possession of an Austin-Healey Sprite (it was more suitable than the Mini for road use and looked good), a kart made by celebrated British racer Barrie 'Whizzo' Williams, and a vast 1929 Bentley 6½-litre landaulette to carry the kart. Not least, I tentatively gained a girlfriend, a long-legged beauty named Marion Ashurst. Things were definitely looking up.

By the end of 1960, however, my ambitions had outgrown the Mini, itself quite worn out by a full season of hard competition, and I had abandoned karting after just one race. When an old Jaguar XK120 became available, I thought, '*Now this will be reliable so I won't have to be a slave to repairs at every event.*' Hmm... Farewell to the Mini, the kart and £350 in exchange for the heady experience of owning what I thought was a proper racing car.

My elation was brief. In just two races at the Catterick and Linton-on-Ouse airfields, my XK120 used up all four tyres, imparting one more costly racing lesson. Ambitions, I discovered, had to be matched by a realistic budget. Since my aspirations

were supported by my slender income, I was forced to fall back on hill-climbs – shorter events that were less demanding on both tyres and expenses. This did have the advantage of allowing me to double up on my motorsport by entering different hill-climbs on both days of a weekend. After one Saturday event at Castle Howard, I fell among jubilant companions and we carried on as if we were professional drivers – i.e. we drank, heavily. As a consequence, I arrived the next day at Catterick, which was also a hill-climb venue, with an industrial-sized hangover, one that may possibly have contributed to my subsequent dramatic performance. Newspaper photos documented my Jaguar airborne as it entered the first corner, landing with an impact sufficient to leave the car's frame slightly bent. To the unfortunate gentleman who purchased my XK120 – sorry.

There was much to be celebrated about 1962, not the least being the Jaguar's exchange for a Morgan Plus Four and, more romantically, my marriage to Marion. True to the time-honoured

ABOVE A 1964 tyre-smoking race in Harry Ratcliffe's British Vita Racing Team Mini, sponsored by Vitafoam, maker of rubber insulation for cars.

Brian Redman collection

BELOW In a 1965 sprint at RAF Woodvale, I set fastest time in Gordon Brown's ex-Stirling Moss Jaguar XK120, bringing me to the attention of Gordon's friend Charles Bridges, my first and best racing patron.

Courtesy of Michael Brown

custom of newly married racers, and the fact that we were penniless, I stepped up to my responsibilities by foregoing competition on four wheels for motocross on two. Still, local memories of my wins persisted and an opportunity arose for me to drive the Vitafoam Mini Cooper for Harry Ratcliffe, king of the Morris Minors. Harry shared with me his brilliantly fast racing car and his philosophical observations, one of the latter proving to be particularly prescient and enduring. '*Brian*,' he advised, '*the poor young racer of today will be the poor old racer of tomorrow*.' Indeed, Harry.

In 1964 Marion became pregnant, occasioning a swift return to the family grocery businesses where I exercised my latent skills as a baker. Scones, bread and biscuits I wrought as our vans dispensed these creations to the Redman shops and regional restaurants. My employment stability threatened to become permanent but I was saved by motorsport temptations that continued to surface. I quietly nurtured each and every one of them. On Easter Monday in 1965 at a Lancashire Automobile Club sprint at Woodvale, a redundant wartime airfield near Southport, I set consecutive fastest times in different cars, first an ex-Stirling Moss XK120 and then the Vitafoam Mini. This attracted the attention of Charles Bridges, patron of Red Rose Racing. The conclusion of my life as a Redman baker grew nigh.

Charles Bridges

Allow me gratefully to state that, but for Charles Bridges and his steady support, you wouldn't be reading this book. He believed in me, even after I had the comical misfortune in my second event to spin off the Aintree motor racing circuit and crash into a Grand National steeplechase jump – driving the famous '4 WPD' Lightweight Jaguar E-type raced by Graham Hill. Things did get better. At Oulton Park I rewarded Charles with an E-type lap record, 1½ seconds quicker than Jackie Stewart's previous mark, and for the rest of the 1965 season I was virtually unbeatable: 12 wins, one second and, of course, the Aintree accident. How easy and natural winning seemed to come to a young, eager driver. I would learn.

Charles, who also raced his E-type from time to time, enjoyed our success and decided to back me in serious sports car racing. In 1966 he purchased a red Lola T70 MkII Can-Am car with an ex-John Surtees 350 cubic inch Traco Chevrolet engine. It was my first taste of absolute power and I was corrupted, absolutely. Once I had survived the Lola's 400bhp learning curve, which included one lurid, rain-induced spin directly in front of a highly animated Charles, I mastered the brute well enough to win every club race we entered and, in spite of mechanical problems, perform well in my first professional events.

Like most young racers, I had few doubts about my abilities but hoped someone important might notice. Recognition came when the Guild of Motoring Writers confirmed me as an up-and-coming driver of 1966 when it bestowed that year's Grovewood Awards upon Chris Lambert, Jackie Oliver and me, presented by no less a racing eminence than two-time Formula 1 World Champion Jim Clark. As attested by this certificate, I was now a total professional, though

BELOW In 1965, I won 12 races in Charles Bridges' Lightweight Jaguar E-type, previously driven by Graham Hill and Jackie Stewart when run by John Coombs.
Peter McFadyen

ABOVE The Tourist Trophy race at Oulton Park in April 1966, driving Charles Bridges' Lola T70 Spyder followed by Peter Sutcliffe's Ford GT40 – the car I raced a month later at Spa.
Ford

BELOW The Red Rose Racing Lola T70 Spyder in the Oulton Park paddock with mechanic Terry Wells. With its 350 cubic inch Traco Chevrolet V8 engine, this car was a fast, powerful winner.
Brian Redman collection

the real racers of the era might have considered my self-assessment a bit of a stretch.

The Bridges were a racing family. After Charles retired from driving at the end of 1966, his equally racing-minded brother David, who as an entrant had lost his driver and racing car to a fiery crash in the German Grand Prix at the Nürburgring that year, decided to put together a new team and asked if I wanted to drive for him. This was my first taste of racing's repetitive syndrome: whenever one driver is killed, another eagerly takes his place. I wasn't thinking that way at the time.

I viewed David's offer as a lucky chance and Marion supported my breakthrough opportunity. My father, however, did not. He stated firmly that, should I accept this job, there would be no return to the Redman grocery business. His ultimatum was uncaring more than unkind. Until that point, he had been generous with his financial support, though we had never developed much of a relationship. He was stationed in India when I was a child and then, immediately after the war

ABOVE At Silverstone
for the 1966 Formula
1 International Trophy
supporting event, where
I finished fourth behind
Denny Hulme (following
me here), Chris Amon
and Bruce McLaren.
Mike Hayward Collection

ended, I went to boarding school for eight years. Curiously, after dismissing any possibility of my returning to the family business, he went on to relate a poignant story about his own youthful crossroads. As a young man, he had been offered a job as a professional actor but didn't take it – and regretted that decision for the rest of his life. I thanked him for his counsel and quickly accepted David's proposal.

The plan was to acquire a new Brabham BT23, equip it with a Cosworth FVA engine and compete in Formula 2, which was the talented driver's stepping stone to Formula 1. Then David dropped a bombshell: Brabham declined to sell him a new chassis and Cosworth refused the necessary engine. The reasons for both rebuffs were identical: these manufacturers had never heard of David's driver (me) and weren't convinced that the results of an unknown would flatter their reputations. Since there was no going back to my father, the only option was to find another way to go racing, and David provided it. He dusted off his two-year-old Formula 2

Brabham B16, hired Charles's excellent mechanic Terry Wells to tend it, strapped the car on an open trailer, and sent us off to race in the UK and on the continent. Soon I found myself in the deep end of the pool driving an old car against such emerging and established greats as Jim Clark, Graham Hill, Jacky Ickx and Jochen Rindt. Being forced to compete with these brilliant talents as an underdog made me tougher and faster.

David Bridges was the owner about whom every driver dreams. Terry and I would be off for a month, racing all over Europe, and return to find him sipping a 10.00am whisky.

'Hello, Spud, where've you been?'

'I raced in Barcelona, at the Nürburgring, France's Dijon and…'

'Eeh, that were a grand trip. How'd you do?'

'We were fourth here and sixth there…'

'Eeh, well that's all right then. Where are you going next?'

That was all there was to it. I greatly appreciated David's hands-off approach but soon learned that it was characteristic of a special man

at a special time. His trusting style was unique in all of my racing experience. Later manipulations by Porsche and Ferrari only magnified the wonder of the absolute faith David Bridges placed in me and the value his gentle kindness brought to my burgeoning career.

The cars, tracks and racing were a young man's dream. This was now my life and, by extension, the life my family shared. Driving became the essence of my existence and winning the most important thing in my world. I revelled in the camaraderie of like-minded drivers, each of us aspiring to beat the other but joyfully sharing the thrill of competition. We were a happy, fluid band of fellow travellers who gathered at tracks across two continents to hone our skills amid shifting rivalries. As seasons passed, I began to learn what might be wrong with this glamorous life. Racing drivers often were killed, many my peers and some my friends. Over the ensuing years, the thinning ranks of racers of my generation proved heart-breaking.

When the late journalist and driver Denise McCluggage wrote her memoir, she titled it *By Brooks Too Broad For Leaping* from a poem by A.E. Housman. While Denise's reminiscences speak eloquently about the companionship and intimacy of international racing, her title hints at a thread of mortality that weaves through her stories about the racers she befriended, much as the same, sad filament wove its way through my career.

With rue my heart is laden
For golden friends I had,
For many a rose-lipt maiden
And many a lightfoot lad.
By brooks too broad for leaping
The lightfoot boys are laid;
The rose-lipt girls lie sleeping
In fields where roses fade.

Racing's propensity for abrupt tragedy forces reasonable people to ask the obvious question. Why *did* these lightfoot boys, me among them, choose to participate in a sport that was so demonstrably dangerous?

ABOVE At Mallory Park for the 1967 Guards International Trophy race driving David Bridges' Formula 2 Brabham BT16, which I raced all over Europe.
Brian Redman collection

LEFT To stay competitive, David Bridges traded his team's year-old Brabham BT16 for a new Lola T100 in mid-1967. Here I am with the Lola at Brands Hatch in August, following John Surtees in his T100 and Jackie Oliver in a Lotus 48.
Mike Hayward Collection

CHAPTER 3
The original Nürburgring

The Nürburgring is a colossus of a circuit in Germany's Eifel Mountains and the home of motorsport writ large. In 1925, when the town of Nürburg's pioneer racing enthusiasts decided to create a new track, they may have looked to the Targa Florio, Europe's most important endurance event, as the model for a proper racing venue. Compared with the Targa's (then) 67-mile ramble through the Sicilian countryside, the Nürburgers' concept for a new 19-mile course looked downright temperate. Whatever inspired the original Nürburgring, it and its successor variants have hosted motorcycle and car racing events for the better part of 100 years, and the largest and most historic section of the track still offers long-distance racing today. The Nürburgring's many days of champagne and podiums aside, the circuit may be best known for defying generations of safety crusaders by remaining scandalously original.

As conceived, the Nürburgring was composed of two loops capable of being used together or separately. The 14.2-mile *Nordschleife* (North Loop) was normally reserved for high-speed racing with the 4.8-mile *Sudschleife* (South Loop) relegated to small events. Rudolf Caracciola won the inaugural race for Mercedes-Benz in 1927 and this marque's famous Silver Arrows cars went on to dominate Grand Prix racing during the period 1934–39.

When racing resumed post-war at the Nürburgring, the guns of the nearby Ardennes still resonated in local memory and the detritus from the Battle of the Bulge lay rusting in fallow fields. It says much about the character of Nürburg's citizens that, just two years after Germany's defeat, they convened an international motorcycle race meeting, and followed up with a non-championship Formula 2 event in 1950. Under the circumstances, they can be forgiven for awarding their Formula 2 race the honorary title 'German Grand Prix', but World Championship Formula 1 came quickly enough. For all but three of the years between 1951 and 1976, the Nürburgring was home to a legitimate Formula 1 German Grand Prix.

In the late 1960s and early 1970s, the seeds of racing safety had yet to germinate but even then drivers were beginning to shy away from the dicier venues. In response, the good Nürburgers began whittling away at the *Nordschleife* to lure back lost international events. By 1970 the *Nordschleife* was shortened to 12.9 miles, bumps were smoothed (a little), bushes removed (some), corners straightened (here and there), jumps modified (though not all), steel barriers added (often quite close to the track) and a chicane was introduced before the main straight. In 1971 these nods towards prudence did indeed seduce Formula 1 to return to the *Nordschleife* following

OPPOSITE A hectic driver change during the 1969 Nürburgring 1,000Kms, me scrambling out after a crucial stint and Seppi Siffert jumping in to drive to the finish.
LAT

a one-year sojourn at Hockenheim. The German
Grand Prix remained at the Nürburgring for the
next five years until the horror of the 1976 race
ended that accord forever.

This tragic race features pivotally in *Rush*, Ron
Howard's film dramatising the rivalry between
James Hunt and Niki Lauda for the 1976 Formula
1 World Championship. *Rush*'s depiction unfolds
from the true facts of a potential Lauda-led
driver boycott that, if successful, would have
aborted the German Grand Prix, and the film's
narrative hinges on the subsequent spectacle of
fire and mayhem.

At a drivers' meeting during practice, Lauda
– the reigning Formula 1 World Champion as
well as the track's record holder – attempted to
convince his fellow drivers not to race, arguing
that he was willing to take a 20 per cent chance
on not surviving, but no more. He contended
that the *Nordschleife* in the rain was a high-stakes
gamble. Niki accepted the track's length and
its myriad corners, known components of the
Nürburgring's challenge, and normally he had

no difficulty with racing in the rain. His fear
was that decades of intermittent resurfacing had
created a patchwork of asphalt surfaces, each
with unique and widely varying levels of grip
when wet, resulting in unpredictable changes
in traction that would turn normal wet-weather
racing into something senselessly treacherous.
Prophetically, the other drivers, led by Hunt,
voted against Lauda.

For reasons never known, Lauda crashed
on the second lap of the race just before the
fast *Bergwerk* kink and his fuel-filled car
erupted in an inferno. The fire consumed his
car, incinerated his ears, ravaged his face and
cauterised his lungs. For precious minutes no
track marshals were even aware the accident
had happened and Lauda would have perished
but for the bravery of four drivers who stopped
to drag him out of the flames – American Brett
Lunger, Italian Arturo Merzario, Englishman
Guy Edwards and Austrian Harald Ertl.
Although the circuit's officials had preened to
the press about their new Porsche 911 rescue

car, they were unable to muster even the basic number of marshals to man this vast track, nor could they provide any specialised vehicles capable of quickly extinguishing a fire. How poignant that the driver who wanted the race abandoned was rescued by four competitors who had denied his pleas for safety. Ironically, Lauda's crash succeeded where his attempted boycott failed – in 1977 the German Grand Prix moved to Hockenheim.

The *Nordschleife* carried on, though Formula 1's departure had as much to do with its growing popularity as safety. Racing was televised internationally, and the 'Ring's vast acreage demanded more cameras and crews than were practical. In the late 1970s the *Sudschleife* was cannibalised to make way for a new, boring Grand Prix-friendly circuit that unfairly hijacked the Nürburgring name. Yet the anachronistic *Nordschleife* remained to uphold the Nürburgring's legend as the tamer of smug bravery and the winnower of minor talents. In the current era of neutered tracks, cramped corners

and Brazil-sized run-off areas, the *Nordschleife* continues to tempt brave drivers to accept its risky challenge. Certainly today's sports racing cars are stronger, better engineered and safer than those I drove in the 1960s and 1970s, but the track is no shorter, the corners no fewer and the barriers no further away.

Today, for about €30 a lap, 'Nürburgring taxis', motorcycles and specialised machines fly around at racing speeds while lumbering tourist coaches and family rental cars circulate as languidly as on a Sunday drive. As a result as many as 12 enthusiasts succumb to mortal accidents every year. The argument goes that it isn't the track that kills them, it's their own hubris.

Learning the Nürburgring – 1967

In 1967 I went to the Nürburgring to share Peter Sutcliffe's Ford GT40 in the 1,000Kms race. Learning the *Nordschleife* by oneself is not the task of a moment, and it was normal for my car owner and co-driver to want a full share of track time. Whilst standing in the pits during a pre-race open

ABOVE Despite a pit-stop for replacement goggles, I hauled my works Ferrari into fourth place in the 1968 *Eifelrennen*, run on the 4.8-mile *Sudschleife*. Taken after the delay, this photo shows me wearing Jacky Ickx's dark goggles.
LAT

Ickx, Piers Courage and Kurt Ahrens. We started the race in that order.

As I passed the pits for the second lap, Kurt dropped a wheel into the dirt and showered me with stones, hammering my car's windscreen and shattering my goggles. Unable to see, I flung one hand in the air to warn cars behind that I was stopping and drove slowly around to the pits.

'*You must go on!*' shouted Mauro Forghieri, Ferrari's team manager.

'*My goggles are smashed,*' I yelled back.

'*Wear your spares,*' he screamed. I had none.

Forghieri promptly fetched a set of goggles from Ickx's bag so I could get back to racing. Unfortunately, these were tinted dark green for use in brilliant sunlight and not the murkiness of the Eifel forests. I was now in last place and conscious of the fact that Ferrari didn't accept excuses for poor performance. Despite being half blind in deep shadows cast by the surrounding trees, I suspended all good judgment and drove as if possessed – passing, passing, passing. By the end of the race, I was closing on the leaders by more than two seconds a lap and finished a creditable fourth behind Chris Irwin, Kurt Ahrens and Derek Bell. Ferrari recognised my tenacity and especially took note that I had set a new lap record.

Ford GT40 – 1968

The following month I was back at the Nürburgring with JW Automotive to drive a Gulf Ford GT40 in the 1,000Kms, paired with Jacky Ickx. On Sunday morning I felt that I still didn't know the track well enough, as I had done only 10 laps in practice, so I decided to caution John Wyer that this might spoil Jacky's chances of a win. He responded by putting Ickx with Paul Hawkins, David Hobbs' regular co-driver, relegating David and me to the second car. The race was run in the Nürburgring's usual wet/dry conditions, with Jacky and Paul finishing third overall (and winning their class) and David and me taking a respectable sixth.

'*Redman, that's the last time I'm taking your advice,*' Wyer huffed. '*If Ickx and you had driven together, we might have won.*'

practice session, a BMW 2002 drew up, the driver obviously noticing a new face on the circuit and recognising the expression of a lost man. Kindly, he asked if I'd like to familiarise myself by taking a lap round the track with him. Thus Stirling Moss became my Nürburgring driving instructor, an acknowledged master conducting a master class.

I had to cancel my 1967 Nürburgring début when I learned that my father had suffered a seizure. I left immediately to be with him and am gratified that I did. He died a week later.

Formula 2 Ferrari – 1968

Early in April 1968 Ferrari invited me to test at the *Autodromo di Modena*, some 30 minutes from the Maranello factory. Typically, the conspiratorial Italian engineers never shared my lap times with me but I must have been sufficiently quick for the team to offer me a Formula 2 drive at the Nürburgring later that month in an older Dino 166, alongside team leader Jacky Ickx in the latest version. My début was in the *Eifelrennen* on the 4.8-mile *Sudschleife* and I qualified fourth behind

Maybe, but no matter; we were the lucky ones. In practice, Chris Irwin, the winner of my 1968 Formula 2 race with Ferrari, was driving the Alan Mann Ford F3L when he took off at the *Flugplatz* jump and went end over end, suffering severe head injuries.

Chris Irwin was 26 years old. He survived but never raced again.

Porsche versus Ferrari

My top-level *Nordschleife* drives were in sports racers and split between Ferrari and Porsche, rivals whose racing histories are legend. For Ferrari, I drove a 312PB and for Porsche a 908/02 and 908/03. Because of Ferrari's and Porsche's huge fan bases and the substantial funding they placed behind winning, drivers dreamed of joining their factory teams.

Coldly commercial manufacturers both, they sought racing victories to inspire the fantasies that spurred the sales of their production cars. Unsurprisingly, the personalities of these two very different manufacturers reflected

their national stereotypes: Porsche logical and organised, Ferrari creative and emotional. In racing terms, however, Ferrari and Porsche were cut from the same cloth. The greatest love of both managements was for their precious racing cars, and their drivers were there to take chances and win, thereby demonstrating their marque's speed, reliability and engineering superiority. If, unhappily, things went pear-shaped, the car could be repaired and, well, there was always another driver eager to move on up.

The Porsche 917 – 1969

In 1969 Porsche was spoiling for the new 917 to make its début and astonish the entire motorsport world. The company's decision makers – led by the imposing motorsport director Ferdinand Piëch – felt that it might be a good idea to prove the 917 at the Nürburgring.

After each of the ten factory drivers had inexplicably turned down this 'opportunity', accusations of faint drivers' hearts and even cowardice were bandied about the Stuttgart

ABOVE For the 1968 1,000Kms I had been due to share this GT40 with Jacky Ickx, but stepped aside in favour of the more experienced Paul Hawkins, a decision later regretted by John Wyer. *Ford*

OPPOSITE Surrounded by trees on the way to sixth place with the Gulf GT40 in the 1968 Nürburgring 1,000Kms. *LAT*

boardroom. If wisdom is cowardice, then it seemed to have infected Porsche's entire platoon of professionals. The company then turned to privateers David Piper and Frank Gardner who, against their better judgement, were persuaded to take on the onerous task of racing a 917 at the Nürburgring. Frank sent me a note describing his initial conversation regarding the race with Huschke von Hanstein, Porsche communications executive and former team manager.

> Frank: '*What about Jo Siffert?*'
> Huschke: '*He's in the hospital.*'
> Frank: '*Brian Redman?*'
> Huschke: '*He's in the hospital.*'
> Frank: '*Gerhard Mitter?*'
> Huschke: '*He's in the hospital too.*'

Gardner, who did the lion's share of the driving, concluded his note with this statement:

'I decided it was a lot easier to settle for what the thing would do and still stay on the road than be a little bit more heroic and throw it all into the undergrowth… It was an animal, structurally wrong. The chassis flexed. You could have jacked up the windscreen wiper and put a new car under it, but even then you'd doubt the windscreen wiper! I've always said that the Nürburgring was the circuit that Hitler designed for Jewish racing drivers, but to be there in a Porsche that didn't handle was an experience. You had 600hp and 10-inch wide wheels, and the track was wet. It was a mess!'

Gardner and Piper qualified in 8 minutes 35.8 seconds, while Jo 'Seppi' Siffert in our car set a time of 8 minutes dead – a huge differential. Still, they did an incredible job to finish at all, and their eighth place (four laps or 57 miles behind Seppi and me) should be regarded as a driving triumph.

My Nürburgring ring – 1969

Having escaped the early 917 duties, I went to the Nürburgring for the 1,000Kms of 1969 to race a 908/02 with Siffert as part of Porsche's five-car onslaught upon that year's International Championship for Makes.

After practice, when the track was reopened to the public, Seppi volunteered to share his

ABOVE Flying at *Flugplatz* during practice for the 1969 Nürburgring 1,000Kms in the lovely Porsche 908/02.
Grand Prix Library

RIGHT In sports car races of my era there was an immense gulf between the slowest and fastest cars on the track. This class-winning Porsche 911 was one minute 45 seconds a lap slower than our 908/02.
Porsche-Werkfoto

Nürburgring secrets with me, demonstrating
corners in his Porsche 911S road car. At a tight
left-hander after the *Fuchsröhre*, some dozen or
so spectators were standing beside the track,
clearly anticipating action. Seppi and I stopped
to learn what piqued their interest. On cue,
with a tremendous wailing of tortured tyres, a
Volkswagen driver left his braking too late, flew
through a hedge and plunged down a steep hill,
all to the unbridled merriment of the spectators,
who guffawed and slapped their *lederhosen*.

Originally, Seppi and I were paired in a
Flunder, Porsche's new 908/02 variant that
observers thought resembled an Atlantic flounder
owing to its flattened shape. Stuttgart had
designed this more aerodynamic bodywork after
noticing that the open-top Matra and Ferrari
spyders could achieve higher straight-line speeds
than the standard 908/02. Two of the team's
Flunders, however, crashed in practice – Siffert in
ours, Vic Elford in another – so a standard 908/02
was borrowed from Porsche Salzburg for Jo and
me to race.

At the first pit-stop I took over from Seppi, who had pulled out a small lead. At about the same time, Pedro Rodriguez replaced Chris Amon in the factory Ferrari 312P that Pedro had qualified a scant one-hundredth of a second slower than Seppi in our Porsche. Many expected Pedro to romp off into the distance but, instead, I pulled out a minute-and-a-half lead over the Ferrari to take the win. At the prize-giving, urged on by Seppi, the organisers awarded me one of the coveted Nürburgring rings, an honour given rarely and only for exceptional drives. I wear it proudly.

The 1970 Nürburgring 1,000Kms

Porsche fielded a dominant juggernaut for the Nürburgring 1,000Kms of 1970, using the light and nimble eight-cylinder 908/03 as it was better suited to that complex circuit than the bigger and more powerful 12-cylinder 917K. Essentially, the race was a Porsche shoot-out between our two JW Automotive 908/03s and those of Porsche Salzburg. John Wyer's team may have been the official factory operation but, as we ruefully

learned, Porsche Salzburg was the ultimate family enterprise.

The owner of the Porsche Salzburg team was nominally Louise Piëch, who was Porsche royalty. She was the daughter of Ferdinand Porsche and married to Anton Piëch, who ran a Porsche factory during the Second World War. Originally his plant was to have manufactured the *Kraft durch Freude-Wagen* (KdF-wagen), Adolf Hitler's 'Strength Through Joy Car', later to be called the Volkswagen Beetle, but during his four-year tenure the factory's output was primarily military. Louise also happened to be the mother of Porsche's racing director, Ferdinand Piëch, at that time the very person to whom Wyer reported. We all marvelled at how an elegant, elderly woman like Louise found the enthusiasm to field a major racing team.

These 908/03s filled the four top spots on the grid. My teammate, Jo Siffert, snatched pole position with a very quick lap of 7 minute 43 seconds, a full 17 seconds faster than his previous year's pole time in the earlier 908/02. Tragically,

A lap of the Nürburgring

Share seven minutes with me in my open-top Porsche 908/03 of 1970. Since it would try your patience (and my memory) if I were to describe all 171 corners, I'll condense this lap into *Nordschleife* highlights.

The Nürburgring's first turn was deceptively easy. After the start/finish line, I flew through the long right-hand *Südkehre* (south curve) without a problem and accelerated past the back of the pits where, for me, the challenges really began. Onward into the 90-degree left-hander followed by an immediate sharp left, then downhill to a right/left/right sequence through *Hatzenbach* and *Hocheichen* – the greatest concentration of bends on the track.

A short straight preceded the *Flugplatz* jump, this apt name taken from a nearby glider airfield and not, as most presume, from flying through the air in a racing car. Throttle to the floor with the road rising, I stayed right for the blind left-hander at the top of the hill and then plunged down again to tiptoe through the fast

Schwedenkreuz and line up on the left before braking into *Aremberg*. Using the entire road, I accelerated hard down the *Fuchsröhre*, straightening the bends as much as possible by clipping the kerbs on each side. The road dipped a bit, then rose into a right-hander followed quickly by a slow, tricky, blind left-hander and then an immediate blind turn to the right.

After a short, fast straight, a rapid left led to two quick rights that left the car pointing downhill. This was the start of the fast, sloping *Adenauer Forst* section where the track wended its way through a series of left/right turns before passing the only vehicle-access gate on the entire course. After *Adenau*, I accelerated uphill through *Metzgesfeld* into *Kallenhard* and then the *Drei-Fach* and *Breidscheid* sweepers that led to the kink before *Bergwerk*, infamous now for Niki Lauda's terrible accident in 1976.

Bergwerk was followed by the uphill *2 Kilometre Kesselchen* straight and *10.5 Kilometre Jump*, which was

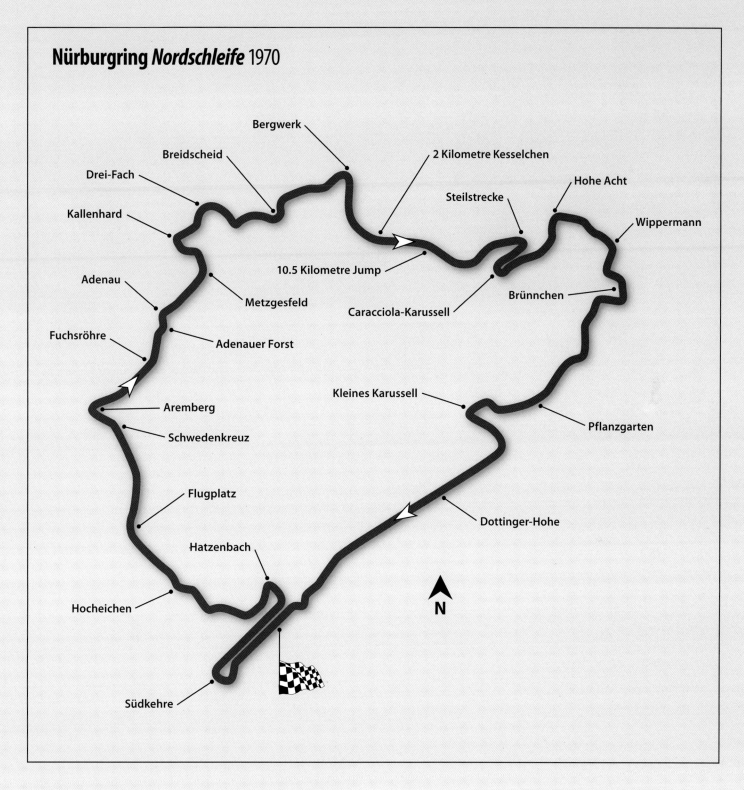

Nürburgring *Nordschleife* 1970

Bergwerk
Breidscheid
Drei-Fach
Kallenhard
2 Kilometre Kesselchen
Steilstrecke
Hohe Acht
Wippermann
Adenau
10.5 Kilometre Jump
Metzgesfeld
Brünnchen
Fuchsröhre
Caracciola-Karussell
Adenauer Forst
Aremberg
Kleines Karussell
Schwedenkreuz
Pflanzgarten
Flugplatz
Hatzenbach
Dottinger-Hohe
Hocheichen
Südkehre

N

taken flat out in top gear, a moment of focused concentration demanding a perfect landing, tyres pointing straight ahead. Next came the right-hander *Steilstrecke*, then the banked *Caracciola-Karussell*, the corner that Jackie Stewart said was easy if you aimed at the tallest tree. Then I turned right at *Hohe Acht*, the highest point on the circuit, right again at *Wippermann*, taking flight at *Brünnchen* and once again

at *Pflanzgarten* before whipping through the *Kleines Karussell* (little carousel). Almost there now – just a right into *Dottinger-Hohe* and a chance to rest on the main straight, leading back to the start/finish line.

The *Nordschleife* was and is the most physically exhausting track in the world and nearly equal to the mental demands of the original Spa.

ABOVE A study in pit-
lane preparation during
practice for the 1970
1,000Kms: Siffert is in
our 908/03, I'm alongside
and team manager David
Yorke is beside me (Gulf
jacket); mechanic Ritchie
Bray is kneeling by the
car. The 'P' identified a
prototype; sports cars
carried an 'S'.
LAT

a 908/02 featured in a terrible accident during
practice. Hans Laine, a young Finnish driver
paired with the experienced Dutchman Gijs van
Lennep, lost control on the fast and undulating
main straight and the car flipped, crashed and
burned. Drivers stopped to help but they had no
fire extinguishers and those used by the marshals
were no match for the conflagration. Laine was
as fresh in his marriage as he was in his racing
career, leaving a young wife and a daughter of
five months. His co-driver, van Lennep, recently
wrote to me about the accident.

*'It was my turn to scrub the tyres for the race after
a successful practice. Laine drove off one spoiler at the
front left in the last practice lap. I did the scrubbing,
21-km! Came on the straight with a mistral head wind.
I went over the first hump and the car went to the right
instead of straight on and became light, so I lift my foot
off the gas completely. (Scrubbing was done!) I came
in, Dunlop checked the tyre pressure – 40 pounds!
Instead of 20 pounds. Laine said, 'The tyres are not
scrubbed right. It is my turn and I do another lap.' So
he did, now with the right pressures. Hans came onto*

*the straight and must have kept full gas and flipped like
a speedboat and burst into flames. Hans could not get
out. A terrible accident and totally unnecessary.'*

The 1970 season was particularly cruel at
the Nürburgring. There were 16 deaths, Laine
among them.

Hans Laine was 25 years old.

Seppi made a good start in the race until a
slow pit-stop dropped us to third. Now it was
my turn. I caught Kurt Ahrens for second place
and closed on the leader, Leo Kinnunen in the
team's sister car, and sat immediately behind
him as we approached the *10.5 Kilometre Jump* in
top gear. Anyone can attack a jump and make
a racing car fly; landing safely is what tests a
driver's skills. When the front wheels first touch
the track's surface, they must do so together and
be pointed perfectly straight or the car will lurch
sideways uncontrollably. Leo, who may have been
distracted by me in his mirrors or by the loss of
his friend Hans Laine, took flight at a slight angle
and I was an eyewitness to the developing crash.
Like a shot, Kinnunen's car went off to our left

and up onto the trackside bank, which launched it airborne back across the circuit. I cringed as the Porsche and Leo sailed directly over my head, missing my helmet by inches. Miraculously and thankfully, neither Leo nor I were hurt. He was out of the race. I carried on.

At half distance I was in the lead, ahead of Ahrens, when I noticed the oil pressure start to fluctuate. I headed for the pits and handed the car over to Jo while the mechanics topped up the oil. Then there was a second bad omen: the engine took a long time to fire. Seppi returned to the track but only briefly before the engine seized. Our race was over and a seemingly certain win had evaporated.

Victory went to Kurt Ahrens and Vic Elford in one of the Porsche Salzburg 908/03s, which, miraculously, showed no sign of lubrication problems. Many years later, I learned the truth from Klaus Bischof, a Porsche Salzburg mechanic in 1971 and later the manager of the Porsche Museum in Stuttgart. Klaus revealed that Ferdinand Piëch had fitted the two Salzburg

908/03s with oversize oil tanks as a precaution against just such a problem. I still find it remarkable that Piëch chose to hide this insider advantage from John Wyer and his own 'factory' team. Blood, it seems, is thicker than oil.

Back to Ferrari

As I became increasingly aware of the poor odds against a racer's longevity, I tried and failed to retire in South Africa and returned to racing in the spring of 1971 only to suffer a devastating accident in the Targa Florio. Painful as my recovery was, the same year's loss of my teammates and friends, Jo Siffert and Pedro Rodriguez, hurt even more. I returned to racing as soon as possible with moderate success but hoped to resume with a major team despite dark thoughts and low expectations. Suddenly my luck brightened.

In November 1971 Ferrari invited me to share a one-off drive in a Ferrari 312PB with Clay Regazzoni at the Kyalami Nine Hours. The team had run the 312PB in almost all the year's races, setting fastest laps and frequently leading, but

LEFT JW Automotive mechanics inspect and refuel our 908/03, I wisely step out while the filler caps are open, and Seppi looks on.
Gulf

LEFT Three weeks after our victory in the Spa 1,000Kms, Arturo Merzario and I finished second at the Nürburgring in our Ferrari 312PB, the class car of 1972.
LAT

never winning. Team leaders Mario Andretti and Jacky Ickx were issued with a new car whilst Clay and I drove an old one. As luck would have it, they suffered a minor problem early in the race and Clay and I won, with Mario and Jacky second. In that era, race wins were celebrated in uninhibited ways but perhaps it is better to draw a veil around most of the party – except the prank that capped the evening.

The rooms at the Kyalami Ranch hotel were separate 'rondavels', round huts with straw roofs. Mario retired just after midnight but, after another hour of full-throttle enjoyment, Clay reasoned that the proper way to end the occasion was to fling a lit newspaper through Mario's door. This was the lesser of two bad judgements. The irate resident who exploded from the burning hut turned out not to be Mario but another hotel guest, and not a race fan. The police were called. Happily, investigations proved inconclusive, but the following day Clay had to be smuggled out of Johannesburg.

Ferrari's 1972 assault on the World Championship for Makes was comprehensive.

ABOVE John Wyer's Gulf Mirage was never really a match for our Ferraris during 1972, but someone forgot to tell Derek Bell – who initially led us at the Nürburgring.
LAT

The team employed nine top-class drivers: Mario Andretti, Jacky Ickx, Ronnie Peterson, Carlos Pace, Tim Schenken, Carlos Reutemann, Clay Regazzoni, Arturo Merzario and me. Schedules were arranged so that we alternated in six identical cars, three of which were fielded in a race while the other three from the previous race were returned to the factory for preparation for the next outing. The 312PB was pretty much a Formula 1 car with bodywork and only Jo Bonnier's Cosworth-powered Lola T280s could match its speed. Other significant contenders in the series were compromised. The Alfa Romeo T33/3s proved to be overweight and John Wyer's new Cosworth-powered Mirage was a late entry, forced to play catch-up for most of the season.

That year's Nürburgring 1,000Kms was held in true Eifel weather, cold and blustery with on-and-off rain. The Gulf Mirage surprised us by suddenly joining the hunt and actually leading until its engine expired. Regazzoni, who was sharing with Ickx, crashed their 312PB at *Hohe Acht*, leaving Ferrari's other two entries to finish

1–2, Peterson and Schenken in the winning car followed by Merzario and me.

Arturo, thin and delicate in his red python driving shoes and white cowboy hat, was as nimble socially as he was on the track. On the way to dinner one evening, Regazzoni and I knocked on Arturo's hotel room door. '*Ciao*,' he called, which we surmised was an invitation to enter. To our amazement, the undersized Arturo was happily bedded between two Viking-proportioned damsels, both unabashed professionals. Clay examined the scene thoughtfully, then enquired, '*Wata-a-you do wis Arturo, gurls? E ees so leetle.*' One of the ladies giggled, '*Oh, ja wohl: sehr leetle, but sehr güt!*' Clay and I went on to a celibate dinner, with our conversation unusually muted.

The 1972 German Grand Prix

At the end of July 1972 I was back at the Nürburgring for the German Grand Prix in a McLaren M19A. It was my third, and last, appearance that year with McLaren's

Yardley-sponsored Formula 1 team, standing in for Peter Revson when he was in America for IndyCar commitments.

There's a short loop behind the pits where a driver can warm tyres in practice before beginning his 14.2-mile journey, and I did exactly that. The tyres, however, decided otherwise, causing me to hurtle through Turn 1 sideways and hit the barrier hard. It took an all-nighter for the mechanics to make repairs, but the crash damaged my confidence as well as the McLaren. With the previous year's Targa Florio in mind and the near-mortal consequences of racing a suspect car, I pedalled around in the race without much heart to a lacklustre fifth place. It's the only time in my career that I remember doing so.

Oh, for the possibility of reliving one's past. Looking back, I should have overcome my concerns and carried on with passion because I loved the Nürburgring and knew every inch of it by heart. With proper effort, I could have had a podium finish – third easily, second perhaps. My Ferrari teammate Jacky Ickx had no

such anxiety, accomplishing a rare 'grand slam' weekend – pole position with a record qualifying lap, an unbroken lead from start to finish, and fastest lap of the race.

Winning again with Ferrari

There's no doubt that Enzo Ferrari wanted to defend Ferrari's World Championship for Makes title in 1973. The *Commendatore* was a driven man, relentless in his ambitions for the *Scuderia*. This year, it wasn't the technologies of others that challenged Ferrari's superiority but workers' strikes that severely cut into the finances of corporate parent FIAT. The budget for endurance racing was slim and there was no money at all to develop the cars.

Without technical progress, the 312PBs – so invincible in 1972 – were at once inferior to the Matra-Simca MS670B in both power and handling. The only change to the Ferrari for 1973 was a much longer tail that made the car difficult to drive, causing it to switch from understeer to oversteer. No budget meant no solutions, so we lived all

ABOVE In 1973, I was back in the Ferrari 312PB and looking appropriately comfortable as Jacky Ickx and engineer Giacomo Caliri confer. *Getty Images/ Rainer Schlegelmilch*

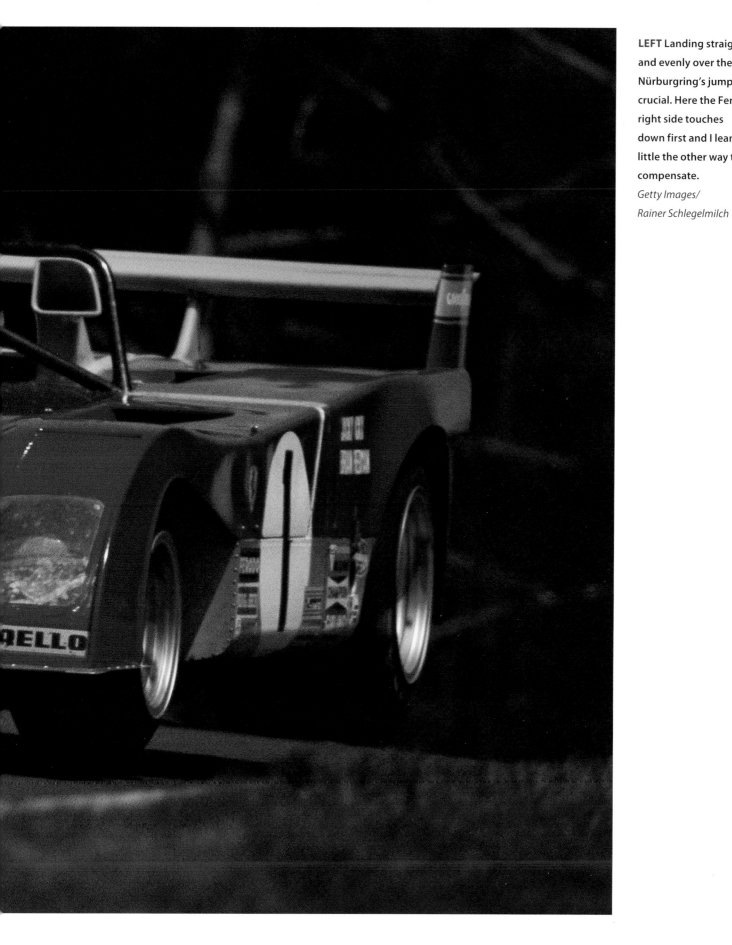

LEFT Landing straight and evenly over the Nürburgring's jumps is crucial. Here the Ferrari's right side touches down first and I lean a little the other way to compensate.
Getty Images/ Rainer Schlegelmilch

LEFT Mid-race pit stops are all commotion. With refuelling done and tyres changed, I'm about to lower my visor and join the 1973 1,000Kms while my partner Jacky Ickx, still helmeted on the right, can relax – a little.
LAT

season with this disquieting understeer/oversteer combination. How Mr Ferrari must have suffered, humbled in long-distance racing and forced by financial need to skip several Formula 1 Grands Prix.

For the Nürburgring 1,000Kms, Jacky Ickx and I were partners again, and Carlos Pace and Arturo Merzario shared the team's second 312PB. Then, as now, Ferrari was not shy about team orders. If, by half distance, one pair of drivers led and the other trailed in second place, positions were to be maintained, thereby eliminating the chance that battling teammates might put both of the Ferrari factory entries out of the race. With Jacky cruising comfortably ahead, Arturo was shown the 'Hold Position' pit board but, astonishingly, chose to blast past into the lead, doing so directly in front of the pits. When he came in on the next lap for fuel and the requisite driver change, he simply refused to get out of the car.

'*Fuori, fuori!*' shouted team manager Giacomo Caliri, '*Out, out!*' With Merzario clenching the steering wheel and refusing to budge, Caliri

ABOVE Compared with 1972, Ferrari faced much stronger opposition during 1973, so my win with Jacky Ickx at the Nürburgring that year was especially satisfying.
LAT

ABOVE Jacky and I celebrate our win with second-placed Carlos Pace, whose co-driver Arturo Merzario refused to mount the podium in protest at his treatment by Ferrari.
LAT

BELOW Mechanical problems plagued my one-off drive with Arturo Merzario for the works Alfa Romeo team in the 1974 Nürburgring 1,000Kms, resulting in a lowly ninth place.
Getty Images/Rainer Schlegelmilch

ordered the mechanics to prise his fingers off the rim and hoist him out of the car, restoring Merzario and Pace to the race in second place, behind Jacky and me in the winning car. A furious Arturo refused to mount the podium to receive his award.

Basta

The first of my Nürburgring farewells (plural, taking a cue from the serial retirements of opera singers) came in 1979, driving a Gelo Racing Porsche 935 with Henri Pescarolo. It was an uneventful race – as much as that can be said of any Nürburgring 1,000Kms – but our third place was very satisfying. My second farewell came the following year, driving with John Paul Sr in his Porsche 935 JLP-2, partnered by Preston Henn. We retired with mechanical problems – not the worst way for me to conclude a relationship with this daunting circuit. In any case, I was done with the Nürburgring forever, grateful to have been spared.

Jackie Stewart famously called the *Nordschleife* 'green hell' and observed that it was '*the most difficult, most treacherous and most demanding*' of all

tracks. '*Anybody who claims he liked the circuit,*' said Jackie, '*is either telling a fib or didn't go fast enough. When I get back to the pits and take a deep breath, I am pleased to be home.*'

Peter Sutcliffe warned me about the Nürburgring's dangers during practice for our aborted 1967 1,000Kms. He pressed two cautions into my mind: '*Brian, first I want you to remember that this is my car. Second, have you seen all those little bushes around the track? Underneath each of them is 100 feet of solid trunk…*' He wasn't exaggerating; the drop-offs were that severe.

For me to be a three-time Nürburgring winner was a great privilege and a record of which I am proud. From the immunity of retirement, I can claim retrospectively that I loved everything about the *Nordschleife* – the fantastic history, the blind corners, the leaps, the hedges, the changeable weather, the enormous crowds and, especially, Hotel Zum Wilden Schwein restaurant's delicious pork chops and fine German beer.

The ultimate *Nordschleife* triumph was Stefan Bellof's still-unequalled record of 6 minutes 11.13

seconds set in a Porsche 956 during qualifying for the 1983 1,000Kms. Stefan was the rising star of racing, appealingly tall, polite, happy and astonishingly quick. He dominated the 1984 World Endurance Championship. Just one year later, in a foolhardy attempt to pass Jacky Ickx's works Porsche 956 on the outside at Spa's *Eau Rouge*, Bellof crashed Porsche stalwart Walter Brun's 956, suffering massive internal injuries.

Stefan Bellof was 28 years old.

CHAPTER 4
The mind of a driver

Between 1965 and 1975, driver deaths were common and racing as a trade made 'living in the moment' a career precondition. It was as if an unseen sniper haunted the tracks and picked off random victims without warning, unsparing of veterans and even legends. Every now and then, a death would occur that gave us pause – 'I never thought that could happen to Jimmy Clark' – but then we'd bottle up our fears and go back to racing.

In that era, the statistics drivers cared about were lap records and podium finishes, not the odds of being killed in their pursuit. No driver I knew tallied up peer deaths or calculated his chances of survival, but we were not naive. Crashes killed; we saw it, we knew it and simply made a conscious decision to ignore it. This wilful suspension of reality was thoroughly institutionalised across the entire racing community: drivers, wives, girlfriends, engineers and team managers – well, maybe less among team managers. I wasn't the only driver in denial. We all shared the same universal bias toward a single preposterous conceit: 'Him, maybe, but not me.'

There was another factor lurking in the background – the practical side of mortal events. Drivers may die but cars are repaired or replaced and racing teams keep going. For up-and-coming drivers and veterans out of a job, each fatality

was a career opportunity – a more prestigious team, a faster car, a fatter cheque. At one time or another, every major driver benefited shamelessly from a colleague's death, including those of teammates and friends. I did so several times. My defence against the morbidity of racing was to keep my friendships few and selective, and honour my vow never to attend drivers' funerals. My protection from thinking too carefully was to spend as much time as possible in a racing car, where the urgent mechanics of competition kept me safe from brooding about unpleasant possibilities. Once I was engaged with a car, irrelevant thoughts vanished, including those involving risk. I suspect that I wasn't alone in this psychological exercise.

Driving fast is both a craft and an art. It takes total concentration to keep a temperamental racing car on the knife edge of the laws of physics and it takes athletic stamina to sustain the mandatory hours of intense effort. On an empty track, all good drivers can set successive lap times that fall within a few tenths of a second, but doing so in close competition takes another level of mental and physical dexterity – fast hands directed by fast thinking reflecting fast judgements. Successful racers aim to establish control – of the tyres' available grip, of the pace required to be a contender, and of their adversaries' commitment. A strategic driver can

OPPOSITE Before a race a professional is composed, focusing his mind on all of the components it takes to win – strong driving to be sure but also car management and teamwork.
BMW

slow the tempo of a race by running comfortably in third, timing his charge for the chequered flag, or he can crush an opponent's confidence with a tough overtaking move and then push hard to open up a discouraging gap.

Winning comes from wanting, and no one wanted to win more than I did. I confess that winning was the best feeling I ever had, in any part of my life. It was the narcotic I craved and I willingly risked health and viability to taste it. When the car, the track and I were perfectly aligned, the sensation of completeness was so exhilarating that I craved more of those addictive moments. As clichéd as these driving platitudes have become, 'feeling in the groove' or 'in a zone' or 'at one with the car' were heady experiences when authentic. This was especially true when competing against the world's best drivers in the world's fastest racing cars on the world's most challenging tracks.

Naturally, there are differences among the top professionals of every era, but in mine it was rare that any single driver dominated all aspects of the sport. If one excelled in the rain, another might be better at dealing with traffic; the master of pre-race set-up might be less effective at getting the most out of a compromised car. Over a season, these differences averaged out and, on balance, the variations among my professional peers were relatively small.

Any reasonably coordinated person can be trained to drive around a track at 90 per cent of a car's potential, and every race concludes with a group of modestly skilled *aficionados* contentedly finishing at the back of the field, usually repetitively so. The middle-of-the-pack finishers are skilled journeymen racers, some seriously fast 'gentlemen drivers' who have worked hard to master the mental and physical techniques of speed and who regularly out-pace the *aficionados*. The more prepared – those who train, care, push and risk – can perform quite well, occasionally even winning races.

Standing out above the most capable journeymen, however, is an extremely small class of drivers who rise to the level of paid

BELOW At the Brands Hatch 1,000Kms, Chris Amon's Ferrari 512 assisted me into an unintentional but substantial accident.
Getty Images/ Rainer Schlegelmilch

professionals. Plenty of time in racing cars helps, but talent helps even more. True pros may not always finish in front but they are always in the hunt, and need to be if they hope to make racing a living. Once or twice an era, a driver appears whose abilities are so sublime that they defy comprehension: Juan Manuel Fangio, Stirling Moss, Jim Clark, Ayrton Senna and Michael Schumacher (plus, perhaps, your omitted favourite). What intangible quality made those drivers exceptional will remain a mystery, but for competitors racing against them, their superiority was an everyday reality. Of course, even the titans of racing could be beaten, and were many times, but more often than not it was due to some constitutional inadequacy in that day's car rather than the superior performances of other drivers.

The racer's professional arc

I began racing because it was thrilling to learn that I could execute a difficult trick and do so at a high level. Things began to change as winning fostered my reputation and racing became my established career. Over time, the actuality of being a high-profile driver swelled in importance until it dominated my life and defined who I was. As the glamour years passed, racing turned from a sport into a trade, a means to sustain my family and support a middle-class life. My dream that a motorsport career might furnish Marion and me with a comfortable retirement proved to be delusional.

By the early 1970s I was growing disturbingly self-aware. Accidents and injuries happened with troubling regularity and the odds against longevity became impossible for me to ignore. Inevitably, there came a time when I could no longer deny that driving for a living had evolved into an increasingly uneasy proposition, and I even attempted retirement – but returned to racing within a few months. I knew it was a risky business but it was the only business I knew. Worse yet, I loved every minute I spent in a racing car and planned to compete forever. In the ethical conflict between racing and responsibility, racing always won.

Hemingway is supposed to have written,

'There are but three true sports – bullfighting, mountain climbing, and motor racing. All the rest are merely games.' This adage was probably penned by someone else, but the author's sly allegation raises a legitimate question: what makes this mugging of team and elite individual sports ring so plausibly true? The answer is self-evident. Errors in tennis, golf and football cause disappointment; errors in bullfighting, mountain climbing and motor racing threaten mortality. As a result, every climber, matador

ABOVE Racing at Spa was always an unsettling experience but with Marion's steady support and James on my knee, I appear to be supremely relaxed.
Brian Redman collection

and racing driver feels a little bit heroic.

Racing didn't suddenly become safe after 1976, but it definitely improved and continued to get better year by year. In my riskiest racing period, 1965 to 1975, hazards were omnipresent, yet I never knew a driver who sought out danger or believed crashes were inevitable. We existed as an elite community that revelled in the manifest benefits of our exotic craft: worldwide travel, the opiate of celebrity, easy companionship, and a life of episodic intensity in which our skills and commitment were constantly measured. The trajectories of our careers were determined by the tick of the team manager's stopwatch, a sponsor's willingness to fund, flattering commentary in the press and the shifting loyalties of fans.

Racing provided top drivers with a decent income in that era, but nothing like today's stratospheric returns. What kept us motivated was competitive success. We were rated continuously against each other by team managers, and we obsessively compared our performances with those of our teammates and our closest rivals. We coveted the respect of the drivers we most admired and gratefully tolerated those a level below. Among equals, competition genially simmered on and off the track. Mexico's great racer, Pedro Rodriguez, once offered me his highest compliment. *'Bree-an,'* he said, *'it was great to have a co-driver almost as fast as me.'*

Going fast

Pedro's ego wasn't as insufferable as it sounds. Every top driver believes he is the best because, in the right car on the right day, he probably is. Nothing makes a driver look more invincible than a racing car perfectly tuned for *that* track, on *that* day, in *those* specific conditions. Pundits have commented that drivers race the track as well as their competitors, and there's some truth in that. Chassis tuning, track surfaces, ambient temperatures, gear ratios, tyre compounds, spring rates, shock absorber settings and numerous other options offer a Rubik's Cube of tuning combinations, with each change affecting many of the other parameters.

There are lots of ways to get things a little bit wrong. Drivers and engineers review previous performances at the same track or a similar one and gauge the ambient differences. Weather, obedient only to chaos theory, makes many decisions sophisticated guesses. When a car is set up perfectly, the driver looks amazingly fast; when it's flawed, the same person is fated to appear to be off his game, not trying or less capable. There are times when a driver begins a race with the wrong set-up and changing conditions suddenly 'bring the track to him'. We tend not to remember these moments of good luck but complain bitterly when chance sends a race in the opposite direction.

Preparation can be a bit transcendental, but the one thing that may never fluctuate is the professional driver's transcendent effort. From the second the green flag drops, a winning driver focuses intently and exclusively on the things he can control: accurate lines, late braking, precise apexes, aggressive exit speeds and, most importantly, gathering and maintaining the momentum needed for

RIGHT Glenda Fox, constant companion of Pedro Rodriguez, became as close to Marion as Pedro was to me. His death engendered a shared sense of devastation.
Brian Redman collection

overtaking. Ruthlessly, he blocks out all thoughts on anything he can't control: understeer, oversteer, unexpected rain, worn tyres and faster competitors. Every nanosecond wasted thinking about uncontrollable circumstances are moments in which performance suffers. The job of a professional driver is to win but, failing that outcome, he is expected to bring the car home in the highest possible position, and to do so without damage to it.

Students of racing theories may learn the technologies that make a car go fast, but what is impossible for non-drivers to appreciate is the skill it takes to process the flood of consequential information and translate it all into repeated fast times, even though each lap is unique in its competitive challenges. Racing requires a million sequential decisions that must flow as seamlessly as the notes of a Jimmy Hendrix riff, with subtle interpretations, a rhythmic cadence and relentless energy.

Risk management

In my era, we may not have been as technically astute as today's racers but we had a firm grasp on the physics behind transitional momentum – if not in theory at least its real-life consequences. A car's mass times its velocity defines the force necessary to propel it to a specific speed, and is equalled exactly by that needed to make it stop. Our typical Formula 1 car with a driver weighed about 1,300 pounds. When travelling at top speed, about 175mph, it generated a great deal of forward energy and, therefore, required an equivalent amount for stopping. When car and driver encountered something as immovable as a large tree, a massive amount of momentum had to be absorbed instantly by everything deformable – the tub, the sheet metal, the suspension, the inflexible fuel tanks, and, of course, the driver's body.

Crashes were inevitable but never welcome. Ironically, the main factor that made drivers

ABOVE Brian: *'Pedro, what were you thinking during your superb 917 drive at Brands Hatch?'* **Pedro:** *'Nothing.'*
Sutton Images

accident-averse was fear of the team manager's wrath, not personal safety. John Wyer, who ran many all-conquering teams, had a disapproving look so severe that he was known as 'Death Ray'. Poor David Hobbs, invited to test a 917 at Daytona with Pedro Rodriguez, Jo Siffert and me, missed a shift and blew the engine – quite an easy thing to do. Porsche's motorsport director, Ferdinand Piëch, took a sufficiently dim view of this driver error that Leo Kinnunen was called in as David's replacement. That was a shame: David was fast and fun while Leo was fast and no fun, especially since he spoke not a word of English.

Team managers jokingly may have referred to their drivers as 'the throwaways', but no such derisive description was ever applied to their vehicles. Racing cars were the team manager's livelihood and the depository of the owner's treasure. Any professional driver who wasted his manager's time and the owner's money on frequent crashes could count on a brief career. The early chassis of that era was either a cat's cradle of tubes – as few, thin and light as the

engineer dared – or an equally delicate tub of riveted sheet metal that formed a monocoque frame. The fuel tanks were inelastic aluminium pods often located on both sides of the driver. The engine was fitted directly behind the driver's back and in front of the rear wheels, a configuration that had the effect of pushing the driver's feet into the car's nose, ahead of the axle line and everything else – with the exception of an oil or water radiator. The package then was wrapped in faired, wind-cheating aluminium, adding little weight and no strength. In a serious crash, all these exquisitely lightweight pieces had the impact resistance of a beer can and offered little protection for the driver. Worse, the rigid fuel tanks habitually split open, spilling petrol around the hot engine. Many drivers burned to death – about as grim an end as can be imagined. Drivers so feared fire that, for my first Grand Prix (at Kyalami in South Africa), half the field wore no seat belts, preferring the risks of jumping out or being thrown out to the chance of being trapped in a flaming car.

The expendable driver

As I rose through the professional ranks with a winning reputation, favourable drives magically appeared. Conversely, when I was recovering from injuries, opportunities dried up, sometimes so completely that I feared one might never come again. For Marion, our children and me, the repetitive cycle of racing, accident, racing, retirement and racing again required each of us to ride an emotional wave of elation and apprehension. There still are spousal tremors.

It's possible that my colleagues experienced the same dread that accompanied my pre-race nights, but there was no way I could ever know. No driver confessed to being afraid and we never discussed the possibility of death. Admitting fear would have been worse than unmanly; it would have been unprofessional. There was, however, a telling ritual following every race that graphically demonstrated the deep-seated anxieties shared by all drivers of my era. Post-race Sunday evenings inevitably erupted into parties, very big parties, usually at the hotel where most

ABOVE AND BELOW Jacky Ickx is amused as his three teammates clown around after the 1968 1,000Kms: Paul Hawkins (concealed by our sponsor's upside-down logo), David Hobbs (with the other Gulf sign) and me (behind a bemused female guest). The lower photo shows Jacky and me later that evening… much later.
Brian Redman collection

ABOVE My gesture demonstrates to Seppi how the back of the long-tail 908 came loose when entering Spa's *Masta* kink at 190mph.
Porsche-Werkfoto

of the drivers stayed. It would have been natural for the top finishers to be in high spirits, yet so ubiquitous was the revelry that a casual observer might have found it impossible to decide who in the crowd actually won. This carousing was alcohol-fuelled and characterised by manic laughter, loud singing and traces of desperation. More often than not, these evenings devolved into food fights and other 'high-spirited' pranks. One doesn't have to be Freud to conclude that our ritual bacchanals weren't celebrating communal sportsmanship. Rather, we were collectively revelling in the ineffable joy of being alive and did so in time-honoured fashion. We became supremely drunk.

Injuries and deaths were not unusual, but they were never overlooked. Each time a colleague was killed, conversations among drivers became offhand and muted.

'Sorry about so-and-so, he was a good lad.'
'Yeah, he was. Brake failure, I heard.'
'Supposedly, but he always was a bit aggressive, don't you think? Um, have you heard anything about who's getting his drive?'

It isn't that drivers are unfeeling. Just as we compartmentalise the on-track things we can't control, we also block out all life events that might compromise our racing performance, and our enjoyment. My way of whistling past the graveyard was to be a cheerful companion to most of my peers but to keep my friendships rare. My vow never to attend driver funerals was compromised by just two exceptions.

Rest in peace

My first driver requiem was involuntary, a matter of Porsche team orders. In August 1969, seven of Porsche's ten factory drivers – Udo Schütz, Richard Attwood, Gérard Larrousse, Jo Siffert, Rolf Stommelen, Kurt Ahrens and me – were instructed to return to Germany to participate in the funeral of company stalwart Gerhard Mitter, who had been killed in a Formula 2 race at the Nürburgring.

For me, the funeral pageantry was surreal and

unnerving. We survivors were to be Mitter's pallbearers, assigned to wear our matching Porsche-embroidered Nomex racing suits, grim reminders that we were lucky and he was not. The parade began with the coffin strapped to a roof rack on the latest Porsche 911 – a ritual of bereavement bizarrely fused to a symbol of immoderation. Gerhard's helmet was fixed to the front of the bier, angled down as it was when he was racing. Seven uniformed drivers flanked the Porsche hearse, marching in procession behind the cortège while an altar boy held a black cross bearing the name 'Gerhard Mitter' in Gothic script. We carried the casket into the cathedral on our shoulders.

I saw that Mitter's wife was sobbing, with the two children at her side. The older was a boy, the younger a girl, roughly the same ages as my children. I couldn't stop the tears from streaming down my cheeks. Afterwards, Udo Schütz approached me.

'Brian, I didn't realise you felt so strongly about Gerhard.'

'Udo,' I replied, *'the truth is I didn't like Gerhard at all. I was thinking that the next funeral is going to be mine.'*

Gerhard Mitter was 34 years old. At the time, I was 32.

The second exception to my no-funeral rule was a deeply felt obligation to participate in the memorial that honoured my magnificent partner, Jo 'Seppi' Siffert. That came later, in October 1971, when I not only permitted dark thoughts but frequently was overwhelmed by them. I was fated to witness Jo's death remotely.

Burns from my Targa Florio accident had forced a three-week convalescence in southern France. Shortly after I returned to England, I turned on our television to watch the so-called Victory Race, an end-of-season non-championship Formula 1 event at Brands Hatch. I was horrified to see Seppi's BRM P160 suffer a suspension failure, swerve into the trackside embankment, overturn and catch fire. The instant inferno sucked the oxygen out of the air and Jo died from asphyxiation. His only physical damage was a broken ankle. Without hesitation, I skipped the final Can-Am race in California to be at his funeral in his home city, Fribourg, Switzerland. Jo Siffert was honoured as a Swiss national hero by more than 50,000 fans who flooded the city's streets to accompany his bier – a stirring tribute to a special man. Seppi's own Porsche 917 preceded his coffin.

My friend Jo Siffert was 35 years old.

BELOW Seven of Porsche's works drivers were ordered to attend Gerhard Mitter's funeral in 1969. On the left Udo Schütz leads Richard Attwood, Gérard Larrousse and me; on the right Jo Siffert is followed by Rolf Stommelen and (hidden) Kurt Ahrens. *Brian Redman collection*

CHAPTER 5
The Targa Florio

Helmut Marko, once a first-rate sports car racer and currently a Red Bull Formula 1 team executive, summed up the Targa Florio with precise economy: 'It's insane!'

Marko was speaking about the circuit on which he and I raced in the late 1960s and early 1970s. What else could you call a 45-mile, 720-corner course that goes through the middle of three villages, skirts 1,000-feet drops and brushes against stone houses? If the rustic terrain weren't sufficient to keep a driver focused, the improvident Sicilians fans were. Young bravos crowded the most dramatic corners, standing and cheering exactly where an errant car might touch down. Whole families amiably picnicked beside the track as we passed at racing speeds in marginal control. Roadside verges and gutters were to be avoided because they were depositories of cast-off nails from horseshoes. Were any sanctioning body or government officials today to suggest a race for 170mph sports prototypes on rural donkey paths they would be locked up. In fact, even the gentlest of the Targa Florio's eccentric features would be enough to disqualify the track from contemporary consideration.

There have been many Targa Florio configurations, some even loonier than the circuit of my era. The original 1906 route was 92 miles long, and a later version set the all-time mark for distance as a 670-mile circumnavigation of the entire island of Sicily. Our *Piccolo* circuit may have been a fraction of the size of the *Grande* courses, but it was still unconditionally mad. It should be noted that, despite Marko's opinion of the Targa's irrationality, he set the fastest race lap in 1972 (33 minutes 41 seconds) at an average speed of 79.69mph and finished second overall. That pretty much sums up the inherent contradictions between how racing drivers think and how they act.

OPPOSITE A rustic scene on my practice lap in 1971 – in the race I crashed before I got this far around the circuit. *Porsche-Werkfoto*

BELOW Action in 1969, Richard Attwood driving our Porsche 908/02. *Getty Images/ Rainer Schlegelmilch*

ABOVE During our recce before the 1969 Targa Florio, Richard Attwood and I try to figure out which way the course went. The locals didn't have much idea either.
Brian Redman collection

The 1969 Targa Florio

In 1969 I was part of a five-car Porsche onslaught and partnered with Richard Attwood, a fast friend in both senses of the words. 'Tatty Atty' was a superb sports car driver who competed at Le Mans every year between 1963 and 1971, winning it in 1970. He also had many good outings in Formula 1, including second place in a BRM P126 behind Graham Hill's Lotus-Cosworth 49B in the 1968 Monaco Grand Prix. As close as Richard and I have remained and as memorable as he is as a driver, it's his wife's observation of racing that always stayed with me. '*During our first years of marriage,*' she said, '*I went to more funerals than weddings.*'

Fortunately, Richard and I didn't add to her burdens in the 1969 race, but luck wasn't with us. While in third place, with Richard driving, our Porsche 908/02 put a wheel on a grass verge. Unfortunately, under the grass was two feet of ditch, and a broken axle finished our Targa Florio. An unsung hero of the day was Herbie Müller whose Lola T70 MkIIIB was delayed at the start

RIGHT Richard looking fast and tidy in our Porsche 908/02... before he investigated a grass verge.
LAT

RIGHT Our open-air workshop in 1969. Sicily usually offered good weather in May.
Getty Images/ Rainer Schlegelmilch

BELOW Most of Porsche's 1969 Targa Florio drivers with the boss: from the left, Umberto Maglioli, Richard Attwood, me, Ferry Porsche, Hans Herrmann, Udo Schütz, someone I can't identify, Rolf Stommelen, Vic Elford, Rudi Lins and Gérard Larrousse. The driver in the car is Gerhard Mitter.
Porsche-Werkfoto

with an electrical problem. He then passed 60 cars on the opening lap, but this splendid effort came to naught when damage from a flat tyre resulted in teammate Jo Bonnier losing the wheel on the straight and retiring the car.

John Wyer, Porsche, Seppi and me

I returned to Sicily and the Targa in 1970 as part of one of the most famous and successful sports car efforts in racing history, the Porsche factory team entered by JW Automotive and directed by John Wyer. Porsche built the powerful 12-cylinder 917s for high-speed circuits like Le Mans, Spa, Daytona and Monza and the nimble eight-cylinder 908/03s for the multi-cornered Nürburgring and the Targa Florio. Wyer's cars were painted in Gulf's iconic blue-and-orange livery and we drivers wore matching driving suits. Walking through the paddock, we looked and felt like gods.

At my request, I was paired that season with Jo 'Seppi' Siffert because I was sure that driving with him was the best way for me to win races. My 1968 drives in Wyer's Ford GT40s and with the factory Porsche 908s in 1969 gave both Seppi and John confidence in my abilities. Jo and I were employed directly by Porsche while Pedro Rodriguez and Finnish rally driver Leo Kinnunen were Gulf drivers. None of us was paid that well. As factory Porsche drivers – the best job in endurance racing at that time – Seppi and I were remunerated at exactly my 1968 John Wyer rate of $750 per race plus expenses, except for Daytona, Sebring and Le Mans for which we received $1,000 each. My total 10-race income from Porsche that year was $8,250.

Before the Targa Florio, the JW Automotive team entered the fast-developing 917K in the first four races of the 1970 International Championship for Makes with generally excellent results for Porsche. For Seppi and me, they were somewhat less successful. At the Daytona opener, Pedro

BELOW A 1969 pit scene: Ferdinand Piëch gets ready to jump off the pit counter, journalist Helmut Zwickl makes notes, I stand looking at the lap times and Helmut Bott records everything. *Getty Images/ Rainer Schlegelmilch*

**ABOVE Porsche had
four 908/03 entries for
the 1970 race – three
Gulf cars and one from
Porsche Salzburg. They
bask in the Sicilian sun
with (from left) Jo Siffert,
John Wyer, Ferdinand
Piëch and Vic Elford.**
Porsche-Werkfoto

and Leo took the win with a single-stint assist
from me, followed by Jo and me in second place.
Sebring was next, a race of multiple mechanical
problems for both Porsches; the sequence of
failures that befell our cars put Seppi and me
out of the race after three short hours while the
less-compromised Rodriguez/Kinnunen duo
soldiered on to fourth place. The BOAC 1,000Kms
at Brands Hatch was run in typically wet British
weather and Pedro – in a race widely recognised
as one of his best drives – splashed to a win with
Leo, while we ran a close second until I was
punted off by the Ferrari 512 of an embarrassed
Chris Amon; I'm sure it wasn't on purpose as
Chris never engaged in dirty racing. At Monza,
the Rodriguez/Kinnunen team continued its
blistering winning streak, leaving Seppi and
me to struggle for 12th place, plagued by
mechanical failures.

The Targa Florio was our fifth race of the
championship season, and the first where

Wyer ran Porsche's new 908/03s. Rodriguez
and Kinnunen were in one, Siffert and me in
another, and Richard Attwood and Swedish
rally driver Björn Waldegård in a third. To John's
surprise and dismay, another 908/03 appeared
in the paddock entered by Ferdinand Piëch's
Porsche Salzburg team, to be driven by Vic Elford
and Hans Herrmann.

The agile 908/03s were perfectly suited to the
serpentine Targa Florio circuit. While Elford did
try a 917 in practice and lapped just a few seconds
slower than his time in the 908/03, the big car
proved to be a handful and was quickly returned
to the Porsche Salzburg transporter. Ferrari, our
major competition, sent one of its mighty 512S
prototypes for factory drivers Nino Vaccarella
and Ignazio Giunti. Nino was a Sicilian from
Palermo, where he was a part-time teacher and
accounting school headmaster. As the local pro,
he trained year round on his home circuit and
was one of very few drivers who knew every

ABOVE AND LEFT Seen passing the pits (above) and out in the Sicilian countryside, my 1970 Targa teammate Jo Siffert entertains the crowd whilst trying to catch Nino Vaccarella.
Getty Images/ Rainer Schlegelmilch

LEFT Carefully balancing the left-front wheel on the edge of the road so as not to drop into the gutter and risk a puncture from debris there.
LAT

one of the Targa's 720 corners. If the Porsche 917 were ill-suited to the Targa, Nino's beefy Ferrari couldn't have been any better. Nonetheless, after Siffert put our car on pole with a lap of 34 minutes 10 seconds and Elford set a time of 34 minutes 37 seconds, Vaccarella – using his intimate course knowledge – qualified third just 36 seconds off Jo's pace.

One of the Targa Florio's few concessions to judiciousness was the staggered start in which competitors were released at roughly 30-second intervals. The race, therefore, was against the clock (as opposed to wheel-to-wheel) so only the team timekeepers could be sure who was in the lead. This start procedure may have prevented first-lap mayhem but it didn't eliminate the hazards of overtaking on Sicily's narrow roads, a necessity given the diversity of entries and their widely differing speeds. Despite the starting intervals, cars bunched up regularly and occasional chaos ensued as multiple drivers attempted to claim the same compact patch of Sicilian tarmac.

ABOVE I thought the oil temperature was getting a bit hot…
Porsche-Werkfoto

The 1970 race was scheduled for 11 laps (495 miles), one lap longer than the previous year. With fuel stops, it would take just over six hours, and fuel economy was Porsche's secret weapon. The thirsty 12-cylinder Ferrari could go just two laps before stopping while the eight-cylinder Porsche could last three or even four if we took advantage of the satellite refuelling station our team had set up in the mountains.

The lead changed numerous times during the race, shifting among Wyer's Porsche 908/03s, the Porsche Salzburg car and the Vaccarella/Giunti Ferrari 512S. Pedro was feeling ill that day, so Kinnunen started the race and jumped into the lead on the opening lap. When Leo handed over the car to Pedro, Vaccarella was able to overtake the ailing Mexican.

I relieved Seppi on lap four and, halfway around the track, I caught Vaccarella. The only logical place to pass the Ferrari was on the long straight beside the Mediterranean but there the 5-litre 512S could use its potent horsepower to establish a 20mph supremacy in top speed. I

did try to pass elsewhere but the Ferrari had Nino aboard, blocking savagely and nearly pushing me off the road in each of my attempts. Prudence and the benefit of better fuel consumption made me patient, and I remained a safe distance behind, waiting for the Ferrari to pit. When I saw Nino getting ready, I closed up fast and we made our usual quick pit-stop for fuel, tyres and driver change. The mechanics' coordinated manoeuvres allowed Siffert to exit the pits in the lead.

At the finish, Jo and I were two minutes ahead of Rodriguez and Kinnunen (Leo setting a new lap record of 33 minutes 36 seconds) and two more in front of the Vaccarella/Giunti Ferrari.

Most races ended with appreciative cheering no matter who won, but not in Sicily, and not for a German car driven by a Brit and a Swiss. As our Porsche triumphantly crossed the finish line for the win, thousands of Italian spectators remained eerily silent, communally crushed that the victor was neither a Ferrari nor an Alfa Romeo, nor any car driven by an Italian.

ABOVE Nicholas Watts beautifully captures the grace, fury and spirit of the Targa Florio in portraying our winning car.

Nicholas Watts

BELOW This striking mosaic, one of several, is in Collesano, which also has the best of the four museums about the Targa Florio.

Brian Redman collection

TARGA FLORIO

54° Targa Florio anno 1970 la competizione tra la Porsche Gulf 908-3 di Siffert-Redman vincitore e la Ferrari 512 S di Vaccarella -Giunti Collesano via Isnello

It mattered not to Seppi and me. After five races together in the JW Automotive team, we finally had our first major victory, and a most satisfying one it was. For nearly 500 miles and nearly 8,000 corners neither of us had put a wheel wrong. That night's celebratory dinner tasted of victory, washed down by copious draughts of Sicily's inky Mount Etna wines.

The 1971 Targa Florio

Returning to racing from my short-lived South African retirement at the end of the 1970 season, I found myself scrambling for any opportunity to drive and rashly accepted a one-off outing in April 1971 for the BOAC 1,000Kms at Brands Hatch in a Martini Racing Porsche 917K, partnering 'Quick Vic' Elford. During a refuelling stop, the tank sprung a leak and sprayed petrol on the undertray just below my seat. When

ABOVE What a relief to win one of the most difficult races on one of the most challenging tracks. Seppi and I share the champagne with John Wyer.
Brian Redman collection

LEFT Porsche made a poster of every FIA race won by its cars. An original copy of this one hangs in my office.
Porsche-Werkfoto

A lap of *Piccolo Madonie*

As my lap of the Nürburgring's 170 corners might have induced sleep if not summarised in highlights, a blow-by-blow description of the Targa Florio's 720 corners would send readers into an unresponsive stupor. Instead, I'll narrate a lap of this Sicilian behemoth in terms of the elevations and contours that kept my hands flailing at the wheel and my feet dancing on the pedals. Not only was the *Piccolo Madonie* the longest course I ever drove, it was also the busiest.

The start of the race took place on route SS 120 at the administrative offices, pit complex and grandstands known as *Floriopolis*. In order to avoid mass mayhem at the start, cars were flagged off at around 30-second intervals. Without today's electronic timekeeping, we had fallible people, mostly family volunteers, scribbling the lap times of 80 racing cars whilst trying to divine their racing order in light of the scrambled start. For the more than 400,000 spectators distributed around the 45-mile circuit, it seemed to make no difference at all. They were certain a red car led, most likely the one driven by local hero Nino Vaccarella.

As I left the startline in my Porsche 908/03 with spinning wheels and high hopes, I reminded myself that the first few corners were always extraordinarily slippery. For five miles, the road twisted and turned upwards towards the town of *Cerda*, at 895 feet, with only short straights providing little in the way of driver relief. Since the road ran straight through the town, hordes of spectators crowded the narrow pavements, and threading through them at speed required a total suspension of reality. The 12 miles between *Cerda* and *Caltavuturo* began with the *Cerda* straight, at the end of which I snapped the car sharply left, through an equally

tight right and onto a mind-numbing series of irregular bends. These meanderings probably began as 'paths of desire', trails created by centuries of human and animal footfall but now corners on a devilish racing circuit.

I attacked the Sicilian hills, climbing to 1,335 feet then dropping to 688 feet, shifting non-stop as I accommodated constantly changing surfaces – rough and smooth, repaired and neglected. The yo-yo continued with a climb to *Bivio Caltavuturoat*, the highest point on the circuit at 1,968 feet, before descending to 820 feet and darting across an ancient bridge spanning the Imera river. Immediately, I zig-zagged back up to *Bivio Polizzi* at 1,870 feet where teams located skeleton crews equipped with fuel, tyres and spare parts.

Now I turned north and entered another series of switchbacks, twists and blind turns. All looked deceptively similar, but varied in subtle, menacing ways. Farmhouse buildings along the roadside flashed words of encouragement for Vaccarella: '*Nino!*' and '*Ferrari!*' Where their beloved Nino might have had a problem in the past, '*Attenzione Nino*' jogged his memory. I heeded their warnings.

At around the 30-mile mark I carved a left between the buildings and then right down a short straight to a 180-degree left-hand horseshoe, a favourite perch for spectators and photographers. I did my best to ignore the houses on the left and the steep rocky hill close by on the right, packed with spectators, before plunging seven and a half miles downhill to *Campofelice de Roccella*, a town perched 200 feet above the sea. For nearly 40 miles there had been no let-up from accelerating, braking, changing gear and assaults on the endless bends, veers, loops and inclines. After *Campofelice* I headed downhill once more through a series of sweeping bends to SS 113, the *Buonfornello* straight. The blue Mediterranean sparkled in the distance.

The *Buonfornello* straight was the first and only time I changed into fifth gear, which was 'out of the gate' in the 908/03; because first gear was in constant use, Porsche built the gearbox with first and third at the top of the H pattern and second and fourth below, with fifth gear to the right of third, out of the way. The temptation to relax on the straight was tempered by the 170mph top speed reached for over five miles. At the end of the straight, I flashed through three extremely quick left/right curves (memorised out of life-saving necessity), then through a tight left into a mile or so of even tighter curves that led back to the pits.

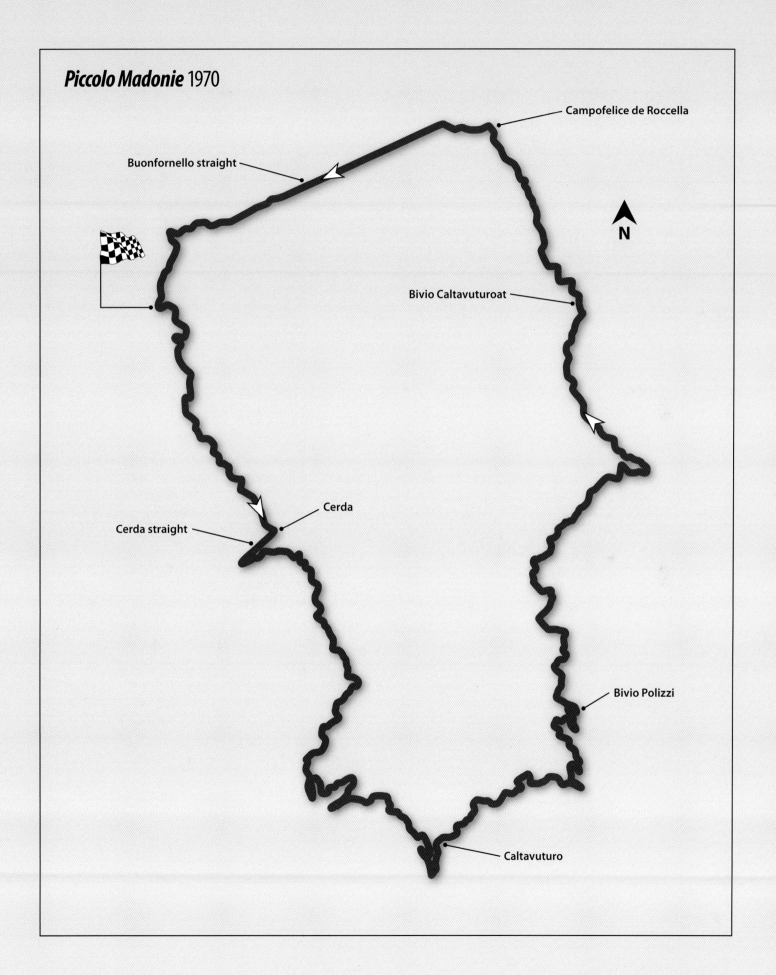

Piccolo Madonie 1970

Campofelice de Roccella

Buonfornello straight

Bivio Caltavuturoat

Cerda

Cerda straight

Bivio Polizzi

Caltavuturo

N

RIGHT The practice
lap is perhaps the
most dangerous of
the entire event. We
were allowed just one
in our racing car, on
public roads open to
everyday traffic – not
to mention donkeys,
sheep and goats.
This is me aboard the
908/03 in 1971 driving
through *Campofelice*
en route to the
Buonfornello straight.
LAT

team leader Reinhold Joest gave the signal to start
the engine, there was a loud bang and the car
burst into flames – and I leaped out. The fire was
extinguished, but we were finished. What a way
to return to racing.

This still left me without a factory ride, but
I gratefully earned a few pounds driving Sid
Taylor's Formula 5000 McLaren M18 until, once
again, John Wyer called. It seemed that Derek Bell,
Jo Siffert's 1971 co-driver, had never raced in the
Targa Florio and John asked if I would consider
teaming up again with Seppi. I saw it as a godsend
and, with visions of a repeat win, jumped at the
opportunity. The Targa Florio of 1971 proved to be
different kind of memorable experience. I drove
the Sicilian classic four times, one more than
I now wish I had.

The Porsche 908/03 hadn't changed much in a
year but the 1971 car had fins on each rear corner
to improve high-speed stability. Wyer remained
his stern, demanding self and Siffert continued
as my fast, mischievous and fun companion.
Practice was uneventful until the very end when
Jo crashed heavily, damaging the entire front end
of the car – wheels, suspension, steering rack and
bodywork. For the mechanics, this meant an
all-nighter for repairs; for the driver who started
the race the next day, it meant racing an untested
car over a long, tough course.

Starts were usually Jo's responsibility, but
on the morning of the race an echo from the
past changed everything. Wyer never forgot
the opening lap of the 1970 Spa 1,000Kms when
teammates Siffert and Rodriguez entered *Eau
Rouge* side by side in the rain, abusing the flimsy
doors of his two precious 917s as they flew up
the hill and out of sight. Determined to avoid a
Rodriguez/Siffert contest of egos and a repeat of
the Spa drama, John decided that I was to drive
the opening stint.

'*If you're going to crash, don't crash on the right side,*'
one Porsche engineer helpfully yelled into my ear
on the grid. '*That's where the fuel tanks are located.*'

Two familiar, conflicting thoughts swam in my
brain: '*The car is untested since Jo's accident so I need
to drive with extra care until I'm confident it's safe*'
versus '*This is a race that can launch me back into the*

top level and I need to be fast.' Conservatism lost the mental war and I committed myself to going flat out.

Almost immediately I realised that something was wrong with the steering, possibly just a little stiffness in the system but more likely a damaged part that our sleepless mechanics missed. In either case, I needed to drive around the problem to get the car back to the pits or at least to our service area in the mountains. Eight miles on, I rushed down a hill that ended in the *Caltavaturo* corner, one I knew well and could round with confidence. Mid-corner, the steering broke, throwing the right side of the car against a stone roadside marker. There wasn't time to heed the mechanic's warning on how not to crash, but it wouldn't have mattered. I was a passenger, no longer in control of the car's direction. The sturdy stone post pierced the right side of the aluminium chassis and ripped open the fuel tank. This released a full load of petrol that saturated my driving suit and poured onto the hot exhaust pipes. Instantly, the car was a cauldron of fire,

OPPOSITE Negotiating one of the Targa Florio's many nameless curves in gloomy weather on my 1971 practice lap.
Grand Prix Library

ABOVE Final preparation in the paddock on race morning; for 1971 our 908/03 had tail fins for extra stability at speed.
Porsche-Werkfoto

BELOW Chatting before the start with Denis Jenkinson, continental correspondent of *Motor Sport* magazine.
Brian Redman collection

with my soaked suit – and me – part of the blaze.

Once a racing car begins burning, even a single second's delay can be the difference between survival and incineration. Drivers are required to practise getting out of their cars in a hurry so Jo and I dutifully performed this precaution. What was easily done when parked in the pits became nearly impossible when blinded by smoke and engulfed in flames. I held my breath, closed my eyes, unbuckled my belts and struggled out of the car. Once free of the burning hulk, I discovered that I had brought fire with me and I was now lit like a human torch. Throwing myself on the ground, I rolled down a slope to smother the flames while helpful spectators beat me with blankets. There was no chance of escaping unscathed.

An oval surrounding my eyes, the facial area not protected by my balaclava, was badly burned, and that shape now remains permanently recorded on my face. My hands and the back of my neck also suffered serious damage but, strangely, I felt no pain during and immediately

after the accident. Sometime later, I remember hearing someone screaming in the distance until I slowly recognised the sound of my own voice. As the shock wore off, the pain took hold. My facial swelling was so immediate that I was blinded within moments. I could hear hysterical villagers around me arguing about how to help, but none was actually doing anything. Finally, one spectator gave me a sip of water and fanned my face with a newspaper.

I waited in increasing pain for 45 wretchedly long minutes before a helicopter came to take me back to the pits. There, a Porsche doctor applied some cream to the burns but decided that I really ought to be in a hospital. Doubtless he envisioned an immaculate facility such as one might find in Stuttgart and not the desolate clinic of Termini Imerese in the Sicilian hills. With no destination mentioned to the team, an ancient ambulance delivered me to that hellhole. What began badly was now a disaster in the making.

At some point after arriving at the hospital, my helmet, shoes, socks and racing uniform disappeared, probably to Sicilian souvenir hunters, leaving me in my long Nomex underwear. After a brief examination, I was wheeled to a bed in a filthy ward filled with the wailing, cigarette-smoking relatives of a boy who had been hit by a car during the race. The sounds and odours were oppressive. I spoke no Italian and no one came near me who spoke English.

Two hours later, they wheeled in another victim, Alain de Cadenet, to join me in the ward. At that time, Alain was an accomplished racer, yet to become a car constructor and television personality. His Lola T210 prototype had broken its suspension and crashed on the four-mile *Buonfornello* straight, knocking him unconscious and immediately catching fire. Predictably, there were no track marshals nearby. A spectator saved Alain's life by dragging him out of the car, hurt but not badly, and fortunately without a spinal injury. In a note to me, Alain described our mutual internment at the clinic this way.

'The room wasn't very big and I remember that you were about 10-to-12 feet from my bed on my

*left against the opposite wall, facing me. You were
bandaged all over like the 'Invisible Man'. I have to
say I barely recollect who else was in that room but I
do remember a kid who'd been hit by an Alfa, I think.
His abdomen was sliced open as I'd seen him in the
operating theatre when I went in for x-rays. He was in
considerable pain and making a lot of noise. Probably
they put the bandaged, repaired and likely-to-survive
folk in our room. I remember it was very white and
quite cool in there and we were both wearing white
cotton over-sleeves. But I only had one eye working so
I probably missed half of it. I think they'd filled you up
with some tasty drugs like morphine as you seemed
quite serene, calm and content.'*

My recollection of that evening was
more disconcerting. Bandaged from head
to foot, including my hands, I found myself
urgently needing to urinate but unable to do
so independently. Reluctantly, with no other
English speaker available, I was obliged to ask
Alain to perform hands-on help. For the past 45
years it has been this charming man's favourite
after-dinner story.

At about 11.00 that night, Pedro Rodriguez
and Richard Attwood went searching for me,
canvassing the island hospitals and clinics,
following clues until they arrived at Termini
Imerese. Bless them, they secured my release and
brought me back to the hotel, where the Porsche
doctor gave me an injection so I could sleep
through the pain. In the morning, a jet hired by
Gulf and Porsche flew me to Manchester where
Marion and a local friend, Howard Lowcock,
were waiting at the airport. When I appeared
in the plane's doorway swathed in bandages,
Howard looked at my burned face and passed
out cold. Marion, as always, simply took charge.

Some years later I ran into Gérard Larrousse,
who drove that year's Targa in the Martini team's
908/02. Gérard explained that, when he saw
the scene of my accident, he was very, very
worried. I replied that I was pretty worried
myself. He then reported on what remained of
the wreckage. *'You know what was left from your
car? Nuzzing. There was a hole in ze road, and inside
ze hole was ze crankshaft.'*

Recovery

Christies, a cancer hospital in Manchester, had a private wing where I was attended by Dr Randell Champion, a superb plastic surgeon whose skills were honed repairing damaged RAF pilots during the Second World War. It took a week for my swelling to subside and then I could see the devastation for myself. The mirror revealed a badly disfigured face bearing a shrivelled nose, with severe burns and thick cream surrounding my eyes. I was horrified, shamed by the possibility of surviving as a gargoyle fearing life in public. Worry was now added to the permanent pain.

Dr Champion was a caring physician who assured me that he could reconstruct my missing parts with skin grafts. By contrast, his officious assistant was a bit of a sadist, and our dislike was instant and mutual. When the time came for me to be 'cleaned up', it was the assistant who performed the torture, with all too much pleasure for my liking. I learned that 'cleaning up' entailed scrubbing away the burnt skin around my eyes and upper face with cotton swabs soaked in alcohol. I'm sure the procedure was designed to be antiseptic, but alcohol on my raw flesh made it feel like the fire had returned. The process seemed to take hours and every second hurt like hell.

When the physician's assistant finished, I threw myself on the floor and began a series of push-ups. *'For heaven's sake, what are you doing, Mr Redman?'* asked the wonderful Scottish nurse who had been assisting. *'Taking my mind off other things,'* I replied. All who witnessed this bizarre exchange thought I had mentally lost it. For me, it was a therapeutic distraction from the penetrating physical pain and unremitting mental misery.

A few days later Dr Champion performed the grafts, removing skin from under my arms, behind my ears and a large section of my left buttock, employing an unpleasant-looking instrument that reminded me of a carpenter's plane. The pain was deep, and when I awoke the following day my bed sheets were soaked top to bottom with blood. Dr Champion's skin grafts were held in place by an ointment covering the raw flesh beneath, and I was told not to wash or touch these areas until the healing had begun. The parts of my body from which the sacrificial skin had been removed were swathed in bandages. Over time, the coagulated blood – especially in my buttock area – became as hard as wood. I lived in fear of another 'clean up'.

'What will you do?' I asked my nurse. *'Put me under to cut off the bandages?'*

'Oh, no, love,' she replied. *'We'll put you in a nice hot bath and pull them off.'*

'I'll do it myself,' I replied.

The following Sunday I sat in the bath for nearly a full day and very slowly – *very, very slowly* – peeled off the bandages. Thereafter, whenever I won a race and received a winner's kiss from the local race queen, I thoughtfully advised her that she had just planted her lips on my left buttock.

As recovery progressed, the need to support my family weighed heavily and I was determined to return to racing as soon as physically possible. Seven weeks after the accident, I was at Mallory Park in Sid Taylor's Formula 5000 car, racing well and finishing third. At my check-up the following week, however, the doctor was horrified to see that my balaclava had rubbed raw the skin graft on my face and warned that, unless I delayed my return to racing, it was sure to become infected. Were this to happen, a fluid build-up underneath the donor skin would prevent the graft from receiving the oxygenated blood needed to attach it permanently. A failed graft then would require the doctor to harvest a new patch of donor skin and undertake a replacement transplant, two painful procedures creating two additional wounds that would need to heal.

'Lovely,' I thought, *'more time off.'* This was exactly what I didn't need. To enforce the no-race ban, Marion and I bought an 18-foot caravan, hooked it to our Jaguar 3.8S, packed up the two children and headed for southern France. The therapy worked, and I improved, but even in that peaceful setting racing intruded. One Monday morning I was returning to the caravan after washing when a fellow Brit, who knew I was connected with motorsport, asked if I knew the driver who'd been killed the day before. He couldn't remember the name, but said, *'Rud, Rud something.'* I filled in the blank. *'Rodriguez?'*

'*Yes,*' he replied. When I returned to the caravan in tears, Marion asked what was troubling me. When I burst out, '*Pedro is dead*', we shared tears in quiet misery.

My teammate Pedro Rodriguez was constitutionally unable to turn down any chance to compete. That weekend he had accepted a one-off drive at Germany's Norisring in Herbie Müller's privateer Ferrari 512M. Leading the race, Pedro was lapping a much slower car when it inexplicably turned in, shoving him off the track and into a heavy crash. Pedro's Ferrari immediately exploded in flames and he had no chance to escape. Painfully, I remembered this fearless Mexican's fatalistic prediction: '*God will decide when it will be the end of the road for me.*' Perhaps God did make the decision but Pedro's death also conformed to racing's poor predictive odds.

As the oldest son of a wealthy Mexican family, Pedro didn't have to race for a living but he lived for nothing else. His precocious younger sibling, Ricardo, had been anointed a factory Ferrari Formula 1 driver when just 19 years old. In 1962 Ricardo accepted a one-off drive in Rob Walker's Lotus 24 at the *Magdelena Mixhuca* circuit in Mexico City because the Ferrari team had declined to participate in this non-championship Formula 1 event, and Ricardo didn't want to disappoint his home fans. During the first day of practice, something happened to his Lotus at the fearsome *Peralta* turn. It was probably a failure in the car's right rear suspension, but it could have been a rare human error from a driver for whom blazingly fast was never fast enough. The car hit the barriers hard, killing Ricardo instantly. Later, after Pedro's death, the Mexico City circuit was named *Autódromo Hermanos Rodriguez* in honour of Mexico's two great heroes.

Marion and I spent many happy times with Pedro and his girlfriend, Glenda Fox. Both were sweet human beings. I wouldn't miss racing against the fiercely competitive Pedro, but I was desolate to lose him as a friend and companion.

Pedro Rodriguez was 31 years old.

Ricardo Rodriguez was 20 years old.

The wisdom of Arturo Merzario

In 1972 I was a factory Ferrari driver but not
assigned to the Targa Florio. That year Ferrari
sent just one car to Sicily, a 312PB to be driven
by Arturo Merzario and rally driver Sandro
Munari. Arturo's comments to the Sicilian
press explained a lot about the Targa's
unique challenges.

*'First, we prepared the car in the right way…
we increased the ground clearance from five to eight
centimetres. That, of course, did not prevent you
from scratching the bottom… but gave you a little
more chance not to be airborne when you had to steer.
The most important point was to lap the track so
many times that you start to remember the trickiest
corners but, more than everything else, to discover
the worst jumps…*

*'Most of the time today, when you look at the
pictures from the past of a crashed car, it usually
shows the front hitting a wall and you wonder how
it could have happened. You look at the corner and
it doesn't seem very tricky, and you assume that the
driver made a big mistake. You're wrong: he simply*

*was airborne and arrived a little too long when he
had to steer to make the corner. We drivers guessed
the length of the "flight" after a certain bump and,
sometimes, we over-estimated our flight control!'*

In a brilliant performance, Arturo and
Sandro won the race.

The 1973 Targa Florio

In 1973 Ferrari sent two cars to the Targa Florio,
Jacky Ickx and me in one and Arturo Merzario
and Nino Vaccarella in the other. Strange as this
may sound, considering the price this race had
extracted from me two years earlier, I was happy
to be there, for several reasons.

First, I was a Ferrari factory driver and wanted
to remain in favour with the team so that I might
continue to be employed. Drivers are a bit like
movie stars: they receive the awards, are written
up in the press and enjoy the fame, while the real
power always lies deeper in the organisation,
close to the money. Hollywood is controlled by
studios, producers and directors; in racing it's
factories, owners, sponsors and team managers.

Second, I was a seasoned professional who, over five years, had accumulated a spectrum of experiences. Racing was a dangerous job and I accepted it as such, but I also truly loved my work. I reasoned that mechanical failures had caused my two accidents and I remained confident in my abilities. In all measurable ways, I was at the top of my game and my career, unthinking of potentially mortal consequences.

Third, I had the feeling that this Targa Florio was going to be an historic occasion. Prodded by Jackie Stewart, the *Fédération Internationale de l'Automobile* (FIA), the sanctioning body governing the International Championship for Makes, was beginning to make some inroads on racing safety. There was a message in the air that the Targa Florio had to change since it was clear to drivers and organisers alike that the risks were unjustifiable. Race fans also must have shared my premonition because they flooded the tracksides, sensing, perhaps, that this might be the last 'real' Targa Florio.

The entry list for 1973 bulged with an astounding 125 cars. Even more impressively, the record crowd topped 400,000, nearly twice as big as the audience for any Le Mans 24 Hours or Daytona's biggest NASCAR gate. Even though the Targa Florio was an event of international importance, its spectators were rabid nationalists, there exclusively to cheer on Ferrari and Alfa Romeo, or at least any competitor with an Italian name. Safety barriers were non-existent so there was nothing to keep this mass of humanity from crowding the track. Historic as the 1973 race proved to be, it was no less dangerous than any other for drivers and spectators.

At the start line, I leaned over to caution my co-driver, the irrepressible Jacky Ickx.

'There's one thing you must remember, Jacky. This is not a race. It's a contest to see who is fastest among those who survive.'

Not heeding my counsel, Jacky set a blistering pace and, predictably, crashed on the second lap. When he finally made it back to the pits I asked, *'Are you okay?'*

LEFT My last Targa Florio, in 1973, was as a works Ferrari driver sharing with Jacky Ickx, making his first visit. Here the mechanics push our 312PB to the start.
LAT

LEFT After three visits to Sicily with a German team, I returned in 1973 as a works Ferrari driver – and so became one of the darlings of the fiercely partisan spectators.
LAT

LEFT In 1973 Ferrari
provided its drivers with
a rare luxury – a spare car
for practice. That meant
I could do two practice
laps – one in each car.
Grand Prix Library

'Yes, thank you, Bree-an, I am fine… but I have
an eenteresting accident. I go down a mountain, a
very long way down a mountain, and there I meet a
donkey.' As someone who loves animals, I never
asked Jacky his definition of 'meet'.

The 1973 Targa Florio was won by Gijs van
Lennep and Herbie Müller driving a Martini-
sponsored works Porsche 911 RSR. Once again,
there were fatal driver and spectator accidents.

These continuing tragedies and a change
in the willingness of fans to accept them
prompted the FIA to mandate full guardrails
around every circuit – an impossibility for
45 miles of rural Sicily. Although the Targa
Florio continued to run as a madcap adventure
for another four years, it did so without the
factory teams and never again as an important
international event. Finally, in 1977, after two
drivers were killed and five spectators injured,
the police stepped in and stopped the race
before the end of the fourth lap.

This time the great Targa Florio was
finished, forever.

ABOVE In the hills on
my practice lap with our
race car – but I didn't
get to drive it in the race
because Jacky crashed
on the second lap.
Grand Prix Library

CHAPTER 6
Stories from the 1960s

The race schedules of top-level drivers of the 1960s and 1970s make most modern professionals look indolent and today's salaries and endorsement packages make me green with envy. In the bad old days we earned our livelihoods by competing at a manic pace at tracks strung across the western world, putting on the show in any race that paid. Cross-continent trips were everyday affairs, and trans-oceanic flights – often in lumbering, propeller-driven aeroplanes – to North America, South America, South Africa and even Australasia were not uncommon. To financially survive, we sold our services to the best racing teams that would take us on, in all kinds of single-seaters and sports cars. If we were entered in Formula 1, our employer might expect similar services for important Formula 2 events with the occasional Indianapolis 500 and *Formule Libre* race thrown in. And, of course, we rarely passed up the odd job from a hopeful privateer owner trying his hand against the major teams. Sometimes privateers had good cars, but often they were last year's equipment prepared to levels that could be anywhere from superb to ratty.

Our weekends rolled into sequenced rotations among different cars, different owners and different tracks, adding up, we hoped, to fiscal stability. Ceaseless travel often required us to sacrifice societal niceties and family milestones;

my daughter Charlotte was born while I was racing at Daytona. Even peers' funerals took a back seat to the need to keep the engines revving and wheels turning. Far too often the thrill of a win and the anguish of a fatality came packaged together. So it was on the day of my first world championship victory in sports cars.

My first big win

The 1968 BOAC Six Hours at Brands Hatch was held on the same April weekend as test days at Le Mans in France and a Formula 2 race at Hockenheim in Germany. Jacky Ickx and I were committed to drive at Brands Hatch in John Wyer's Gulf Ford GT40 but, typically of the era, John had also entered a GT40 for the Le Mans test weekend. Jacky practised at Brands on Friday then flew to Le Mans, where he put in 44 laps on Saturday before returning for Sunday's race in England. As Jacky set the fastest time at Le Mans during that testing, our hopes for a win in the 24 Hours were high, but they were dashed when he broke his leg in practice for the Canadian Grand Prix and I broke my arm at Spa. Pedro Rodriguez and Lucien Bianchi inherited 'our' Le Mans GT40 and drove superbly to take the win.

As I waited nervously in the Brands Hatch pit before my first stint of the race, a journalist edged into my line of sight to ask if I had heard about Jim Clark. '*Killed at Hockenheim, mate,*' he reported.

OPPOSITE Sharing the 1968 Spanish Grand Prix podium with two World Champions, Graham Hill (centre) and Denny Hulme, was a heady moment at only my second race in the Formula 1 World Championship.
National Motor Museum

ABOVE The Brands Hatch
Six Hours of 1968 was
my first win in a world
championship sports
car race, shared with
Jacky Ickx in a John
Wyer Ford GT40.
Ford

I acknowledged the news with a nod but tried to keep my mind on my upcoming responsibility of racing to win.

Compartmentalisation is self-protection. When my turn came, I put everything else out of my mind and bore down on racing with all of the finesse and determination I could muster. Jacky drove brilliantly, as usual, and we won the race, just 22 seconds ahead of the factory Porsche 907 piloted by Gerhard Mitter and my Cooper Formula 1 teammate, Ludovico Scarfiotti. The Brands Hatch Six Hours was my first win in the International Championship for Makes but the taste of victory soured in my mouth as I numbly absorbed the loss of the great Jim Clark.

In my early days of traipsing around Europe with David Bridges' Brabham BT16, Jim Clark was my mentor and idol. He set the standard for excellence with grace and was the role model every racer tried to emulate. It was said of Jim that his driving was so naturally effortless it looked as if he were only half trying – as he rocketed off to win after win after win. He was the era's

superstar, a hero as worthy of peer esteem as he was of the adulation of millions of race fans. He was also my earliest and only fitness instructor, dispensing training guidance characteristic of the era. Clark's routine? '*I lift my legs each night as I get into bed*,' he said, and I have followed Jim's exercise programme without missing a day since 1968.

It's a bit of a shame that Clark's gentlemanly reputation masked the fact that he was also a lot of fun. It was Jim who introduced me to the fine art of the 'bunfight' at the inevitable bacchanal following *Il Gran Premio de Barcelona* in 1967. Balancing a dab of butter on his knife, he gave it a quick flick, propelling it across several tables and onto the forehead of an attractive young woman. That was the signal for all of the assembled drivers and team personnel to uncork their tensions, turning dinner into chaos until every bread roll had been launched. As always, plentiful amounts of alcohol had been consumed before and during the meal in keeping with our post-race ritual of communal self-medication. Even cool Jim Clark was not immune

to the private thrill of finding himself alive.

At the behest of Colin Chapman (boss of Lotus) or perhaps Firestone (with whom Clark had a contract), Jim opted out of the Brands Hatch Six Hours in favour of driving a Formula 2 Lotus 48 in the *Deutschland Trophäe* at Hockenheim. During the first heat Clark's car lurched off the track at very high speed and into the trees lining that part of the circuit. He succumbed to multiple injuries before reaching the hospital. We all believed that some mechanical failure must have occurred – possibly the result of a deflating rear tyre – as Jim simply didn't make mistakes, and later our tyre theory was proven to be true.

This gentle Scottish sheep farmer, twice Formula 1 World Champion and winner of the 1965 Indianapolis 500, was undoubtedly the outstanding driver of his era. When Jim Clark died, we realised that, if the unthinkable could happen to him, it could happen to anyone. No death ever shook us more.

Jim Clark was 32 years old and at the peak of his career.

Mr Ferrari and me – *prima occasione*

Any serious driver of the 1960s and 1970s will admit that, as often as he fell asleep feeling moist for some tempting pit bunny, he spent many more hours fantasising about receiving the ultimate racer's phone call. In April 1968, my call came.

'It's Franco Gozzi, with Ferrari, and I'm calling to ask if you would like to test Formula Due *in Modena. Can you be free on Tuesday?'* Could I somehow tear myself away to test for Ferrari? Wife in labour? Need to bury Grandma? Scheduled to accept the Nobel Peace Prize? No problem. *'Yes, yes Signor Gozzi, no trouble at all. In fact, I can leave this minute if that would suit you better.'*

In every driver's black heart was a willingness to sacrifice sensitive body parts for a drive with Ferrari. Moreover, there isn't a racer alive today – as proven by Ferrari's Formula 1 revolving door – who wouldn't do the same: *anything* for a shot at racing for the *Scuderia*.

I flew to Milan (although I was prepared to walk) and checked into a Modena hotel from which I was collected by *Ingegnere* Mauro Forghieri the following morning. At that time, Ferrari used the *Autodromo di Modena* for car development and I was taken there immediately for my day of testing. Things seemed to be going well, although with Ferrari one never really knew. When we stopped for a short lunch break, Forghieri pointed out a figure in a black overcoat with dark glasses sitting under a tree at the end of the circuit, a perch sited so that he could survey every corner.

'See that man over there?' he whispered reverentially. *'It's* Commendatore *Ferrari. He has come here to watch you.'* The unspoken message was clear, *'Redman, you ambitious fool, try harder.'* I had heard about Ferrari's penchant for manipulating drivers. Now the *Scuderia*'s infamous pressure tactics were being brought to bear on me.

The test continued through the afternoon, as did Forghieri's lack of feedback. The next day, I was summoned to lunch in Maranello at *Ristorante Cavallino*, where I was to meet Enzo Ferrari and his large entourage. As I entered the restaurant's private dining room, the old man himself stood up from the table and walked slowly towards me. Slightly behind, one on each side, were Forghieri

and Gozzi, the PR manager. I froze: the restaurant fell silent. *Signor* Ferrari was tall and physically imposing with the self-assurance of a famous industrialist who was also the world's premier racing car manufacturer. Yet, to me, he was humble and charming. He smiled warmly, extended his hand, looked me in the eye, and voiced these words with kindness and respect: *'Finally, Mr Redman, I am deeply honoured to meet you.'*

Actually, that never happened except in my fantasies. In Enzo Ferrari's world, drivers were like children, expected to be ornamental outside a racing car and useful only for bringing glory to the Ferrari name. As my hand hung in the air anticipating his, *Il Commendatore* reached up and seized my left cheek between his thumb and forefinger, squeezing firmly as he shook my face. Then he addressed me with this memorable tribute: *'Niz-a-boy!'* Although I drove Ferrari's cars in many events, these were the only words *Signor* Ferrari ever directed towards my inconsequential presence.

At lunch there was a place at the table for me, not that it mattered much to *Signor* Ferrari or the other guests. Since Ferrari spoke no English and I had no Italian, I kept silent during the meal and tried to lose myself in forking down the excellent pasta. Ferrari chatted amiably in Italian with those all around me, and I did hear my name mentioned several times, but no one offered to translate. It was a complete mystery what Forghieri reported about my test or if any of the discussion around the table included my future as a Ferrari driver. Even as I was returned to the airport, no hints were offered. Over time, I learned that this was consistent with the way Ferrari controlled all drivers.

Not many days later, I received a call from Gozzi inviting me to race the team's older Formula 2 car alongside team leader Jacky Ickx in the newest version at the Nürburgring on 21 April. At last, I knew that my performance at the *Autodromo di Modena* had been sufficient.

In writing earlier about my Ferrari début, I recounted the debacle that led me to drive obsessively – even insanely – in the race, going from last place to fourth at the finish, and setting a new Formula 2 lap record. There's another story

about that Nürburgring weekend that says a lot about Ferrari's ambitions and, equally, my own.

Having given my all during Saturday's practice, I pulled into the pits with 15 minutes remaining in the session.

'*Why you a-stop, Bre-an?*' enquired Forghieri.

'*Well… I've gone as fast as I can,*' I replied.

'*Bre-an, you are only in tenth place. Now go back out and try harder.*'

Stunned by my sub-standard showing and wanting badly to make an impression on Forghieri, I went out and drove like a madman, taking far more risks than were wise. When I returned to the pits, Forghieri smiled.

'*Good, Bre-an, now fourth!*'

As was my habit after every session, I consulted the lap charts to assess my relative competitiveness and was shocked to see that my new times were only one tenth of a second faster than those I'd set earlier. Moreover, the team's lap charts showed that I had been in fourth place all along, before I took those unnecessary chances. Forghieri had lied to me or, at best, craftily given me misleading information. His 'fine Italian hand' would have made the Medicis proud.

Nonetheless, my drive during the race made a strong impression on Forghieri. After dinner that night, he excused himself from the table, returning 10 minutes later to sit beside me.

'*Bre-an,*' he whispered conspiratorially, '*I speak with* Signor *Ferrari and he say* Formula Due *for you this season and,*' his voice increasing dramatically, '*at Monza's* Gran Premio d'Italia *in September,* Formula Uno!'

In a burst of self-protective honesty, words came tumbling out of my mouth uninfluenced by any rational thought: 'Ingegnere *Forghieri, I'm sorry, but no thank you.*'

ABOVE Enzo Ferrari listens cautiously to Mauro Forghieri, as did I when I turned down his offer to drive for Ferrari in Formula 2 and Formula 1. Later, I made the most of my second chance with Ferrari, driving sports prototypes in 1972 and 1973.
Getty Images/ Rainer Schlegelmilch

'*WAT?*' he shouted. '*Wadda you mean, no thank you?*'

Still not thinking, I gave my answer. '*If I drive for Ferrari,* Ingegnere *Forghieri, I'll be dead before the end of the year.*'

Later that night, I sat on the edge of my bed with my head in my hands staring at the floor. What in the world had I done, turning down Ferrari and Formula 1, the one job in racing that fulfils every driver's dreams? Somehow, the synapses that still resided in the logical part of my mind recognised that wanting to live was a worthy emotion and, however painful this decision, I had done the right thing. Well, maybe.

Mr Ferrari and me – *possibilità secondo*

Three years later, following my brief retirement, emigration to South Africa and the disastrous fire at the Targa Florio, I found myself the owner of a career deeply in the doldrums. Luck appeared in the person of my old patron, Sid Taylor. In September, BRM loaned the well-connected Sid a freshly designed P167 Can-Am car for him to quietly test at the Interserie race at Imola, Italy. Interserie racing was essentially *Formule Libre*, with rules devised to allow a variety of dissimilar cars to race as equals. Sid's cars were often last year's model, but the factory BRM was a Tony Southgate design and, therefore, likely to be very good. It rained hard at Imola and, predictably, Southgate's car was superb in the wet. In fact, it was so superior that I was able to lap the entire field, including the factory Ferraris.

Soon my old pal *Ingegnere* Forghieri appeared at my side. Leaning forward, he affected theatrical sincerity.

'*Bre-an, what you are doing next year?*' Moving closer, he continued, '*You are the only driver* Signor *Ferrari ever ask twice.*'

Magnifico! I was back in the racing business at senior level.

Cooper duper

During 1968 I contested my first three World Championship Formula 1 Grands Prix, for Cooper, as well as one non-championship Formula 1 race.

BELOW My best result in 15 Formula 1 World Championship races was third place in the 1968 Spanish Grand Prix at Jarama, driving a Cooper-BRM T86B. *Sutton Images*

For the first race, the South African Grand Prix at Kyalami, I drove a T81B equipped with a Maserati V12 engine, but thereafter I had a new T86B with a BRM V12. In March, in the non-championship Race of Champions at Brands Hatch, I qualified a disappointing tenth but managed to drag the car up to a respectable fifth place at the finish.

For May's Spanish Grand Prix, my teammate Ludovico Scarfiotti and I qualified at the tail end of the field, 12th and 13th respectively. We worked our way up the order, mainly because of the alarming attrition rate, and, with a podium position looking possible, I nipped past Ludovico to claim third place behind winner Graham Hill and runner-up Denny Hulme, Ludovico bringing his reluctant Cooper home fourth. I wasn't the only one surprised by this result. The victory celebrations for the three podium finishers included a lap of honour and when I joined Graham and Denny perched on the back of an implausibly small SEAT convertible, Hill – fully familiar with the abysmal nature of the Cooper – did a double take. '*Christ Almighty, Redman,*' he exclaimed, '*don't tell me* you *were third!*'

Who was I to mention that my good fortune was due largely to attrition? While Ludovico and I were one lap down on Graham and Denny, fifth-placed Jean-Pierre Beltoise was a whopping nine laps behind the leaders – and there were no other finishers. It's permissible to get lucky once in a while, and I'm grateful whenever it happens.

The 1968 season was going splendidly: a third place in the Spanish Grand Prix, two wins with Jacky Ickx in the Gulf GT40, and an excellent second to Jochen Rindt in David Bridges' Formula 2 Lola T100 car at Crystal Palace. Sweetest of all were an offer from Ferrari and a competing invitation for a 'talk' with Colin Chapman at Lotus.

I arrived at Spa for my third Grand Prix flush with hope and promise. I left on a stretcher, body broken and dreams shattered. On top of the world one minute, at the bottom the next. As the saying goes, '*That's racing*'.

ABOVE On the lap of honour following the 1968 Spanish Grand Prix, a locally built SEAT 850 Sport Spyder labours around Jarama carrying winner Graham Hill, runner-up Denny Hulme and third-placed me.
Sutton Images

ABOVE Just a week after my 1968 Brands Hatch 1,000Kms victory, I won my first race for Sid Taylor, at Oulton Park in his Lola T70 MkIIIB.

Mike Hayward Collection

BELOW Over the years I raced a lot in sports cars and Formula 5000 for Sid Taylor (left), an independent entrant on the edges of the establishment.

Peter McFadyen

Sid Taylor

Sid Taylor, an Irishman from Rathfarnham, was 50 per cent businessman, 50 per cent hustler and 100 per cent motor racing enthusiast. He played helpful roles in my life on several occasions, and had an extraordinary reputation as a talent-spotter. Over the years Sid became famous for employing racers on their way to great careers (Alan Jones and Patrick Tambay), talented-if-quirky characters (Peter Gethin and Tommy Byrne) and emerging young drivers (Tony Brise and me).

I first encountered Sid as an aspiring professional in 1968 when he hired me for one race in place of Denny Hulme – one of his favourites whom he regarded as a true pal – in his 5-litre Lola T70 MkIIIB sports racer after the rough, talented New Zealander found a permanent home with Bruce McLaren's team. The race was at Oulton Park, my home circuit, and I won it. The following season I raced Sid's big Lola coupé nine times and took three wins. My first win was at Thruxton against Jo Bonnier

in a T70 that was purportedly similar, but not so. It was pretty clear to me that Bonnier's car was powered by what is euphemistically known as a 'big' engine, one whose capacity has been stretched illegally. This happens in racing among even the most gentlemanly of competitors. At the subsequent non-FIA event at the Norisring (a converted Nazi parade ground on the edge of Nürnberg), by no coincidence we, too, had a 'big' 5.7-litre engine. This time, I had an easy win.

Sid Taylor intersected with my career twice more, as I relate in other chapters. After my return to England in March 1971 from my ill-advised South African retirement, Sid gave me the chance to resume racing in Formula 5000, and the following year his carefully cultivated industry contacts led to the fortuitous opportunity in Interserie racing that relaunched my professional prospects.

Between 1976 and 1983, Sid went on to run Teddy Yip's troubled Theodore Formula 1 effort, employing a series of desperate drivers. Few of these could push the Theodores to lap times fast

ABOVE In 1969 I won three races in Sid Taylor's Lola T70 MkIIIB, the first here at Thruxton where Jo Bonnier's similar car can be seen following.
Mike Hayward Collection

BELOW It's always a relief to walk away from an accident, as I did at Oulton Park after a tyre failed on Sid's Lola T70 in the 1969 Tourist Trophy race.
Peter Doran

enough to qualify, a record that says more about the car than those behind the wheel.

Sid's racing career mirrored the up-and-down cycle of his business history, beginning with a small fortune earned in the plant-hire business, moving on to asphalt paving, and then striking gold by renting heavy machinery to dispose of cow carcasses during the 1967 outbreak of 'foot and mouth' disease. Later he converted a barn on his parents' Rathfarnham property into a hotel/pub/disco called Taylor's Grange, the latter a regular 'sponsor' of Sid's teams. The final Taylor enterprise of which I am aware is a chain of lap-dancing clubs in Birmingham, through which I'm sure he is cheerfully enjoying life.

Taming the Porsche 917

After Bruce McLaren and Chris Amon won Le Mans in 1966 with Ford's ground-shaking 7-litre MkII and then Dan Gurney and A.J. Foyt followed up with a second Ford win in

1967 with the even more brutal MkIV, Ferrari and Porsche petitioned the *Commission Sportive International* (CSI) for a rule revision. Their excuse was that speeds on the *Mulsanne* straight had become too high, a surprising change of heart by manufacturers who suddenly and inexplicably had become concerned about driver safety. Perish all suspicions that Ferrari and Porsche were tired of being beaten by Ford.

Needless to say, the CSI accommodated its two most important teams by reducing the engine capacities of all manufacturers competing in the International Championship for Makes. As of 1968, prototype engines would be allowed to displace a maximum of 3 litres, with one seemingly unachievable exception. As a token gesture to those still enamoured of the old rule, the CSI declared that factories producing 50 identical cars would be permitted to equip them with engines of up to 5 litres – 50 versions of any racing car model were more than the most

popular ever achieved. A year later the CSI, with no new takers and no existing 5-litre cars other than the GT40 and, somewhat doubtfully, the Lola T70 MkIII, reduced the homologation number further to a still-unlikely 25 cars. Porsche took up the challenge, and Ferdinand Piëch proceeded to drive his radically new 4.5-litre 12-cylinder Porsche 917 right through the CSI loophole.

On 20 April 1969 Herr Piëch presented the CSI inspectors with a line-up of 25 identical Porsche 917s, even offering to let them drive a random sample to prove that all were real cars. By 1 May the 917 was accepted as legal and ready to race, at least in theory. Conforming to a rule does not a racing car make, and the new 917 hadn't been tested for either handling or reliability.

In the first days of April 1969 I was enjoying being at home despite the icy blasts coming down from the Lancashire moors. Four-year-old James was playing quietly in front of the fire and baby Charlotte was just six weeks old. The phone rang.

'*Herr Redman,*' said the voice from Porsche, '*please to come and test ze new 917.*'

Strange, I thought, why ask me when they have six factory drivers within easy reach of the Stuttgart headquarters? Caution made me hesitant. '*I'll just check my calendar and call you back in an hour,*' I said with sincerity, as if I were touched to be so honoured. Immediately I telephoned my Porsche co-driver, Jo Siffert, in Switzerland. '*Seppi, have you tested the 917?*' A long silence followed. Finally, '*No no, Bre-an, we let the others find out what breaks first.*' I suddenly found my calendar completely full.

Cars with unresolved aerodynamics tend to wander at high speeds, 'hunting' in the vernacular of racing. At around 200mph a hunting car is beyond disconcerting. When a car lurches from side to side, the weighting and unweighting of the tyres continually changes their relative grip, requiring frantic steering inputs to keep the car going more or less in a

ABOVE Porsche staged a press-call at Hockenheim to launch the 917 with (from left) Rico Steinemann, Pedro Rodriguez, Dr Ferry Porsche, me and Jo Siffert.
Porsche-Werkfoto

RIGHT Flawed
aerodynamics created
directional instability
in the original 917,
making it difficult
to drive – yet we all
knew it was Porsche's
racing future.
Porsche-Werkfoto

straight line. The chances of the driver finding the car pointing in the right direction at an approaching corner become exactly 50/50.

Gradually I became acquainted with the troublesome 917. I tried one briefly (and circumspectly) in practice at Spa. At the Nürburgring 1,000Kms, I with the other factory drivers lobbied to drive the 908/02, and were vindicated when Jo Siffert and I won. Another encounter came at Le Mans where Seppi and I found our 917 so terrifying on the *Mulsanne* straight that we got permission to race a long-tail 908/02 *Flunder*.

I finally had my first race in a 917 at the Österreichring 1,000Kms, the last round of the 1969 championship. There were two cars entered for factory drivers, Siffert sharing with Kurt Ahrens, Richard Attwood with me. Although both cars were well off the pace during practice on this fast, swooping circuit, our steady work during the race paid off, Jo and Kurt taking the win – the first for a 917 – while Richard and I were third.

Two months later, Porsche decided it was time, finally, to get to grips with the 917. I got a call from David Yorke, John Wyer's team manager, to test the 917 at the Österreichring. Wyer's operation, JW Automotive Engineering, had been named to run the official Porsche factory team for 1970, and I had been hired as one of the drivers – strong motivation for serious work. Since Wyer couldn't attend this test session, he relied on the competent Yorke to run the shakedown process, supported by his brilliant engineer, John Horsman, and mechanics Ermanno Cuoghi and Peter Davies. Representing Porsche's Stuttgart-based design and engineering contingent were Helmut Flegel and Peter Falk. Kurt Ahrens and I were there as test drivers along with Piers Courage, who was invited to do some laps because Wyer was considering him for a seat in 1970. One additional team candidate, Finnish rally ace Leo Kinnunen, was to arrive later.

Our mission was to spend three days finding out how to turn the 917 into a winning car before we took it to the first race of the 1970 season.

Porsche had three 917s on hand for the test, two factory-fresh coupés and one open-top 917PA spyder, the latter an early 917 variant raced in the 1969 North American Can-Am series by Jo Siffert. All three 917s were meant to be shod with Firestone tyres, the supplier with whom Wyer had contracted for the 1970 season, but to our bewilderment the Firestone engineers stayed firmly in the background by their truck, showing no interest in becoming involved in our testing. When asked, they asserted with unassailable logic that Firestone was aware of the 917's reputation for treacherous handling and the company chose not to be associated with the car until it was properly sorted. Right! So the test was run on Dunlops.

Ahrens and I alternated between the new chassis, numbers 006 and 008, while Piers mainly drove the spyder. After a modicum of testing work, Courage received 'an urgent call' from Formula 1 team owner Frank Williams and quickly disappeared, limbering up his contract-signing hand.

The 917's handling lived up to its demonic reputation and displayed the same instability Kurt and I had experienced personally in previous outings. I found that the car hunted alarmingly even on the Österreichring's smoothest straights, requiring fingertip corrections to keep it on the track. Through the corners the car's grip was like bananas on glass, making it impossible to add power anywhere near an apex. We both complained that the chassis flexed disturbingly, and I couldn't rid myself of an unsettling feeling that the car was about to disintegrate.

Kurt and I arrived mutually at a damning conclusion: the 917 was dangerous and, even worse, it was a pig. Our best Österreichring lap times were a full 1.7 seconds slower than Jacky Ickx had managed when winning in Wyer's year-old Mirage-Ford at the same circuit just two months earlier. As I considered the discouraging test results, I began to write off the entire 1970 season and descended into a deep gloom. Horsman and the mechanics were as frustrated

ABOVE The 917's first success came in the 1969 Österreichring 1,000Kms, Siffert and Ahrens first, Attwood and me third. After John Horsman's changes a few months later, the 917 was five seconds a lap faster on the same circuit.
Getty Images/ Rainer Schlegelmilch

ABOVE An open-top
917PA and a long-tail
917 await testing at
the Österreichring
in October 1969 as
Ermanno Cuoghi (orange
overalls) talks with Piers
Courage. The cars' poor
handling depressed
the 1970 drivers –
Kurt Ahrens (Porsche
Salzburg) and me (John
Wyer's Gulf works team).
Porsche-Werkfoto

as the drivers. If team manager Yorke feared for
Wyer's relationship with Porsche, Kurt and I
feared for our reputations, and our bodies.

As the test progressed it became increasingly
evident that the 917's aerodynamics weren't
working. The fact that the car was nervous and
the rear tyres lacked grip suggested that the
boundary layer of the airflow was detaching
from the bodywork well before it reached the
rear of the car, creating negative pressure (lift).*
Horsman quietly observed that the front of each
917 at our test was spattered with dead gnats,
crushed by the dense layer of attached air that
created downforce on the front wheels. He also
noted that the rear bodywork remained clean
until the very tip of the tail where turbulence
sucked the insects back onto the car. In brief,
something was detaching the boundary layer
from the bodywork before arriving at the 917's
long tail, making it aerodynamically ineffective.
Horsman's dead gnats raised the right questions;
now he needed to supply the answers.

At the end of the first depressing day of

testing, Horsman and the mechanics sprang into
action borrowing tools and materials from the
Porsche truck. To the horror of Porsche engineers
Flegel and Falk, Wyer's three men set upon one
sacrificial 917's rear body with hacksaws, cutting
off everything behind the trailing edge of the rear
wheels. Destruction accomplished, they utilised

*Aerodynamics is as much of an art as it is a science. When a
car flows through atmosphere, molecules compress at its nose,
blunting the car's progress until these particles find paths of
lesser resistance around the bodywork, tyres, suspension and
mirrors. If the shape of the car is aerodynamically favourable,
the molecules remain compressed in a thin boundary layer
as they flow over and around the car's surfaces, streaming
without interruption onto and past the tail. The goal is to
keep that thin river of molecules tightly attached to the car at
all times since any separation reduces downforce and creates
drag. Additionally, performance suffers when the turbulence
created by this vacuum at the car's tail exceeds the downward
frontal pressure, acting like a dragging anchor that degrades
the car's forward speed. Good aerodynamics is why racing car
shapes tend to be graceful.*

a combination of sheet aluminium, plywood and duct tape to fashion a stubby, wedge tail that rose to an abrupt cut-off crowned by a couple of tacked-on rectangular spoilers.

There was no streamlining of any kind. Porsche's profoundly elegant 917 racing car now resembled a ham-fisted hot rod. Traditionalists are fond of asserting that 'what looks fast is fast', which I now qualify with 'sometimes'. Horsman was grateful that Piëch wasn't present as he never would have allowed such improvisation.

In the morning, I was to be the first out in the patched-together car and arrived more than a little sceptical about Horsman's cosmetic surgery. If Porsche factory aerodynamicists couldn't make the car handle, why should bodywork cobbled together by an engineer and a couple of mechanics radically improve this sophisticated car's aerodynamics?

After about a half a lap, my opinion was transformed. The car felt stable, fast and willing. The effect of the reconstructed tail was nothing short of miraculous. Not only had the 917 ceased

to hunt on high-speed straights, but it allowed me to relax at flat-out speeds. Even better, the rear of the car felt planted, encouraging me to attack the corners with confident aggression. Greedily, I stayed out for seven laps to enjoy the fun and to be 100 per cent sure I was right.

Ahrens followed me in the car, immediately loving the handling and confirming my

ABOVE AND BELOW
John Horsman butchered the original long-tail body style (seen at the Österreichring 1,000Kms) into a cobbled-up short-tail.
Peter Davies

ABOVE Fully sorted, the definitive 917K (shown testing at Sebring) dominated the 1970 International Championship for Makes, with Jo Siffert and me taking our first win at Spa.
Michael Keyser

RIGHT Porsche's Ferdinand Piëch (standing) and JW Automotive's John Wyer (with clipboard) were two of the key figures behind the 917's eventual racing success.
Getty Images/ Rainer Schlegelmilch

judgement. Even running on the less effective Dunlops, our lap times fell by almost three seconds, from 1m 48.2s to 1m 45.3s, more than a second faster than the 1m 46.6s set by the Mirage two months earlier. So efficient was the new tail that Horsman needed to balance its downforce by tweaking the nose to increase front-end grip.

On the third day of testing, now equipped with the superior Firestone tyres, we lit up the time charts, gaining another two full seconds a lap. Thanks to the ingenuity of Horsman and his crew, the JW Automotive operation could field a Porsche team that would make the factory proud, and we drivers now had a potential winner for the 1970 season. Glorious!

On that last day of testing a group of German-speaking gentlemen in suits landed on the track in a private airplane. First they consulted with Porsche engineers Flegel and Falk, and then they carefully measured the crudely fashioned tail. Without a congratulatory word to John Horsman or consultation with any

driver, the executives departed on their waiting plane to report back to Porsche headquarters. It appeared that, in transforming the 917 from a failure to one of racing's all-time most admired cars, John Horsman and two guys with fibreglass under their fingernails had unintentionally wounded the pride of Porsche's aerodynamic brains trust – a bittersweet resolution for the wizards of Zuffenhausen. Strange, no?

In April 1970, Kurt Ahrens was testing a revised long-tail 917 in the rain at Volkswagen's Ehra-Lessien proving ground near Wolfsburg when the car aquaplaned. Somehow its back half got caught under a steel barrier while Kurt and the front section carried on down the road. A month later Willi Kauhsen had a similarly frightening experience that ended with a second 917 completely destroyed. These accidents made me reflect on Seppi Siffert's original warning about letting others discover what would break first. Ultimately, Kurt, Willi and the factory learned the answer – it was the chassis.

BELOW In April 1970, after John Wyer's team had sorted out the 917K's handling, Kurt Ahrens aquaplaned when testing a new long-tail 917 in the rain at VW's Ehra-Lessien proving ground, thankfully without serious injury. *Porsche-Werkfoto*

CHAPTER 7
Le Mans:
Le Heartbreaker

The cinema was dark, so the cadre of young males transfixed by the movie could simmer in their fantasies knowing they were cloaked in communal anonymity. Each watched the screen intently, eyes glazed, cheeks flushed, lips parted and hearts beating in sympathetic cadence. One year before, the sad woman above them had lost her husband at Le Mans in a crash that involved the driver she had now followed to his caravan. With the tangled emotions of painful loss mingled with stirrings of unforeseen yearning, she pleaded for understanding from the handsome driver facing her.

'*But what's so important about driving faster than anyone else,*' she implored? Every male in the audience held his breath as the man in the Dunlop overalls crinkled his eyes and answered with the painstaking tenderness credible only from the truly tough. '*Lotta people go through life doing things badly,*' he said. '*Racing's important to men who do it well. When you're racing, it's life. Anything that happens before or after is just waiting.*'

In validating his obsession, the film's hero, Michael Delaney (Steve McQueen), revealed how every driver is, himself, a driven man, hooked on a life of such intensity that normal human activities become, well, just waiting. At that moment, every male in the audience (and not a few females) believed they could feel the same way about racing. Few ever would. While no driver of the 1970s would have described his job with such melodrama, we all silently recognised the germ of truth in Delaney's corny denouement. The phrase '*anything that happens before or after is just waiting*' arrives steeped in loneliness – and there was some of that in real racing too.

Steve McQueen's *Le Mans* was meant to be the most authentic racing story ever filmed and came very close to succeeding. While critics justifiably raised their eyebrows over the Hollywood plot with its soulful stares and sparse dialogue, enthusiasts and escapists across the world soaked in every last frame of manifest driver cool, the commotion of glorious engines, the furious door-to-door action and, yes, even the overblown competitor and love interest dependencies. For many young and older dreamers, *Le Mans* was a private reverie whose ethos embodied their hidden aspirations.

In cinematographic terms, the first 45 minutes of *Le Mans* are magnificent, richly conveying the authenticity of the intensive pre-race experience, shot in real time leading to the 1970 start. In the cold eyes of the era's professionals, McQueen's cinematic portrayal never quite captured the bite of real competition but it did serve to flatter our motivations. In its simplistic way, it reinforced why we committed our lives to this trade. The film also offered quite a few of us well-paying jobs.

OPPOSITE Steve McQueen, like Paul Newman, had a real love for racing. If they had made motor racing their professions, they would have been as good as anyone.
Porsche-Werkfoto

My (very brief) movie career

The day after the finish of the real 1970 Le Mans 24 Hours, Steve McQueen geared up to document his film tribute to long-distance sports car racing. When former Lotus team manager Andrew Ferguson invited a clutch of professionals to join the *Le Mans* production, many race participants quickly accepted. Answering the call were Jo Siffert, Vic Elford, Richard Attwood, David Piper, Hughes de Fierlant, Derek Bell, Jonathan Williams and me, all of us exhausted from the preceding four days of the real contest. Richard had won with Hans Herrmann, driving a Porsche Salzburg 917. Hughes was the best of the rest of us, finishing fifth, and not far behind in ninth place were Jonathan Williams and Herbert Linge driving McQueen's Porsche 908/02. This was an exceptional achievement for a camera car with its aerodynamics compromised by protruding photo equipment and with pit-stops requiring the exchange of film cartridges as well as drivers. This genuine on-track action provided many of the film's best moments. Although Siffert and I failed to finish the real race, the film's story centred on our Gulf Porsche 917 – car number 20.

Since Porsche had constructed 25 917s, there were plenty left over for other purposes. Those used in the film's production were new and authentic, numbered to match the cars that actually raced. Jacques Swaters, the Belgian Ferrari dealer and racing privateer, orchestrated the necessary allocation of Ferrari 512Ss. It seems that when *Il Commendatore* learned that a Porsche triumphed over a Ferrari in the movie, he declined to offer factory cars and have his Le Mans entries humbled twice in the same year. It made little difference since Swaters' Ferraris were very similar to the works entries and the actual competitors' numbers were easily replicated.

The remuneration McQueen offered to each driver was good by our non-demanding standards, but clever Jo Siffert found a way to turn this modest opportunity into a spectacular financial killing. Seppi owned a Porsche dealership in Switzerland and had developed

BELOW The drivers gather for a Le Mans production meeting to prepare a staged driving sequence: from the left, Jack Reddish (producer), Herbie Müller, me, Vic Elford, Hughes de Fierlant, a film technician, Jonathan Williams and Derek Bell (in the chair marked 'SCRIPT').
Brian Redman collection

a knack for wheeling and dealing in used racing cars, of which McQueen's production needed many. When the props department produced a list of specific models, Seppi's eyes grew wide. Shoulders raised in astonishment, he simply had to confess that each and every one of the desired cars was waiting in his Swiss garage, ready to take to the track. Of course, Jo had nothing like the sort of collection he professed to own, but he knew he could procure the entire fleet and then rent the cars to McQueen's production at Hollywood prices. When the filming was complete, Jo also realised that his enterprise had an Act II. He persuasively promised that each car he sold bore McQueen's famous fingerprints, and more than one 917 became the actual Delaney/ McQueen car. Then, as now, the resale values of racing cars were burnished by the lustre of stardom.

A little later, in a moment of good fortune, the genuine McQueen 917 became mine. Yes, really! Following my neck-breaking accident in Canada, however, I sold it to an unimpressed Richard Attwood, who had won the real thing in a 917 and had little need for the additional McQueen stardust.

Working on location was exceedingly painstaking. The crews took forever to set up their cameras. The light had to be just right, and then all the little details needed to be perfect. Given McQueen's fastidiousness, they were. Each day the crew would examine film of the real pit-stops and then match the action so precisely that, when we watched the rushes every evening, it was hard to tell the movie version from the original. The on-track sequences were staged with faster and slower cars mixed together and we were instructed on where, when and how to pass. In the final edit, these sequences were woven artfully into footage shot during the race, resulting in majestic distance views and vivid close-ups of exciting cars doing battle.

This next statement will begin to sound familiar, but I soon learned that working in the movies was another job for which I was unsuited. I found all the constraints counter-intuitive and,

ABOVE In Steve McQueen's *Le Mans*, Michael Delaney's 917 number 20 sacrificed a win so Porsche could have a 1–2 sweep. *Porsche-Werkfoto*

Le Mans was filmed in
the weeks following
the race with we
well-paid professional
drivers simulating the
racing action.
Porsche-Werkfoto

to me, following McQueen's scripted scenarios
was unnatural. After several weeks I could
no longer take the tedious pace or the travel
back and forth between England and France.
I resigned from the *Le Mans* crew – one more
career opportunity tossed aside.

The genuine tragedy in the creation of
Le Mans was how David Piper, a top sports-car
driver, sustained a deep leg cut in a crash that
destroyed the Porsche 917 he was driving. While
David was being removed from the wreckage,
brake fluid and other debris got into the wound,
causing a severe infection. The lower section
of his leg had to be amputated to save his life.
A lesser man would have moved on to a sport
with fewer physical challenges, but not Piper.
While his professional career was finished, he
continued to compete successfully in historic
racing for over 40 years, often in his own green
Porsche 917. David also endures as a fixture in
many racing paddocks, often upstaged – as we
all are – by his incredibly funny wife Liz, from
whom I learned my best after-dinner jokes.

The 1967 24 Hours

Long before Lord Alexander Hesketh spiked
the Formula 1 punch bowl with champagne,
Rolls-Royces, starry-eyed lovelies and a Teddy
Bear-emblazoned racing car driven by the
colourful James Hunt, there were team owners
whose approach to competition would shock
the stern professionals in today's paddocks.
My first Le Mans appearance was steeped in
that indulgent style.

In 1967 the Yorkshire landowner and City of
London businessman Viscount Downe (John
Dawnay) invited me to drive his Ford GT40 at
Le Mans. The team was entered by the
formidable John Wyer who, with John Willment,
had just formed JW Automotive Engineering
to take over Ford Advanced Vehicles. (The 'JW'
initials in the company name actually stood
for John Willment, not John Wyer). In addition
to building a Ford variant called the Mirage,
JW Automotive continued to supply parts
and services to existing GT40 owners such
as Viscount Downe, but was too busy with

ABOVE Despite the cumbersome camera boxes, Herbert Linge and Jonathan Williams raced McQueen's 908/02 camera car to an estimable ninth place in the 1970 24 Hours, all the while recording the film's superb live racing action.

Porsche-Werkfoto

its own Le Mans entry to run another team. There were probably some Wyer workshop personnel among our band of mechanics and, after the Mirages were halted early in the race by head-gasket failures, I think a few of the pit lads lent us a hand but a disciplined Wyer-run operation the Downe team was not. Wyer wouldn't have tolerated the laid-back atmosphere of Downe's *équipe*, run from the Hôtel de France in La Chartre-sur-le-Loir.

On the Thursday before the race, the team's commitment to eating, drinking and fine living was in full flow at this classically traditional establishment when, at about 3.30pm, the good Viscount finally turned his attention to business. '*What time is practice today,*' he enquired? As 14 diners looked at each other in bemused, semi-stupefied silence, I meekly volunteered, '*It's at 5 o'clock.*' The suddenly aroused John Dawnay turned to his brother James and roared, '*Get Brian to the track, as quickly as possible.*' I came to wish he hadn't.

Dawnay's enormous old Rolls-Royce, of Second World War vintage, could only proceed with any vigour when centrally positioned above the crowned French country roads, which James attacked at 75mph. Inevitably, a small Citroën *Deux Chevaux* appeared through the windscreen, driven by a native who was determined to claim his highway patrimony. As I was about to dive under the dashboard, James stood up. Steering with one hand and waving with the other, he shouted, '*Get out of the way, you bloody peasant!*' Miraculously, the peasant did.

For the race, I was paired with veteran sports car driver Mike Salmon, who was the designated starter. When, after 20 laps, Mike stopped for fuel, I opened the door expecting to get in. '*I'm terribly comfortable, old boy,*' Mike said, claiming his senior right to remain in place. After every refuelling stop, it was the responsibility of the *Automobile Club de l'Ouest*'s official *plombeur* to secure the filler cap with a lead seal to prevent a mischievous driver later topping up the tank himself. Unfortunately in this case, the seal wasn't fastened properly. As Mike stamped

ABOVE My first Le Mans, an all-British effort in Viscount Downe's GT40, ended with my co-driver, Mike Salmon, escaping a 200mph fire.
LAT

BELOW The burned-out wreckage of our GT40 lies abandoned at the *Mulsanne* corner after Mike Salmon baled out with painful burns.
Getty Images/Rainer Schlegelmilch

on the brakes at the end of the *Mulsanne* straight, fuel surged from the tank, popped open the cap and flowed onto the hot exhaust pipes. Immediately the car erupted in flames. Salmon was able to extricate himself but not before becoming badly burned, while the car was totally consumed. Were it not for Mike's insistence on continuing, it would have been me in the car that day and me in the hospital that night. Surely Marion must have thought the same thing.

I returned to the Le Mans 24 Hours many times but never won in 14 attempts, even though I usually had fast, well-prepared cars and strong co-drivers, some of whom did win in other years with other partners. If the shortage of triumphs in the rest of this chapter bothers you, I can assure you it bothers me much more. It is painful to know that Le Mans is the only major world championship sports car race missing from my résumé, and writing those words still wounds my pride. It is small consolation that I took firsts in the IMSA class in 1978 and 1980, and frustrating to know that I led the race overall on five different occasions, four of them in works cars: with Jo Siffert in 1969 in a Porsche 908/02 and again in 1970 in a 917K; twice also with Jacky Ickx, first in a Ferrari 312PB in 1973 and then in a Porsche 936 in 1979; and, finally aboard Dick Barbour's Porsche 935 in 1980. Every Le Mans without a win was crushing but the five that I now go on to describe were particular heartbreakers.

The 1969 24 Hours

During practice for Le Mans in 1969, Jo Siffert and I tried one of the Porsche 917s, understanding that the company's prestige and fortune hung upon its success and that it was destined to be in our future. On the *Mulsanne* straight the new 917 became downright terrifying, hunting at 225mph in a way that made sequential fast laps difficult and exhausting. For the race, Jo and I lobbied for and got permission to use a special, new, long-tail 908 *Flunder* that we found infinitely

ABOVE Porsche's overriding ambition for the 917 was to win Le Mans, but for the 1969 race Jo Siffert and I preferred a well-proven 908/02. *Porsche-Werkfoto*

BELOW Jo and I contemplate the race ahead confident in the reliability of our Porsche 908/02. We were disappointed to be proven wrong. *Getty Images/Rainer Schlegelmilch*

ABOVE The 1969 race was the last to start with the drivers sprinting across the track to their cars. The driver walking slowly is Jacky Ickx in his lone, brave – and, it transpired, successful – protest against this traditional start procedure.
LAT

LEFT Our Porsche 908/02 long-tail *Flunder*, with Siffert at the wheel, leads the pack off the start, with the 917 of Vic Elford and Richard Attwood tucked behind.
Porsche-Werkfoto

more stable and, therefore, more comfortable for a long, fast race. We led during the third and fourth hours until the transmission overheated and melted the plastic piping that delivered oil from the pressure sump to the main shaft and differential, probably because the enclosed tail section made the ducts in the rear bodywork inefficient. The *Flunder* may have let us down, but it kept us safe. A wealthy Le Mans aspirant wasn't so lucky.

In a moment of regrettable business judgement, Porsche sold one of its unsorted long-tail 917s to John Woolfe, a modestly talented English privateer who had achieved some success driving a Chevron B12 and a Lola T70 in domestic competition. Sadly, Woolfe's inexperience was such that either he didn't recognise that his new purchase was diabolical or wouldn't accept that it was unsuitable for a 24-hour race. His co-driver, Digby Martland, was even less experienced but exercised better judgement. During practice, Martland rode out a lurid spin over the crest near the end

of the *Mulsanne* straight, just before the 90-degree *Mulsanne* corner. Returning to the pits, he immediately announced his unconditional retirement – from Le Mans, from the Woolfe team and from all future racing.

Porsche, concerned by the mistake of selling an undeveloped car to an unprepared owner, supplied factory driver Kurt Ahrens to qualify the car (in an estimable ninth place) and a second factory regular, Herbert Linge, as Martland's replacement. They then begged Woolfe to let the experienced Linge take the start. Woolfe, eager for his family to see him behind the wheel and fearful of the car's early retirement, became adamant. '*It's my car and I'm going to drive it,*' he said, nominating himself to start the race.

This was the last year of the traditional Le Mans start where cars were arrayed side by side in front of the pits with drivers lined up on the opposite side of the track, facing their cars. At the signal for the four o'clock start, all drivers dashed across the tarmac, jumped into their

ABOVE In the early stages of the 1969 race, Jo and I led for a couple of hours but dropped out with transmission failure – frustrating for the Porsche team but even more so for us.
Porsche-Werkfoto

ABOVE Our 908/02
Flunder for the 1969 race
was a special long-tail
version that proved to be
very stable at speed and
comfortable to drive.
Porsche-Werkfoto

cars and charged off in a chaotic mêleé – that is, all except one. Jacky Ickx, critical of the obvious dangers inherent in this colourful bit of theatre, made it a point to stroll across the track after everyone else and carefully fasten his safety belts before starting his car. Jacky may have joined the 55-car queue last, but 24 hours later he finished first, even if only by 100 yards. Point emphatically made!

Habitually, most drivers were in such a hurry to get underway that they charged from the line with seat belts unbuckled. The conventional practice was to let the field sort itself out and then, on the second or third lap, hold the wheel with one's knees down the *Mulsanne* straight while belting in.

On Woolfe's first lap, he lost control of his 917 in the fast, tricky *Maison Blanche* (White House) section, crashing heavily. Not incidentally for the Porsche team, he took most of the rival Ferraris with him. Without a seat belt, he was thrown from his car and died from his injuries.

John Woolfe was 37 years old.

The 1970 24 Hours

By 1970 the 917 had been developed and proven, and Porsche was determined to hammer out a Le Mans victory. Seven 917s formed a Porsche steamroller, four with the new (since Monza) 4.9-litre engine and three with the older 4.5-litre motor. Two were new long-tail cars specially designed for that year's Le Mans and the other five were short-tail 917Ks, which were more forgiving to drive but not as fast on the straights. Porsche's might was arrayed against no fewer than 11 Ferrari 512s in short-tail and long-tail configurations, all with 5-litre V12s.

John Wyer opted to run short-tail 917Ks rather than any new Porsche-supplied long-tails because his cars were proven and prepared by his own people. His usual drivers – Pedro Rodriguez with Leo Kinnunen, and Jo Siffert with me – were given cars with the upgraded 4.9-litre engines, and for this event Wyer opted to add a third Gulf entry with 4.5-litre power, for Mike Hailwood and David Hobbs. Porsche Salzburg brought one of the new 917LH long-

tail versions for Vic Elford/Kurt Ahrens and a 917K for Richard Attwood/Hans Herrmann. The Martini *équipe* ran Gérard Larrousse/Willi Kauhsen in the other new long-tail car, and Finnish privateer Aarnio Wihuri entered his 917K driven by David Piper/Gijs van Lennep.

As always, the JW Automotive team headquartered at that lovely old bastion of French *laissez faire*, the Hôtel de France, and, as always, John Wyer's favourite retreat proved the perfect place for his drivers to relax and enjoy the camaraderie of their peers. The mechanics would drive our racing cars to and from the track and it became normal to find a trio of 917s with noses thrust against the front entrance as if arranged by a proud parking valet. Off the track, our lives were simple, with race strategies, car set-ups and driver rotations discussed with John and the engineers in informal conversations, often during meals. Without today's tsunami of telemetry data, there were no marathon decoding sessions with superimposed drivers' laps, G-load analytics,

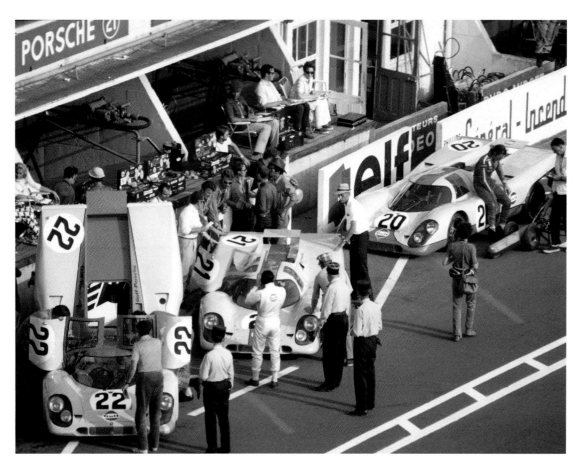

and print-outs tattling on every second of a driver's performance. We managed to race without masseuses ministering to knotted muscles, or personal trainers imposing biometric rigours, or nutritionists prescribing leafy diets, or mindset coaches firming up wobbly resolves, or, God help us, oxygen-infusing hyperbaric chambers. Essentially, we drivers were the most technological components of the entire effort, with much of the burden for the team's success on our shoulders. Racing wasn't better than now, just different. I suspect that most of us would be quite fast in the current racing environment as the best of today would have been in ours.

During the 1970 race, Porsche's vaunted 917 juggernaut began to become undone in alarmingly quick succession. Our team's Rodriguez/Kinnunen car was the first out with a broken connecting rod, after just 22 laps. They were quickly followed 27 laps later by Wyer's Hailwood/Hobbs entry after Mike failed to stop when called in for rain tyres and slid his Porsche into a stalled Alfa Romeo. This excused Mr

Hailwood permanently from the bother of any
future calls from Mr Wyer.

As rain fell in the early evening, Reine Wisell,
struggling to see through the oil-smeared
windscreen of his Filipinetti-entered Ferrari 512S,
was driving slowly through *Maison Blanche* as he
headed for the pits. Three factory 512s arrived
on the scene, nose to tail. Derek Bell, in the first,
managed to swerve and avoid Wisell's car but, in
doing so, selected the wrong gear and blew his
engine. The second, with Clay Regazzoni aboard,
didn't miss: not only did Clay take out Wisell but
he also gathered up the following Michael Parkes.
In one fell swoop, four top-rated Ferraris were out
of the race, leaving the Jacky Ickx/Peter Schetty
512 as the marque's only serious contender.

All this left Seppi and me with a very nice
five-lap lead and in control of the pace. At 2.00am,
while on our 157th lap, Seppi missed a shift,
disintegrating the engine and shattering my
dream of victory. Nobody is perfect, though Seppi
came pretty close.

Elford/Ahrens in Porsche Salzburg's long-tail

A lap of Le Mans

Le Circuit de la Sarthe is one of the world's most compelling tracks, combining the pit straight and first corner of the permanent *Course Bugatti* with the municipal roads that bear the region's commerce, except on a certain June weekend when racing cars rule.

In its 1970 configuration, the Le Mans circuit matched everything offered by the world's finest venues, even the majestic Spa, plus racing's most seductive straight. With a Porsche 917 on a dry track, I rounded the course's 8.5 miles every 3 minutes 25 seconds at an average speed of 145mph, without a moment of boredom. To me, the cadence and grace of a fast lap in a fast car was so rhythmically hypnotic that only Bach could score the video. On each tour, I glided over gentle undulations, negotiated lightning-quick switchbacks and flicked through the gears on long straights. I elbowed around one corner in first gear, then flew through the next flat out. The *24 Heures du Mans* was always emotionally intense, mentally draining, physically tiring and, for me, eternally frustrating, but I eagerly anticipated every one of my 14 annual rendezvous.

The lap began at the start/finish line about halfway down a pitlane stuffed with 55 hopeful driver crews and their teams. Having exited the chicane in first gear, I crossed the line in third at 120mph and found fourth as I swept through the Dunlop curve, an uphill right-hander, until my windscreen filled with a bridge resembling a segment of Dunlop tyre. I crested the hill there at 170mph to find the track dropping away beneath me as momentum lifted the car until the wheels extended in full droop, barely touching the surface. When gravity returned the car to its dampers, the wheels had to be perfectly straight or the car would lurch to either side of the track. I braked as soon as the tyres developed bite, just enough to gain control, leaving sufficient momentum to zip through the 120mph left/right Esses and attack the short straight preceding *Tertre Rouge*. Now the fun began.

Tertre Rouge was a straightforward right-hand turn but, because it launched the car onto the legendary *Mulsanne* straight, it was far and away the circuit's most critical corner. All cars achieve maximum speed on the 3.7-mile *Mulsanne*, so the faster I exited *Tertre Rouge*, the sooner I reached terminal velocity, and the longer that speed

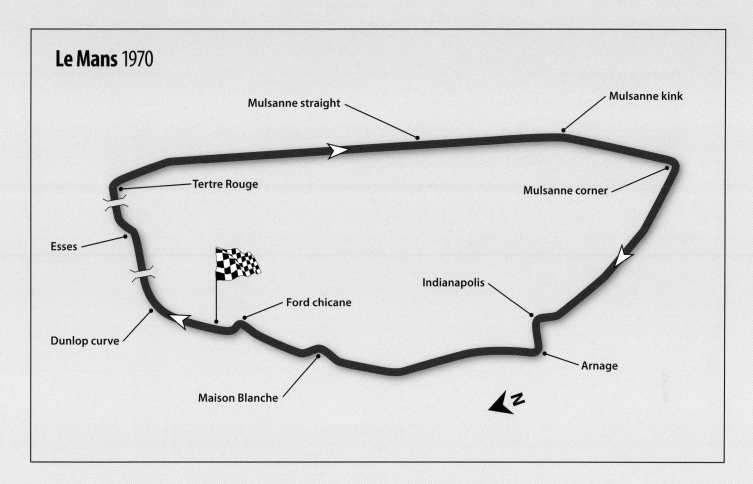

Le Mans 1970

Mulsanne straight

Mulsanne kink

Tertre Rouge

Mulsanne corner

Esses

Indianapolis

Ford chicane

Dunlop curve

Arnage

Maison Blanche

N

advantage was sustained. About a third of the way down the *Mulsanne* is the *Hunaudières* restaurant where diners accompanied their digestifs with Gauloises cigarettes while I breezed by cars huffing along at two-thirds my speed. What put the disquiet in the *Mulsanne* wasn't just the sustained high speed but also its right-hand kink, at about three-quarter distance. Taken at 215mph without lifting, it required every shred of commitment. It wasn't an exercise for the faint-hearted and the kink's intimidation factor has shortened many careers.

The *Mulsanne* ends with a pronounced drop towards the 90-degree right-hand *Virage Mulsanne*, taken in first gear and requiring very heavy braking, plus an abundance of caution. On the approach I always looked ahead to observe the crowds: flashes of yellow or circles of black – umbrellas – signalled rain; lots of people on their feet meant there was an accident. Since both rain and accidents were common, I learned to take the approach dead centre, avoiding crashed cars to the left and right that couldn't control their braking, or landed with wheels pointed the wrong way, or plunged into an unexpected patch of rain-slicked road. My signalling crew was among those lining the rail after the apex of *Virage Mulsanne*, close enough for me to pick

out our team's pit board reporting my position, the number of laps to go, and the number of seconds I was ahead of or behind my nearest competitor.

What followed *Virage Mulsanne* can only be described as a frighteningly fast passage that included two blind, flat-out right-handers. I considered this to be the most dangerous part of the track and it was the scene of many accidents. I braked hard for the third-gear *Indianapolis* left-hander, then turned into a short straight followed by a sharp second-gear right called *Arnage*. As the track unwound, I accelerated through the gears and into top before another blind, fast, dangerous kink at *Maison Blanche*. A short, quick straight led back to *Virage Ford*, the first-gear chicane that practically stopped the cars before releasing them to power up the pit straight to begin another lap.

In 1990 the FIA, governing body for all World Championship motor racing, decreed that no race track could include a straight longer than two kilometres, requiring Le Mans to introduce two chicanes into the *Mulsanne*. I can only say that I'm glad my racing at Le Mans was on the classic circuit, one that offered speed, grace and satisfaction like no other on this planet.

ABOVE Jacky Ickx usually took the start when we were paired together, but not at Le Mans in 1973. My Ferrari 312PB leads a pack of Matras that includes the eventual race winner, number 11 driven by Henri Pescarolo and Gérard Larrousse.
Getty Images/
Rainer Schlegelmilch

OPPOSITE In the 1973 race we experienced various pit delays, but this stop was for routine refuelling – with me calmly (and foolishly?) remaining belted in.
LAT

car soldiered on until lap 225 before expiring, leaving just two of the 4.5-litre 917s remaining. To the collective relief of Porsche's engineers and executives (Ferry Porsche, as the honorary Grand Marshal, had dropped the starting flag), not only did both finish but also they came home a glorious 1–2. Second with 338 laps was the Martini entry of Larrousse/Kauhsen and standing on the top step of the podium, and the world, was the underdog team of Attwood/Herrmann, who finished with a five-lap advantage. The only thing better for Porsche than a Wyer win with a Gulf car was one by Porsche Salzburg, the family's private entry. With the Rudi Lins/Helmut Marko 908/02 picking up third place, the Porsche brand earned not only its first win at Le Mans but also a podium sweep.

Richard Attwood is a lifelong friend and no one deserved a Le Mans win more. As serendipity would have it, Richard's 1970 victory was to have an unexpected and positive effect on my recovery from the devastating 1977 Can-Am accident in St Jovite, Canada.

The 1973 24 Hours
Ferrari skipped Le Mans in 1972 because of concerns about the reliability of the Formula 1-based engine powering the 312PB. It was the only major race that year that Ferrari didn't win. For 1973 the *Scuderia* entered three cars in the 24 Hours, one for Arturo Merzario and Carlos Pace, the second for Tim Schenken and Carlos Reutemann, and the third for Jacky Ickx and me. I was asked to test the car at Paul Ricard, at the time a new state-of-the art circuit in sight of the *Côte d'Azur*'s Mediterranean waters. Every driver loves the chance to try fresh ideas without the pressure of a race weekend's limited practice. I happily agreed that southern France's warmth, lyrical landscapes and roasted lamb rinsed in Bandol's purple wine created the perfect environment for serious racing car development.

Among the concepts that team manager Mauro Forghieri wanted to explore was lowering the airbox that feeds oxygen to the engine and he asked me to gauge the effect on

ABOVE My Ferrari works drive with Jacky Ickx in 1973 was my fourth visit to Le Mans, and my closest brush yet with achieving a good finish. The car failed with just half an hour to go.

Grand Prix Library

the airflow by loosening my belts at top speed and lifting my head. The immediate effect was that my helmet was sucked against the air intake and suddenly I was looking at the sky in a racing car doing 170mph. Emergencies unleash hidden strength and I managed to drag my head out of the airstream and control the car. It made for interesting dinner conversation. More wine, please.

Before the start of the 1973 race, Jacky came to me and said, *'Bree-an, I wish not to start and do battle with Merzario.'* Their animosity was well known and mutual. I reminded him that one of the nine prototypes in the race would win, and that Le Mans was about survival. I warned Jacky that, at the end of the first lap, he should expect to see me in ninth place. *'Good,'* he answered, a very un-Jacky-like sentiment.

By 7.00pm, just three hours into the race, we had been lapped by our teammates. Unexpectedly, I received an out-of-sequence signal to pit. Forghieri wanted to examine our brakes as the backing plates on Merzario's

car had welded themselves to the discs. The decision was that our brakes were fine and we were good to go until midnight. At about that time, the other Ferrari developed a fuel leak and we inherited the lead. Late on Sunday morning we also developed a fuel leak similar to the one that delayed our sister car, and we suffered a broken exhaust that the mechanics tried in vain to repair. By Sunday afternoon Jacky and I had slipped into second place behind the Matra-Simca MS670B of Henri Pescarolo and Gérard Larrousse, but still with a slim chance of pulling off the win.

I had finished my final stint and was resting when Jacky delivered the news that our engine had failed as he was entering the pits. It expired at 3.27pm, 33 tantalising minutes from the finish. We had run for 332 laps and had we been able to cross the finishing line under our own power, a Le Mans requirement, we would have placed third. Ferrari's exhausted mechanics were in tears as they pushed our car from the pits. The grandstand gave our team a standing ovation.

The 1976 24 Hours

I've struggled with how to do justice to my 1976 race in the beautiful (and now immensely valuable) turbocharged BMW CSL Art Car. After we blew three engines in practice, the least damaged one was reinstalled for the race. Jochen Neerpasch then issued the most welcome instructions of any team manager, ever.

'Brian, I vish you to start the race and drive as fast as possible. The engine vill not last.' It managed to survive for two glorious hours.

Twenty years later I met chief engineer Martin Braungart, who asked, *'Do you remember the turbo CSL? Do you know what was the power?'*

'Yes,' I replied, *'it was 750bhp.'*

'Ah, zis is vat vee tell ze drivers – actually 950.'

As with my similar 1975 Sebring-winning CSL, the turbo Art Car was hugely fast, but luck wasn't with any of the BMW competitors that year. Two of seven finished, the best in tenth place, and mine was the first to drop out. That lovely Art Car remains one of my favourites but will always be best known for its striking Frank Stella graphics.

ABOVE The BMW Art Car of 1976 had an unfortunate taste for engines, blowing three in practice. I started the race with the least damaged.
Getty Images/Rainer Schlegelmilch

BELOW Instructed to race flat out, I did so for two glorious hours. American artist Frank Stella based his design on a drawing he created on graph paper.
Grand Prix Library

The 1979 24 Hours

In 1979, opportunistic Porsche was so confident
it could win Le Mans for the second year
running that it entered a pair of well-travelled
936 prototypes, one for Bob Wollek and Hurley
Haywood and the other for Jacky Ickx and
me. Both had been resuscitated from Jochen
Mass crashes, the second accident at the 1979
Silverstone Six Hours being one in which I
played a supporting role.

With six laps remaining in my stint at
Silverstone, I felt the brakes fading. Knowing
that Jochen wouldn't be ready and not eager
for back-to-back sessions, I decided to nurse
the car to our scheduled stop. Three laps later, I
hurtled into Club corner at 180mph to discover
that the brakes were completely absent. Disaster
imminent, I came off the pedal and tried to
spin. There was a bang as the rear bodywork
hit a wooden catch-fence post and, unhurt, I
found myself pointing in the right direction.
With good pit work and a new rear body,
Jochen rejoined the race, still in the lead. While

approaching Woodcote on his opening lap at
tremendous speed, the new rear body flew
off the car, involving Jochen in an enormous
accident. Thankfully he also was unhurt.
Sorry, Jochen.

So cocky was Porsche that the two 936s
were repaired but not tested before Le Mans.
Bob Wollek, borrowed from Georg Loos's Gelo
team, put one 936 on pole, only to shed a tyre
on the *Mulsanne* later in practice. More bolts
were deemed necessary to hold the tyres to the
wheels; personally, I couldn't have enough bolts.

The race began well and we were leading
when I took over from Jacky at the end of his
first stint. Then, as now, the tight, S-shaped Ford
chicane slowed the field to a walk just before
the start/finish straight, and at that time the pit
entry came immediately after this chicane. As I
pivoted through the chicane, the 936 didn't feel
quite right but I couldn't identify any obvious
problem. With just an instant to decide whether
or not to pit, I chose to carry on. Thus began the
most frightening of my Le Mans experiences.

ABOVE It wasn't until 1978 that I could claim my first Le Mans finish, fifth in Dick Barbour's Porsche 935. About to lap our IMSA class entry is the race-winning Renault Alpine prototype of Didier Pironi and Jean-Pierre Jaussaud.
Courtesy of Thomas Horat

LEFT I was happy to have completed a Le Mans 24 Hours at long last, but thoroughly exhausted.
Larry Peterson

ABOVE Perhaps my
best chance to win Le
Mans came in 1979,
when I resumed my old
partnership with Jacky
Ickx in a Porsche 936
– the class of the field.
Jacky leads away on the
warm-up lap, ready for
the 2.00pm start.
LAT

RIGHT Jacky eases our
936 through *Mulsanne*
corner, possibly during
one of our spells in the
lead before disaster
struck in the third hour.
LAT

The tiny instability I'd felt in the chicane turned out to be a deflating left rear tyre. Entering the Dunlop curve at 160mph, the 936 spun without warning. I heard the rear body come off and saw the barrier flash by. Only the combination of a desperate swerve and a miracle kept me from smashing into it.

The Porsche carried a substantial tool kit that included a 'pad saw', a hacksaw blade with one end covered in duct tape. After pulling off at the entry to *Tertre Rouge*, I cut the remains of the tyre off the rim and then slowly drove the seven miles back to the pits, keeping the left rear wheel on the grass as much as possible. Amazingly, after a lap lasting 38 minutes and repairs in the pits costing a further 53, we carried on, in 35th place.

We had worked our way back to seventh place by one o'clock in the morning when, amidst thunder, lightning and pouring rain, the small television on the wall of our pit announced, '*Jacky Ickx is stopped on the Mulsanne.*' Undaunted, Jacky was able to fit a spare fuel-pump drive belt and, 20 minutes later, the TV reported, '*Jacky Ickx is going again.*' After just five more minutes it informed us, '*Jacky Ickx is stopped at the* Mulsanne *corner.*' Now, I was sure we were out of the race.

Wrong. Half an hour later, Jacky appeared in the pits and team manager Norbert Singer waved me into the car. After 45 minutes of frenzied driving in torrential rain, I received a signal to pit. '*Brian, you can get out of the car,*' Herr Singer said. '*We were disqualified an hour ago.*'

It seems that a mechanic had taken a 'sandwich' and thrown it across the track to Jacky. A vigilant marshal spotted the drive belt in Jacky's 'lunch' and we were disqualified for receiving outside assistance. The next day's French newspapers accused Porsche of cheating.

ABOVE After a 160mph tyre failure in the Dunlop curve, I kept my bare wheel on the grass where possible for nearly an entire lap to get back to the pits – singularly frightening with cars passing at over 200mph.
Automobile Club de l'Ouest

CHAPTER 8
Family matters

During the 1968 Belgian Grand Prix at Spa, the bottom right front wishbone broke on my Cooper, causing the car to veer off the track and vault a steel barrier. My right arm was momentarily caught against the guardrail and the radius and ulna were snapped.

The husband whom Marion brought home from the Liège hospital wasn't quite the person who had kissed her goodbye. I remained no less zealous a young racer, but I had been blooded and I found it sobering. Although Marion remained her usual efficient and helpful self, tending to the children and me, things had changed for her as well.

People find it hard to believe that Marion and I never discussed my professional risks, either before or after any of my injuries. The ability to 'keep calm and carry on' was the motto of Londoners during the Luftwaffe's *blitzkrieg* of the Second World War, and that unflinching spirit was perpetuated in the Redman household. As Londoners endured their plight without drama, so, too, did we. This very British trait so infused our personal relationship that there was no dwelling on the potential family and financial repercussions of my accident at Spa, or its implications for our future. That didn't mean that Marion was unmindful of them. After I had been home for about two weeks, she decided to break her code of silence, addressing me in a

firm and steady voice. '*Brian, I would like you to stop racing.*'

Marion was so definite and I was so nonplussed that I remained completely mute. What was I to say? Racing wasn't just a part of my life, it was my whole life, the place where I felt most in control, most satisfied and most alive. I stayed silent, suppressing any suggestions of my intention to continue. To my astonishment, Marion never followed up on her warning but kept calm and carried on. Yes, we are British.

A few months later I had my arm X-rayed at a local hospital and was pronounced healed. When Derek Bennett telephoned to invite me to drive his delightful Chevron-BMW B8 2-litre sports car in South Africa's Springbok Trophy series in the early winter of 1968, I accepted immediately. I suppose it was clear to Marion that I craved racing as much as I did domestic approval, and my return to the competitive circus was accompanied, on my part, by joy and relief. It was now Marion's turn to remain silent.

Retirement in South Africa – 1971

By 1970, too many drivers I knew well had been killed, broken, crushed or burned to death, one after another. That year alone we lost (what an offensively innocuous word) Bruce McLaren, Piers Courage, Hans Laine and Jochen Rindt,

and these were just from the top tier. Many more could be counted in the lesser ranks. For three years I had spent the night before every race sleepless with anxiety. Increasingly I found myself secretly looking for a dignified and financially viable way to quit racing.

Ironically, my experiences during South Africa's Springbok Trophy series with Derek Bennett's Chevron B8 created the opportunity. Whilst racing there in 1968 I met Franz Richter*, a BMW and Volkswagen dealer in Johannesburg who became both a friend and a father confessor. Since Franz was not from the racing world, I could share my apprehensions without shame, and without endangering my job. He listened sympathetically and, after absorbing the instability of my situation, suggested that I move to Johannesburg for a good position in one of his automotive dealerships. '*The climate is great here, Brian, and the living is easy.*'

South Africa is a dazzling country and I particularly loved my experiences at Kyalami, near Johannesburg and the country's premier

ABOVE My first visit to South Africa was to drive a Gulf Mirage at Kyalami in 1967. Three years later, I tried (and failed) to retire in South Africa.
David Pearson

BELOW The Kyalami outing in the Mirage, here displayed in a London showroom, was my first race for John Wyer and my first drive with Jacky Ickx.
Courtesy of John Horsman

circuit. In 1968 the South African Grand Prix was held on New Year's Day. Our Formula 1 entourage was gloriously indulged and largely insulated from the heinousness of apartheid, a system of racial discrimination that was accepted as normal by Afrikaners and most visitors, but now recognised as monstrous. We drivers unthinkingly, and in retrospect shamefully, enjoyed the benefits of our privileged status.

Franz's job offer gave me the chance to escape from racing and, at the end of the 1970 season, I took it. As a hedge against just such a move, I had purchased a house in Johannesburg the year before, justifying it as a rental investment. Now we left our three-bedroom detached home in Colne and flew in to take possession of our new bungalow while our worldly possessions followed by ship.

In the manner of one unwilling to admit the truth, I positioned my retirement as a decision reluctantly taken for the sake of my family. Posing as the responsible *pater familias* allowed me to wrap my insincerity in tissues of thoughtfulness and honour. I suppose I knew what made life in South Africa so effortless but, as with my pre-race anxieties, I chose to compartmentalise. Marion quietly supported my decision to move our family: inside she may have been popping a champagne cork but, just as when life was going the opposite way, she contained her emotions and accepted victory gracefully.

I undertook my apprenticeship at the Volkswagen dealership with optimism and diligence, but it was soon obvious that I was

ABOVE In late 1968 I drove this factory Chevron B8 in five South African races, this the first of them, with Tim Schenken in the Kyalami Nine Hours, where we finished fourth overall.
Brian Redman collection

Violence continues in South Africa. Later in life, Franz Richter sold his car dealerships and embarked on his real love, the game-park and safari businesses. In November 2007 Franz was on his way to pay dancers at his Heia Safari ranch in Mulderdrift, outside Johannesburg, when he was killed by a gunshot to the chest. Richter's common-law wife, Celiwe Mbokazi, was convicted of orchestrating the murder. Daughter Gaby, who as a young girl stayed with us at Taira House, married and later divorced ranch manager Paul Schultze, but continued to own and, with him, manage the property. In November 2013 Schultze was shot dead by intruders.

a terrible salesman and even worse at collecting the money. When sent to secure payment from a tough Afrikaner, I was kept waiting for three hours and then berated for my efforts. What stunned me most was the fury unleashed by the man's elegant wife, who cursed me mercilessly because I had sent a young black boy from the dealership to deliver their invoice. Over the ensuing weeks, I discovered that life in Johannesburg was like that all the time, creating a new reason for me to be frightened. At my insistence, my family had moved from the safety of Lancashire to a country poised to explode into ethnic violence. Nothing about apartheid had touched our family, yet, but I understood that we were not immune. Soon, apartheid changed our lives.

The country's endemic racial problem became personal when, at 1.00am one night, we were wakened by pounding on our front door. A 6-foot 5-inch Afrikaner policeman stood beside an equally imposing policewoman.

'Good evening, sir. We need to see your servants' passes.'

Reluctantly, Joseph and Grace crept from their quarters behind the house. Joseph turned out to be a paperless immigrant from Rhodesia. Grace had a legal pass, but for a different neighbourhood.

'What happens now?' I asked.

'Trial at 7.00am in the morning,' the policeman declared as he spirited Joseph and Grace into the night.

At 7.00am I found myself in a large, tin-covered building where more than 200 black people were incarcerated. One by one, the offending parties were marched before an Afrikaner judge, who was the only white person in the courtroom. 'Guilty' he pronounced on each without ever looking up, followed by the punishment. In the case of Joseph and Grace, it was a fine of 1,000 Rand (about £50), which I paid.

Back at the house, I was unnerved by the dilemma of whether to chance becoming responsible for their repeated arrests or turn away two helpless people, committing them to lives of joblessness and hiding. As the weeks passed, my mind became a cauldron of anxieties as fierce as those that made me quit racing. I, personally, had been subjected to police menace and had witnessed the

ABOVE In 1969 local racer John Love shared my third Kyalami Nine Hours in Sid Taylor's Lola T70, reliveried to Team Gunston identity. Unfortunately, we didn't finish.
David Pearson

BELOW Although in my mind I was retired, in January 1971 I did two single-seater races, at Killarney and Kyalami, in a factory Chevron B18C sponsored by my local employer.
David Pearson

discriminatory injustice of an Afrikaner court. It was clear to me that South Africa was a racial tinderbox and, if and when a conflagration erupted, it would sear everyone in its path.

'*We have to leave now*,' I told Marion. '*One day soon, the black people are going to get fed up and kill all the whites.*' Bloodshed seemed inevitable and I believe it would have come but for the grace of the magnificent Nelson Mandela.

So brief was our stay in South Africa that the container with all of our furniture and other possessions never left the dockside in Durban. I arranged for it to be returned, unopened, to England on the next ship.

Racing, again

I still had to get my family out of South Africa so my return to racing for the 1971 season was no longer a choice but a necessity. As has happened at other difficult moments in my life, good fortune turned up, this time in the form of a call from John Surtees, who invited me to drive his TS7 Formula 1 car in the South African

Grand Prix in March. Thrilled, I immediately accepted the opportunity to earn £1,000 and was especially grateful for the chance to get back in a racing car to scrape off my mental rust. I qualified 17th in a competitive field and finished seventh. This wasn't bad for a retired driver although definitely not good enough for me to regain my place in the professional pecking order.

Marion and I had been so optimistic about South Africa that we had let our house in Colne for an entire year, so there was no home to which my family could return. Worse, I had no paying drive waiting for me. Our lodging problem was solved when Marion's parents volunteered to share their gracious Victorian residence.

Slowly, new racing possibilities began to find me. First a one-off drive in a Martini Porsche 917K with Vic Elford at Brands Hatch, then a race in Sid Taylor's Formula 5000 McLaren M18. Welcome as these two income opportunities were, neither would help me climb back into the

ABOVE In March 1971 my brief retirement ended with a fortunate invitation from John Surtees to drive his Formula 1 TS7 in the South African Grand Prix. I started 17th and finished seventh.
Sutton Images

top ranks. Out of the blue, a stroke of serendipity changed everything.

John Wyer called asking if I wanted to share a Porsche 908/03 with Jo Siffert in the 1971 Targa Florio. Yes, I wanted it desperately. A Wyer drive would confer an immediate stamp of legitimacy and ease my return to big-league status.

At the time, Wyer's offer was life altering and I was fired with enthusiasm. Retrospectively, the 1971 Targa Florio proved to be life threatening and nearly ended my career. Racing is like that.

Aftermath of the 1971 Targa Florio

Both my body and my remaining illusions of indestructibility were shattered by my horrendous crash on the first lap of the 1971 Targa Florio. Gulf Oil and Porsche chartered a Lear jet to return me to England where Marion, as always, was the essence of care and efficiency but reluctant to become another racing widow. One day as I was beginning to recover, she repeated with conviction the precise sentence

that shook me after the crash at Spa. '*Brian, I would like you to stop racing.*'

I had practised my response in 1968 – studied silence. Even swaddled in my bandages, I knew that I had to return to racing because history proved I wasn't suitable for anything else. Neither Marion nor I spoke of her warning again. Perhaps she realised our situation and quietly accepted the sacrifices she had made by marrying a racing driver. Even after two serious accidents, discussions about injury and mortality remained unspoken in the Redman household.

Conscious of my responsibilities as a breadwinner, I was determined to return to racing as soon as medically possible. Seven weeks after the accident, I was back in Sid Taylor's Formula 5000 McLaren, finishing a credible third at Mallory Park and feeling pretty good about my competitive return. At a check-up the following week, my doctor warned that my balaclava had seriously chafed the skin grafts around my eyes and there was a significant danger of infection, which would cause the grafts to fail, necessitating harvesting new skin and a replacement transplant. Nightmare! Marion and I packed up the children and headed for a campsite in southern France, where my healing progressed nicely.

It was becoming clear to me that careers in racing vary like the seasons, with winters when opportunities went cold and my mood became gloomy, yielding (with luck) to promising spring contracts and golden summers of podium finishes. Now a fully established professional with a reputation that attracted well-paying drives, I slid easily into what Paul Simon portrayed as 'the age of miracles and wonder' with wins in world championship sports cars for Porsche and Ferrari, and American adventures that included three Formula 5000 championship titles. Sprinkled among these high-profile successes were satisfying wins in 2-litre sports-car events for Chevron.

I drove with unalloyed joy.

ABOVE In November 1971 Kyalami played another significant part in my career – my first race as a works driver in Ferrari's sports-car team. After I qualified our car on pole, Clay Regazzoni and I went on to win.
David Pearson

BELOW My last race at Kyalami, in 1972, echoed my first, driving again with Jacky Ickx. Sharing the track with mundane opposition in front of a sparse audience, our factory Ferrari 312PB failed to finish.
David Pearson

ABOVE Family life
took on a new level of
happiness and splendour
in 1973 when we moved
to Taira House in
Gargrave, on the edge of
the Yorkshire Dales.
Brian Redman collection

Taira House idylls

Prosperity makes everything easier. The years from 1973 to 1977 generated a long string of steady employment. My nagging fears were quelled as favourable opportunities boosted my career and the Redman family slid effortlessly and contentedly into a bountiful way of life.

Emboldened by my strong racing performances and proportionately wholesome income, Marion and I purchased a property in Gargrave, a village on the southern edge of the Yorkshire Dales, near the bustling market town of Skipton. Our new home was Taira House, a large 18th century stone dwelling set in two acres. It was a beautiful place to live and country life beguiled us completely. Our lives blossomed. Marion remained the cheerful centre of our family's Arcadian lifestyle. I became agreeably pastoral.

James and Charlotte, nine and six respectively when we moved to Taira, became absorbed in the country bustle and, inevitably, horses. After performing my parental duty by escorting them to a local stable, I became sufficiently intrigued about riding to start again myself.

The timing, balance and mental discipline learned in motor racing allowed me quickly to improve my horsemanship. I discovered a magnificent sense of freedom in my gallops across the farmland and was invigorated by the thrill of jumping walls, hedges and ditches. As in all sports, the camaraderie among riders was strong, but these were relationships I could enjoy without the cautions that tempered my racing friendships. The easy give and take of our post-ride ritual echoed racing's manic bashes but in an infinitely more gentile way. Instead of becoming imprudently drunk, my fellow riders and I gathered around a farmhouse table growing quietly mellow from dusky coffee generously laced with whisky. There was no bravado, no inebriated antics, and no reason to drink away the fears. Heaven!

Competitive spirit to the fore, I grew increasingly serious about my riding. Just as a fast car tends to flatter a competitor's talent, so, too, a hunting horse gifted with 'a big jump'. I attended a local auction and observed a mare that cantered steadily, taking five-foot obstacles without hesitation. Also on the paddock rail was John Whitaker, the famous showjumping rider and trainer. John, I concluded, wouldn't be there without a reason. Each of us bid for the mare that had caught my eye. When I raised the ante to £900, Whitaker said nothing and walked away. Lovely Willow (*Willow-Wood Sunshine*) became mine.

Willow was a little on the small side, just 15.3 hands at the withers, but she had a heart as big as Red Rum, the legendary Grand National winner. Confident in my equestrian skills and my new mount, I joined the Pendle Forest & Craven Hunt club, one of over 300 across Britain, more than half of which had existed for over a century. Our members hunted hares across a craggy landscape interrupted by the ancient dry-stone walls that separated parcels of land. The five-foot high hurdles were shortened to a more manageable three feet in key places, ensuring that the terrain was traversed expediently by both hares and huntsmen. Every Tuesday and Saturday, from the first weekend of November to the first weekend of March, the Pendle Forest & Craven members met, often with 70 or 80 mounted huntsmen creating a wave of black and scarlet riders. Masters and Whippers-In wore scarlet coats with yellow collars festooned with Pendle buttons, their breeches traditional white, their hats and boots classic black. Members such as me wore black top hats, black three-button hunting jackets and beige hunting breeches tucked into plain black boots.

On days crisped by the frosts of winter, I rose at 7.00am, breakfasted on coffee and porridge, fed and watered Willow, led her into the horsebox hitched to my ancient Land Rover and headed to whatever stately home was hosting that day's event. Once mounted, I assumed the role of gentleman huntsman, reaching down from Willow to accept whatever libation the house butler proffered in stirrup cups from his silver tray. Marion always provided a hip flask filled with invigorating brandy that served me well over five or six hours of cantering, galloping and jumping. Oscar Wilde defined hunting as '*the unspeakable in pursuit of the inedible*', but for me it was bracing exercise for the riders, the hounds and even the hares – which always got away.

Our Taira idyll – family tranquillity interrupted only by the reality of racing – lasted for four glorious years. Supporting our country lifestyle required me to drive in rather a lot of events; sleek Formula 1 cars, rude Can-Am brutes, delightful 2-litre greyhounds and the rapidly rising Formula 5000 class in America, a category I pretty much came to own. In each of these I did the job, so I was offered more jobs, quelling my disquiet about the dangers. Our lives were blessed.

Of course, given the vicissitudes of racing, there was no chance that this blissful existence would last forever.

BELOW Taking a jump on wonderful Willow.
Brian Redman collection

CHAPTER 9
Daytona International Speedway

In 1967 John Wyer invited me to drive his formidable GT40-based Mirage with Jacky Ickx in the *Daily Mail* Nine Hours at Kyalami, South Africa's leading circuit. That solid win together paved the way for our partnership in the 1968 season, beginning with the 24 Hours of Daytona.

I had raced on a banked track twice before, in Nick Cussons' Ford GT40 at the 1966 Monza 1,000Kms – my first race abroad – and at Montlhéry with David Piper's Ferrari 250 LM in the 1967 Paris 1,000Kms. In fact the latter event, in which Richard Attwood and I finished sixth in pouring rain, was the prompt for Wyer to contact me for the Kyalami drive. Whereas the huge banked bowl at Montlhéry dates back to 1924 and remains active as a proving ground today, Monza's high-speed oval was fairly short-lived. First used in 1955, it was abandoned by Formula 1 after the 1961 Italian Grand Prix, the race blighted by the death of Wolfgang von Trips and 15 spectators, but continued as a sports-car venue until 1969. It also featured stirringly in *Grand Prix*, John Frankenheimer's fine 1966 racing film. Now just one section of Monza's banking remains, truncated by grandstands perched above the modern track's Turn One.

All the same, learning Daytona's steeply banked curves was a new challenge, and I found the process unnerving. Despite considerable determination, I couldn't seem to keep my foot hard on the throttle in the steeply angled turn known as NASCAR 3, *the critical corner for a fast lap time*. My hesitation had a lot to do with approaching a steep wall at about 195mph. Even more daunting was the incredible compression on the chassis, and my body, as centrifugal forces pushed the car up the embankment towards the looming concrete barrier. Suitably embarrassed, I asked my younger co-driver if he were flat out all the way through NASCAR 3. *'Yes, of course, Bree-an,'* Jacky replied, *'but each time I sink zat I fly to ze moon.'*

If you can imagine what it might be like to drive around the inside of a cereal bowl, you have a pretty good idea of the bizarre attitudes a racing car takes on Daytona's high banks. Still, with all due respect, until you have ticked off a couple of hundred day-and-night laps tilted at this unnatural angle over the course of 24 hours, your imagination still has room to stretch. There's more to Daytona than its high banking, of course, but the slingshots they provide onto two long straights are what make this track fast, difficult and dangerous.

Think of the Daytona International Speedway as a broad, upright, elongated oval with the vertical stretch on the right-hand side pulled out in a graceful arc to form a shape that is, whimsically enough, like a giant capital 'D'. This arc is banked at 18 degrees, enhancing a car's grip and, therefore, its speed, but actually angled to give grandstand

ABOVE Prior to my racing on Daytona's high banks, I had experienced Monza's rain-soaked inclines in the 1966 1,000Kms driving Nick Cussons' Ford GT40 with Richard Bond, finishing in ninth place.

LAT

spectators a close-up view of the cars in profile. Daytona's start/finish line crosses the centre of this arc and has prime seating above for tens of thousands of fans. Jutting out over the hallowed stripe is a platform that has hosted a spectrum of flag-waving celebrities, including several serving American presidents, enlisted to drop the green flag on the starting marshal's command.

The only flat surface of the tri-oval, directly opposite the start/finish line, is the long back straight that connects the two sets of nearly identical banking. On this 1,000-yard stretch, a driver has time to check his gauges and relax a little, albeit while accelerating towards 200mph. The aforementioned two sets of banking are in fact the four celebrated 31-degree corners that give the circuit its special character: NASCAR 1 and 2 at the top, NASCAR 3 and 4 at the bottom. Each is angled about as steeply as San Francisco's most vertical hills, with one crucial difference – traffic on Daytona's inclines runs sideways. From within a racing car, the road ahead seems to soar away in a continuous uphill curve.

NASCAR

Daytona is the beating heart of the National Association for Stock Car Auto Racing and the premier venue for this massively popular racing series for *faux* street sedans that resonates among millions of white-collar, blue-collar and no-collar American fans. NASCAR was launched in 1948 by 'Big' Bill France as a way to gather together a scattering of individual events for 'stock' cars into a championship series. It turned out to be a billion-dollar idea.

There's an old story about this beginning that undoubtedly is apocryphal, but too amusing not to repeat. France, frustrated that former bootlegger and top driver Junior Johnson was reluctant to sign up for the complete series, invited him to a Southern breakfast of bacon, eggs and grits.

'Junior, you need to be committed to the entire series.'

'Well, Bill, I plan to enter all the major races so I really will be involved.'

'Junior, there's an important difference between

involved and committed. *Consider what it took to produce your breakfast. The chicken may have been involved, but the pig was committed.'*

From 1936 until 1959, races were held on a thin 4.2-mile loop alongside the Atlantic Ocean. The main straight was two miles of Highway A1A connected by a quick U-turn onto Daytona's hard-packed sandy beach, where competitors duelled for two more miles along the water's edge before swinging back onto the highway for another lap. Even today, you may still drive your street car along these very stretches of road and beach, although more carefully: the current speed limit is a sedate 10mph.

By 1959 stock car racing was becoming a significant spectator sport. Forward-looking Bill France invested $3 million (about $25 million in today's money) to create a huge uptown speedway that could seat thousands of fans. By the time I arrived some nine years after the bulldozers had departed, little about Daytona had changed. Over the years attendance grew in parallel with NASCAR's increasing popularity

and in its heyday the Daytona International Speedway could accommodate 150,000 fanatically partisan supporters of larger-than-life superstar drivers, fans parking their cars in reserved single-marque corrals. NASCAR events have always featured 'stock' cars, their facsimile bodies shaped to resemble family sedans, but with little or nothing about them off-the-shelf stock.

Daytona is home to two race tracks. From the speedway's inception, all sports racers, including our exotic prototypes, have raced on a layout that interrupts the tri-oval to incorporate an infield section, extending the track's length from 2.5 miles to over 3.5 and includes three of the four high-banked curves. Unlike most of the circuits I've raced on, Daytona runs anti-clockwise.

For the stock cars, the arcing front straight rises to enter NASCAR 1. Sports cars, however, skip NASCAR 1 and join the road racing circuit just beyond the pit exit and follow a boomerang-shaped track through six corners before re-entering the tri-oval between NASCAR 1 and NASCAR 2.

ABOVE We heroes of the 1968 Gulf GT40 team survey our world, me at left (on my first visit to the USA) with Jacky Ickx, David Hobbs and Paul Hawkins.
Courtesy of John Horsman

Daytona's driving demands

Visitors to Daytona may amuse themselves by trying to walk up the 31-degree banking without help from their hands, but in doing so they are one small slip away from scuffed palms. While ordinary road cars touring the high banking at speeds below 90mph are likely to slide to the lower apron, a racing car circulating at the limits of adhesion is shoved the opposite way, towards the outside concrete wall, experiencing the same centrifugal forces as astronauts launched from nearby Cape Canaveral. This unforgiving barrier, added in 1964 to prevent cars from occasionally departing the circuit, brings the unfortunate consequence that contact with it usually causes a crashed car to rebound across the track, much to the fright of its helpless driver and the distress of any racers bearing down on him. One accident often leads to another, and sometimes many.

Drivers were rewarded when we were fast, and we were fast when we probed the edges of the physical limits of both car and tyres. So probe we did, and violent wrecks in NASCAR 3 became increasingly common. By 1973 blow-outs from over-stressed tyres were causing too many severe crashes, inducing the track management to add a broad U-shaped chicane just before NASCAR 3. (NASCAR races excluded this chicane because their cars ran quite a lot slower.) This speed-arresting complex looked a lot like a bus stop and immediately became known by that name. No more did our cars arrive at the end of the back straight at about 200mph directly facing the entry to NASCAR 3 but were down to about half that speed by the time they exited the chicane. The 'bus stop' did its job, and the number of crashes in NASCAR 3 was significantly reduced.

Drivers negotiated the chicane by braking reasonably hard on the approach – just enough to find the entry – and then flowing the car left into the first part of the U. There was room for a short burst of acceleration along the chicane's mini-straight before one touched the brakes for the hard right leading to the left-hand final turn. Until the mid-1980s, this exit from the chicane

pointed the car directly at the outside wall just 60 feet away, requiring a demonic commitment to open the throttle while changing direction by 90 degrees. The arc from the chicane exit into the apex had to be as aggressive as it was graceful, and the bigger and smoother the radius, the more speed a car could carry; but the harder the acceleration, the more the car pushed towards the wall at the top of the banking. NASCAR 3 was where races were won because even a small speed advantage gained in this curve was sustained for a full mile, all the way to NASCAR 1. There was a pressing incentive to be fast.

The Daytona traffic jam

The 24 Hours of Daytona (now known as the 'Rolex 24 at Daytona') has always been a race stuffed with competitors. Daytona takes 75 or more cars on the 3.5-mile sports car course, whereas Le Mans accommodates just 55 on its 8.5-mile circuit. The French race also takes place near the summer solstice when daylight hours are at their maximum, while Daytona's endurance race is run in late January. Although Daytona is now softly illuminated for the Rolex, races before 1998 forced drivers to rely on headlights for 11 hours of the 24. The distance an incandescent headlight reaches at 200mph is the same as at 20 but, while the beam illuminates the same amount of track, the interval is covered 10 times more quickly.

Throughout the history of the 24 Hours of Daytona, the most dangerous hazard has been the huge differential in speeds among the various racing classes. In a Porsche 917 we were often 70mph faster than the slowest cars – MGBs, Volvo 122Ss and Fiat 124s – and we passed as many as 15 competitors every lap. Off the start, we would catch the stragglers on our fourth lap, less than eight minutes into the race, and lap them another 150 times over the full race distance. Nonetheless, we still had to set consistent times that pleased the team manager's merciless stopwatch.

In the 917 we changed drivers at every fuel stop, more or less once an hour. After seven intense stints each between the noon start and

2.00am, drivers tire and mistakes are inevitable,
especially in the hours before dawn. Before
racing cars became reliable (a relatively recent
miracle) at least one-third of the field either
crashed or broke. As the pits of eliminated teams
went dark, the lights in the medical hut burned
all the more brightly.

The 1969 24 Hours

In January 1969 I arrived at Daytona for the
24 Hours with very little use of my right arm,
which had been badly fractured seven months
earlier in my crash at Spa during the 1968
Belgian Grand Prix.

My radius and ulna were reconnected by
steel pins and after the surgery I exercised
regularly until a single X-ray at my local hospital
pronounced the bones healed. At the end of
that season Derek Bennett hired me to drive his
lovely 2-litre Chevron-BMW B8 in South Africa's
Springbok Trophy series, which began with
the Kyalami Nine Hours. My arm hurt like hell
during that race and got progressively worse in

the subsequent three-hour races in Cape Town,
Bulawayo and Lourenço Marques. Providentially,
Alex Blignaut, organiser of the South African
Grand Prix, knew a great orthopaedic surgeon
named Dr David Roux, who saw me quickly and
took a barrage of new X-rays.

*'I have two bits of bad news for you, Brian. Your
bones never knitted together.'* When I asked about
the second unpleasantry, Dr Roux replied, *'Well,
there's an experimental procedure I could try but I'm
going on vacation tomorrow.'*

This indeed was very bad news. A week earlier
I had been contacted by Rico Steinemann, the
Porsche team manager, offering me a contract
to drive one of the five 908s being prepared for
the factory's campaign in the 1969 International
Championship for Makes. If I ever were to
race for Porsche, or anybody else, I needed that
operation. The good-hearted Dr Roux agreed to
delay his holiday and operated the next morning.
He opened up my arm, cleaned it out, cut some
bone from my right hip and glued it into position
above the radius and ulna. For reasons never

explained, he chose not to encase his repair in plaster, providing a sling instead. '*Don't use your arm until it's necessary,*' cautioned Dr Roux. As promised, I rested it as much as possible through the winter break, mindful that it was exercise that had prevented the bones from healing in the first place. At Daytona, I would need both arms.

All the Porsche team cars were 908LH long-tail coupés and I was paired with 'Quick Vic' Elford, so my lap times needed to be good. I found that I could move my damaged right arm forwards and backwards well enough to shift gears, but the rotational strain of turning on the high banked curves obliged me to jam the steering wheel with my left knee. In the infield, I relied heavily on my left arm. I managed to fake my way through practice and qualifying but worried that I wouldn't survive 24 hours of hard racing. This was especially concerning because my continued employment depended on a strong performance in the first event of the season.

Early in the race, Vic and I were nearly rendered unconscious by an exhaust leak but,

unfortunately, that was fixed. Then, blessedly, the titanium teeth on each of our cars' timing-gear drive shafts began breaking and, one by one, all five factory Porsches were forced to drop out. Vic and I were finished just past the halfway point, to my unspoken relief.

In that year's race an unusually high number of cars had problems and a little-known underdog,

ABOVE AND BELOW In 1969 Vic Elford put our long-tail Porsche 908 on pole, but we retired from the race at half-distance with an engine problem. *Getty Images/RacingOne & Porsche-Werkfoto*

LEFT Jo Siffert, my partner at Daytona in 1970, rests his injured ankle, sitting in his removable 917 seat.
Michael Keyser

RIGHT Our splendid Gulf Porsche 917s sparkle in the spring sunshine ahead of their début race. The roof of each car was fitted with an oval-shaped window to allow the drivers a better view of the banking as it soared ahead of us.
Michael Keyser

a Lola-Chevrolet T70 run by Roger Penske and driven by Mark Donohue, was the winner even though it had spent over two hours in the pits. Never before had a car powered by a General Motors engine won a major endurance event and the names Penske and Donohue went on to rock the racing world.

Daytona's woes aside, Porsche triumphed in the 1969 season, with Seppi Siffert and me winning four races in a sequence of five – the Brands Hatch Six Hours and the 1,000Kms events at Spa, Monza and the Nürburgring. The gearbox of our long-tail 908 Spyder failed us whilst we were leading at Le Mans, overheating after 60 laps. In the next race at Watkins Glen, Seppi and I won again.

The 1970 24 Hours

The 1970 24 Hours of Daytona was a legendary battle. It was also the début of the JW Automotive team's formidable Gulf Porsche 917Ks, Pedro Rodriguez and Leo Kinnunen in one of them, Seppi Siffert and me the other. John Wyer's team was the official Porsche entry, with full

ABOVE The 24 Hours of Daytona in 1970 was the first round of a much-anticipated, year-long Ferrari/Porsche battle. In fact Porsche won nine of the ten championship rounds, four of them with me at the wheel.

Porsche-Werkfoto

RIGHT In 1970 John Wyer was rightly disturbed about the Daytona presence of a rival to his works 917s – this unexpected competitor from within Porsche itself.

Porsche-Werkfoto

ABOVE The Ferrari of
Andretti/Merzario/Ickx,
fastest of the works
cars, challenges my
Porsche – perilously
close racing on Daytona's
bumpy banking.
Getty Images/
The Enthusiast Network

factory backing – purportedly. When our team showed up in Daytona at the end of January, we were surprised to find another factory 917K for Vic Elford and Kurt Ahrens entered by Porsche Konstruktionen, essentially the factory development department. Wyer queried this with Ferdinand Piëch, the director of Porsche motorsport, who disingenuously assured us that he and Porsche Konstruktionen flew their car, spares, drivers and mechanics to Daytona just for some fun in the sun. It appeared that we would be battling not only a team of Ferrari 512s but also racing against ourselves.

Seppi turned up with a still-healing ankle, broken in a bizarre off-season go-kart accident that says everything about the competitive nature of my friend. The previous month Porsche had invited all of the factory drivers to celebrate its championship year with other successful German sports stars at the Berlin Sportpalast. The venue included a velodrome configured like a big teacup, flat at its base but sloping increasingly sharply upwards until its sides were

nearly vertical. We were to take part in a race for fun (mostly Porsche management's) but, instead of bicycles, we were issued with go-karts. The team's usual clear and strict instructions were to confine ourselves to the flat track at the bottom of the velodrome because a sizable door in the banked wall had been left open. Seppi, true to form, ignored team orders and shot up the wall to take advantage of the additional grip. Almost immediately he had to choose between the yawning void of the doorway and the narrow bit of track above it. Picking the latter, Seppi found his go-kart wouldn't fit through the space, tumbling him to the bottom of the track with his machine on top, breaking his ankle – and catching fire. If Seppi's mending ankle bothered him at Daytona, it certainly didn't diminish his performance.

Our chief competitors, the imposing Ferrari factory team, introduced the new 512S and had three cars for six seriously talented drivers: Mario Andretti with Arturo Merzario, Jacky Ickx with Peter Schetty, and Nino Vaccarella with Ignazio Giunti. Not to be ignored was the supremely

RIGHT Porsche 917 number 2 won the 1970 race, crewed by Pedro Rodriguez and Leo Kinnunen – plus, for one stint, Redman. *Porsche-Werkfoto*

BELOW After 2,758 miles of racing, the winner has earned its battle scars. *Getty Images/ RacingOne*

capable Dan Gurney, partnered by Chuck Parsons in another 512S run by the North American Racing Team (NART).

Andretti in his Ferrari took pole position with Siffert in our Porsche on the outside of the front row. Shortly after the start, Seppi jumped Mario for the lead and our 917K stayed in front for three hours, until we had problems. First there was an ignition fault, then a puncture, then a loose brake line. The last failure was the most memorable. At 2.00am, with me driving, the car hit the notorious NASCAR 4 hump hard enough to break the right rear shock absorber, causing me to spin helplessly down the front straight. Drivers of racing cars experience almost no sensation of speed, even at 200mph, except when the car is out of control. That night, as I watched the infield lights and outside wall swap places half a dozen times, I found the velocity terrifying.

A total of 20 laps were lost fixing all of these problems and we dropped to third place. Meanwhile, the Rodriguez/Kinnunen Porsche had assumed the lead and was running flawlessly. Rejoining the race after repairs, we followed our teammates through the night until, at 7.00am, our car's clutch gave out. Our mechanics were ready to push the car to the garage but Ferdinand Piëch insisted that the team fit a replacement. That was a major job and dropped us from 20 laps behind the leaders to over 50, but, amazingly, we still retained third place.

Whilst the mechanics were working on the clutch, Wyer called the leading 917K into the pits because Kinnunen wasn't following his instruction to slow down and conserve the car. Either Leo didn't understand team orders or he refused to obey them; it was hard to know which as he spoke no English and our cars had no radios. I took Leo's place with strict instructions to run calibrated times, fast enough to win but slow enough to protect the car. To my surprise, a delighted Seppi passed me on the banking in our own 917K, waving at me as he swept by. Not only was the Porsche factory team racing its competition director, I found that I was now racing myself!

ABOVE I watch (foreground) as Seppi impatiently waits while mechanics repair our car after I slid on the 'marbles' coming onto the banking, striking the wall a glancing blow.
Michael Keyser

A lap of Daytona

Let me share the sensations of lapping the 3.5-mile Daytona circuit in my 1970 Porsche 917K.

After rocketing out of NASCAR 4, I reached the start/finish line at about 210mph, staying in the middle of the 18-degree banking in order to set up for the smoothest possible entry into the tight left-hand corner leading to the infield section of the course. Hard braking, snatch second gear and accelerate into third, then ease off the throttle a little in the quick right/left before braking hard for Infield Turn 3.

This is the Horseshoe, which required careful car placement because the gravel on either side of the track contained shells sharp enough to cut a tyre. Exiting, I would squeeze on speed in second gear, grab third and fly through the next left-hand bend at 160mph with as small a lift as my courage and the tyres' grip would allow. More hard braking and then it was second gear for the 180-degree Infield Turn 5 right-hander, then up to third and back to second for the final turn of the infield section, a left that squirted the car back onto the speedway about halfway between NASCAR 1 and NASCAR 2. Because Infield Turn

6 widened at its exit, I could open the throttle aggressively as the car made its abrupt transition to the banking and climbed the 31-degree gradient.

Now the 917K was accelerating rapidly and angled towards the outside wall with only 20 yards to bend it back to the direction of the track. As I progressively added speed, I needed to leave exactly enough grip in the tyres so that they continued to obey steering input. NASCAR 2 was bumpy enough to make my eyeballs rattle and the car wandered slightly in response, but after a few laps I was used to it. I kept the throttle buried, selected fourth gear (top in a 917K), flashed through the banking and onto the 1,000-yard back straight, arriving at NASCAR 3 at about 210mph.

The key to a fast lap at Daytona lay in keeping the car on the ragged edge through NASCAR 3, the corner Jacky Ickx likened to a moon-shot. Flying into that quick-transitioning banking, I dived for the apex at the bottom and stayed on the throttle as centrifugal forces pushed the car sideways up the slope until it skimmed the wall at 180mph.

Good entry speed was important and hitting the apex

Daytona International Speedway 1970

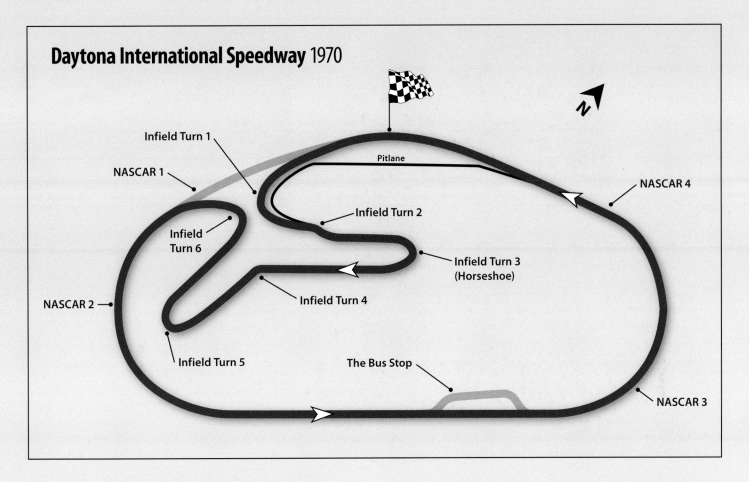

Infield Turn 1

NASCAR 1

Pitlane

Infield Turn 2

NASCAR 4

Infield
Turn 6

Infield Turn 3
(Horseshoe)

NASCAR 2

Infield Turn 4

Infield Turn 5

The Bus Stop

NASCAR 3

was critical, but fast exit speed was paramount. At the apex I pressed my foot to the floor, throttle wide open. As the car accelerated, the increasing velocity demanded more and more of the tyres' grip, so I progressively unlocked my arms and straightened the wheel. If I timed the exit perfectly, my hands were level and the car was pointed straight, inches from the concrete wall. An early apex tightened the radius of the exit and, under maximum acceleration, caused the car to arrive at the outside wall with more turning required. The inexperienced driver instinctively would lift his throttle foot, inducing an unfortunate phenomenon called trailing-throttle oversteer where the front bites, the rear lifts, the car rotates, and – bang! Despite the alarming proximity of solid concrete, it was critical to lift as little as possible and better not at all. One-tenth of a second faster in NASCAR 3 yielded a full car-length advantage by the end of the start/finish straight. After just five matching laps, the gap could stretch to 100 yards.

My Porsche 917K hammered into NASCAR 3 in anything but an orderly way. Once beside the outside wall, it was disconcerting to realise that looking straight ahead is no good at all since there was nothing out there

but curving asphalt. To see where the car would travel over each next half second, I focused exclusively on the top left-hand corner of the windscreen since that was where the car was headed next. In 1970 Porsche fitted each 917K with a small half-moon Plexiglas window above the driver's head for better visibility.

Throughout all my years of racing at Daytona, there was an unexpected complication between NASCAR 3 and NASCAR 4 – a severe bump in the track above the tunnel that gave cars and trucks access to the infield. Drivers get used to instability caused by a track's washboard surface – a condition certainly not unique to Daytona – but it took some time for me to become comfortable with the way this mid-corner hump abruptly tossed a car four or five feet towards the outside wall. At 210mph, it was critical to stay low on the banking and leave a clear lane between my car and one being passed. Four feet apart could quickly become inches – and potential trouble.

Coming off NASCAR 4, I bent the car once more towards the infield as the banking slowly flattened to 18 degrees. From there to the start/finish line, it was flat out, with more than 200mph sustained for nearly a mile.

One lap done – just 700 or so to go.

Back in my car, I drove flat out to the end of the race, as did Seppi. Near the finish, he managed to pass the Andretti/Merzario Ferrari for second place, giving Porsche, Gulf and JW Automotive a splendid 1–2 finish on their collective début. Since I contributed to the win, I was expected to join Rodriguez and Kinnunen on the top step of the podium but I chose not to do so, content to stick with Seppi one level lower.

The lesson we all learned that night was that Piëch may have misled us on our factory exclusivity but, in insisting that we repair the car, he made an intelligent decision. When things go wrong, fix the car and don't give up.

Daytona with Ferrari

My ill-considered retirement to South Africa meant no Daytona for me in 1971. By the following year's 24 Hours, I was driving for Ferrari and 1971's disappointments vanished as the season unfolded. It was a magical year of podium domination and a driver's dream – if he were in a Ferrari 312PB.

The *Scuderia*'s lightning-fast 3-litre machines were essentially Formula 1 cars with bodywork, and no other manufacturer's sports racer came anywhere close. Peter Schetty, the team manager, was a Swiss ex-driver who, unlike some of his emotional and occasionally draconian Italian predecessors, ran the operation with the precision of his home country's watches. For good measure, Ferrari's driver line-up was racing's Murderers' Row: Mario Andretti, Jacky Ickx, Carlos Pace, Carlos Reutemann, Ronnie Peterson, Tim Schenken, Clay Regazzoni, Arturo Merzario and me. Moreover, our competition that year was seriously compromised. Carlo Chiti, a talented engine designer but an old-school team godfather, was at the helm of Autodelta's Alfa Romeo team. John Wyer, always a force, was fielding an *équipe* of still-teething Mirages and could only muster sporadic challenges. Jo Bonnier's Lola T280s proved to be quick in the corners, but their detuned Cosworth Formula 1 engines were underpowered.

In deference to America's looming energy crisis and the millions of cars lined up at fuel pumps, the 1972 Daytona race was cut to just six hours. Not unexpectedly, the Ferraris were the class of the field, taking the top three grid spots in qualifying. In the race I was paired with Regazzoni and we were very much in the hunt when, with Clay driving, a tyre blow-out on the banking tore up the rear bodywork. He was able to limp to the pits, but extensive repairs put us many laps behind. Mario and Jacky took the win with Ronnie and Tim second. Vic Elford and Helmut Marko were third in one of the Alfa Romeo T33s while Clay and I hobbled home in fourth place.

That year the Ferrari team ruled the World Championship for Makes, winning six of its 11 rounds, with my indisputable highlight the victory with Merzario at Spa. The year's saddest moment was the death of Jo Bonnier at Le Mans when his Lola T280 tangled with an amateur's Ferrari Daytona and flew over the trackside barrier into thick woodland, out of sight of any track marshals. Vic Elford saw the burning Ferrari and stopped to rip open the door and free the driver, not realising that he already had escaped.

ABOVE The field bunches up on Daytona's infield, Regazzoni in our number 4 Ferrari in company with Andretti's number 2.
Bill Warner

LEFT I'm at the wheel during the 'easy' 1972 Daytona race, shortened to six hours by the energy crisis.
LAT

As Vic looked around, he spotted Bonnier's car nestled among the trees. He called for help, but it was too late. Vic's heroics cost him valuable time and, while he carried on in the race, his Alfa ultimately broke down and he had to retire. Later Vic's valour was recognised when the French President, Georges Pompidou, awarded him a *Chevalier de l'Ordre National du Mérite*.

Ironically, Bonnier was the sitting president of the Grand Prix Drivers' Association, a group specifically organised to promote driver safety. While not a friend, he was a talented racer and my respected competitor in many thrilling battles.

Jo Bonnier was 42 years old.

Daytona with BMW

Daytona, Sebring and Brands Hatch fell off the world championship trail in 1973 and the following year I was busy with Formula 1, Formula 5000 and Can-Am. By 1975 Daytona had been restored to a 24-hour event and was now the opener for John Bishop's superb IMSA series. I was hired by BMW and paired with Ronnie Peterson in

LEFT The BMW entries demonstrate team driving as Ronnie Peterson in our car leads the sister CSL of Sam Posey and Hans Stuck early in the 1975 race. *BMW*

RIGHT Ronnie Peterson blew our BMW CSL's engine during his first stint, leaving me with nothing to drive. Work done, Ronnie and I watch as team manager Jochen Neerpasch (centre) keeps tabs on his other car. *BMW*

ABOVE The Sebring 12 Hours in 1975 was the scene of a fabulous BMW victory. Although the CSL bears Ronnie Peterson's name, my real co-driver was Aussie Allan Moffat, with Sam Posey and Hans Stuck contributing stints after their sister car failed.
BMW

RIGHT The fast but fragile CSL makes a night-time pit-stop, with me crouching in the foreground.
BMW

a 3.0 CSL. Alas, our race lasted all of 29 laps before the engine convulsed. If drivers are destined not to finish an endurance race, it's preferable to get it over with quickly.

For the 1976 24 Hours of Daytona I again drove a BMW 3.0 CSL, a lovely car, this time with Peter Gregg, an American driver who was known for many unflattering reasons as Peter Perfect. I suppose partisanship played a role when Saturday's *Daytona News Journal* proclaimed '*Gregg Wins Pole*' but I was less understanding about Peter's race contribution over the next 24 hours. It seemed that Peter was feeling less than perfect at the start of the race and he elected to drive just two brief daytime stints. This was the year when water somehow found its way into the Union 76 fuel truck patrolling the pits and one by one cars began to falter, including ours. IMSA stopped the race for two hours 40 minutes to allow teams to purge their tanks and take on fresh fuel. With Peter retired to his motorhome, I drove 14 brutally long stints, occasionally assisted by John Fitzpatrick whose sister BMW had failed.

ABOVE Drivers Hans Stuck, Sam Posey, Allan Moffat and Brian Redman test the strength of the winning BMW CSL's roof as they celebrate BMW Motorsport North America's historic victory at the 1975 12 Hours of Sebring.
BMW

LEFT BMW sets out its stall during practice for the 1976 24 Hours of Daytona, my car in the foreground.
Getty Images/ RacingOne

ABOVE Rain adds to
Daytona's hazards,
especially if some of
the many competitors
have dropped oil on
the track's surface.
*Getty Images/
RacingOne*

At 4.00am our CSL went from six to five cylinders but, by using the maximum 9,000rpm, I was still faster than the fastest Porsche RSR. Grit paid off, and John and I claimed victory.

As we approached the winner's circle, we were dumbfounded to see Peter there ahead of us, looking fit in an immaculate driving suit and revelling in the rewards of victory. His arms only left the two race queens' waists to shake hands and accept congratulations. Dirty and completely drained, I looked and felt like Peter's grandfather. Fitzpatrick was so offended by Peter's preening that he refused to take part in the ceremonies.

At breakfast the next day, our team manager, Jochen Neerpasch, said, *'Brian, you missed ze victory dinner.'*

When I apologised that I had fallen asleep in the bath, Jochen responded, *'No worries, Brian, it does not matter. Peter Gregg gave a fantastic speech, thanking all of the mechanics in German.'*

How perfectly Peter Perfect!

I shouldn't have been surprised at Peter's self-interest. In 1970 he had collected David Piper's

RIGHT Matching
numbers, as the
Daytona scoreboard
shows car number 59
leading the 1976 race.
*Getty Images/
RacingOne*

917K from the Miami port and, without David's knowledge, entered it in the 24 Hours for Tony Dean (another character) and himself. That time Karma prevailed and the car broke in practice.

A Daytona coda

To me, Daytona was, is and always will be one of the world's greatest circuits. Yet it earned its 'killer track' sobriquet honestly: 22 racing drivers,

nine motorcycle racers, three go-karters, one powerboat racer (on the infield lake) and one track worker. In an oblique way, Daytona also killed Peter Gregg.

In June 1980 Peter crashed his road car near Paris while *en route* to Le Mans, where he had been due to practise a Porsche 924 Carrera GTS as a member of that year's works team. His injuries prevented him from racing at Le Mans but the following month he returned for the Paul Revere 250 at Daytona. There he struggled with what was said to be double vision and his impaired condition was obvious as he slipped back, passed by lesser cars driven by lesser drivers. Later, hearing that Peter was preparing a team for the 1981 24 Hours, the IMSA sanctioning body investigated. When tests showed that Peter was suffering from severely compromised vision, the IMSA officials had no choice but to withdraw his competition licence. Unable to race, Peter wrote a note that said, '*I just don't enjoy life any more…*', and took his own life in December 1980.

Peter Gregg was 40 years old.

RIGHT Jochen Neerpasch (left), the largely missing Peter Gregg and an unidentified crew member display the winners' trophies while, after the toughest race of my career, I get to hold the banner.
Bill Warner

RIGHT Peter Perfect embraces the race queens while the driver who did most of the work does his best to fit in.
Getty Images/ RacingOne

CHAPTER 10
The 2-litre sports cars

The 2-litre sports-racing cars of my era were the whippets of motor racing, renowned for their superb grip, precise handling and forgiving nature. All were modestly powered, few had a rear wing, and none was tricked out with aerodynamic aids to abet their downforce. While a 2-litre car may have lacked the swagger of a Ferrari 312 sports racer or the athleticism of a Formula 1 Lotus, professional drivers of the 1970s celebrated them for a quality often missing in their everyday rides – fun. Top drivers of my period rarely passed up the chance to add 2-litre racing to their competition portfolios, as often as their day jobs allowed. Today's historic racers prize 2-litre Chevrons, Porsches and Lolas because they're straightforward to drive and a safe way to go quite fast, as well as being relatively inexpensive to run. It's ironic that the very qualities that made 2-litre sports cars pleasurable to race also made it difficult for me to dominate in them.

Any fit driver could race a Chevron B16 comfortably for hours and still feel fresh – but not at the front of a high-quality field. In 1970, winning races in the European 2-Litre Sports Car Championship for Makes took enormous concentration and sophisticated race-management skills. With just 235bhp and very little torque, the B16 was a 'momentum' car. The tiniest of lifts was punishing, sacrificing painful

seconds before the car returned to speed. Gear-shifting needed to be strategic and constant to keep the engine in the optimum power bands for horsepower and torque. Braking for corners had to be late and light, and the throttle opened early so the engine reached its maximum revs at the end of the longest straight. Passing required logistical planning, maintaining forward momentum when dispatching slower cars, especially when entering or exiting a turn.

Through most of the 1960s, 2-litre sports cars raced against more powerful Ford GT40s, Lola T70s and Porsche 908s in the International Championship for Makes, so there was little chance of an outright victory. By 1969, however, there were enough 2-litre sports cars in Europe to warrant a separate championship and so the first European 2-Litre Sports Car Championship for Makes was held in 1970. Most competitors raced Chevron B16s, Lola T210s or Abarth 2000SPs, with sporadic appearances of Porsches, Alfa Romeos and the Ferrari Dino 206S. Over the next few years, these marques were joined by Astra, March, GRD, Nomad, Redex, Taydec, Martin, AMS, Nomad, RPA, Martin, Gropa, TOJ, Alpine, Jerboa, Crossley, Cox and Mercury.

All of my 2-litre experience was in Derek Bennett's practically perfect Chevrons, racing cars that delivered more smiles-to-the-mile

OPPOSITE My number 15 Chevron B16 leads away at the Hockenheim round of the 1970 European Sports Car Championship. Lurking behind me is Dieter Quester in a B16 powered by a works BMW engine, courtesy of father-in-law Alex von Falkenhausen, head of engine development! I finished second to Jo Bonnier in the striped Lola T210.
McKlein

RIGHT My first
experiences with Derek
Bennett's Chevrons
came in 1967, when I
raced David Bridges'
giant-killing B5, here
flanked by big-engined
Lola T70s on the grid for
the Anerley Trophy race
at Crystal Palace. I won.
Chris Beach

BELOW At Crystal
Palace later in 1967,
David Piper's Ferrari
P3/4 spins with brake
failure while I go on to
win in Derek Bennett's
BMW-engined B8 after
my BRM-powered B5
developed a misfire.
Jay Gilloti

enjoyment than any other, and I'm not alone
in this opinion. Derek Bennett, Chevron's
genius owner/designer/builder, was a fellow
Lancastrian who began racing Midgets on dirt
ovals, built his own cars and then sold replicas
of them to his competitors. He moved into
road racing in an Austin-based 750 Formula
car followed by an 1,172cc special with a Ford
chassis. In 1959 Derek had a very bad crash at
Oulton Park in a car with race number 11 and
he spent 11 days in Ward 11 at Chester Royal
Infirmary. That number was never used for a
production chassis.

Over the next few years Derek Bennett
won many events, always using his innate
engineering talents to improve his cars. In 1965
his friend Brian Classic asked him to build a car
to beat the successful Lotus 7s and the outcome
was the first Chevron – the B1 Clubmans car.
Derek won the B1's first race, at Kirkistown,
Northern Ireland in July 1965, and orders
followed. Over the next few years Chevron
produced a series of GT cars in ascending model

numbers (all beginning with B for Bennett),
followed by contenders for Formula 3 and
Formula 2. Derek's breakthrough came with
the drop-dead-gorgeous B16, a racing car as
competent on the track as it was heart-stopping
in the showroom.

The Nürburgring, 1969

Derek Bennett invited me to drive his beautiful
new B16 coupé for its début in the Nürburgring
500Kms in September 1969. The car's bodywork
was designed and fabricated by Peter Jackson's
Specialised Mouldings Ltd, in Huntingdon,
Cambridgeshire and looked like a Ferrari-styled
version of the Lola T70 MkIIIB coupé. A 1,600cc
Cosworth FVA engine provided the power. As
usual with Derek, the first B16 was finished at
the 11th hour but, as usual with most Chevrons,
it was good from the start.

We tested at Oulton Park, just an hour away
from the Chevron works in Bolton, Lancashire.
After I arrived at the best set-up, Derek would
listen to my comments, drive the car himself

ABOVE In the 1969 Nürburgring 500Kms the works Abarths were our biggest threat – one is right behind my B16 on the pace lap – but I led them all the way.
LAT

BELOW My spanking new B16 prepares for the 1970 European 2-Litre Championship at Oulton Park, home circuit for both Chevron and me.
Brian Redman collection

and hurtle back to Bolton. With right-hand man Paul Owens and mechanic Steve Sheldon, he would work on the car until the early hours of the morning. By 8.00am, car and team would be back in the Oulton Park paddock.

Derek, the mechanics and I set off to conquer all at the Nürburgring, fully prepared and certain of our superiority. The ancient Greeks characterise over-confidence as *hubris*, an offence to the Gods, and possibly our attitude annoyed some Germanic deity. In Friday's practice I was horrified to find that the handling was terrible. No matter what adjustments we made, the B16 was a dog. It was aerodynamically unstable, hunted badly at speed and became alarmingly unpredictable over the track's dozen jumps. At the end of the day we were 22 seconds slower than the three factory 2-litre Abarths.

All day Saturday we were in and out of the pits every lap, changing anything we suspected might be the culprit. We altered the ride height, swapped the Armstrong

shock absorbers for Bilsteins, and varied the camber of the front and rear wheels to achieve maximum rubber on the road when the car leaned into a corner. We even tried different wheel rims and tyres of different sizes. In racing, timing is literally everything, and as the end of practice drew near I finally had a car that I could trust. Late in the session I drove my heart out and set the fastest lap. The Abarth drivers ran for their cars but they were too late – we were on pole.

Our strategy for the race was to conserve the car by running behind the Abarths through what we expected would be a long, hot afternoon, and then use our superior speed to attack the tired drivers during the last few laps. In spite of my promise to Derek that I would shadow the Abarths, I went straight into the lead at the start and was never headed for the 500 kilometres. The real winner, however, was Derek Bennett, who very quickly received a stream of customer orders for his wonderful B16. Abarths were second, third and fourth.

The European Championship – 1970

In the first year of the European 2-Litre Sports Car Championship for Makes the races were normally two hours in length, sometimes run in two heats. The 1970 series came down to a fight between Swedish driver Jo Bonnier in his Lola T210 spyder and me in Derek Bennett's Chevron B16 coupé.

Bonnier, Lola's European distributor, entered what was a factory team while I was royally sponsored by Prince Jorge de Bagration's *Escuderia Montjuïch*, named after the race circuit set in parkland on the edge of Barcelona. Both the Lola and the Chevron had 1,800cc Cosworth FVA four-cylinder engines, but the Lola was lighter, at 550kg *versus* our 590kg. I won the first outing at the Paul Ricard circuit in southern France's Bandol wine country, but only because Bonnier's throttle cable broke.

It was immediately clear to me that because the Lola was lighter, it was bound to be faster, and that without a lightweight car my season was going to be a long and disappointing one.

ABOVE Our *Ecurie Montjuïch* Chevron B16 at the Paul Ricard circuit in southern France, venue for the first round of the new European 2-Litre Sports Car Championship in 1970. *LAT*

I begged Derek to lighten the B16 coupé by cutting off its roof and converting it to a spyder. Derek didn't want to do that: he was delivering coupés to happy customers and was reluctant to render obsolete the model that was paying his company's bills. By August he relented and removed the beautiful bodywork, although cautioning that he had no money for wind-tunnel testing. I had the answer.

'Just copy the Porsche 908/03. Porsche's engineers have already done the testing for you.'

That's exactly what Derek did. Unknowingly, Porsche contributed both to the fabulous handling of the Chevron B16 spyder as well as the now-classic look that characterised all later Chevron sports racers.

Once again our new Chevron was fast in testing at Oulton Park, and once again we departed for the Nürburgring for the 500Kms race, the penultimate round of the nine-race series. I was fastest in practice in the B16 spyder and, in the race, held a two-minute lead at the halfway point. At the top-gear 14km jump,

where I always backed off the power while in the air to avoid over-revving, the engine began to misfire. When I opened the throttle again the fuel pressure gauge started fluttering erratically. I switched on the electric pump – normally used only to start the engine – and heard a loud bang accompanied by flames from the back of the car. A fuel line had broken, spraying petrol onto the hot engine. In an attempt to save the Chevron, I continued to the nearest marshals' post nearly a mile up the road, arriving with the car merrily ablaze. The marshal there instantly disappeared, fortunately without his fire extinguisher, so I was able to contain the damage and prevent a complete loss. Vic Elford in our team's B16 coupé saved the day, winning the race and accumulating valuable manufacturers' points for Chevron.

My spyder survived the fire but was badly damaged. By working furiously, Derek and his crew performed a miracle and the car was ready two weeks later for Spa's 500km *Trophée des Ardennes*. This, the final event of the 2-litre

ABOVE Derek Bennett
(left) and Eric Broadley,
whose Chevrons and
Lolas dominated the
European 2-Litre Sports
Car Championship of
1970, appear in deep
conference, with me
appropriately attentive.
LAT

RIGHT The chequered
flag at Spa waved for my
Trophée des Ardennes win
and Chevron's inaugural
European 2-Litre Sports
Car Championship.
LAT

ABOVE There's a winning team behind every winning driver. Chevron's team leader, Paul Owens, stands in front of a group of hard-working 'Lancashire Lads'.
Brian Redman collection

series, found Chevron one championship point behind Lola.

Amazingly, the repaired Chevron was as balanced and sure-footed as always, and so perfect at Spa – with its fast, flowing corners and one very tight turn – that I consistently ran more than three seconds a lap quicker than I had in the previous year's 1,000Kms, in which I'd set fastest lap driving a much more powerful Porsche 908LH. In the race Jo Bonnier's Lola T210 and my Chevron B16 spyder were never more than a second apart. When I finally passed him after the *Masta* kink on the last lap, I was sure the job was finished, but clever Jo got me back in the run-up to *La Source*, the first-gear hairpin just before the finish line. We arrived at the corner side by side with me in the unfavourable outer position. I braked at the very last second – or, more correctly, half a second after the very last second – and ended up having to take the escape road. Deflated, I turned the car, expecting to see

Jo gliding past the chequered flag. Instead I saw a driver even more frustrated than me: Bonnier was a beached whale, sitting sideways across the track, having spun his car and stalled it. There was just enough room for me to sneak past the inert Lola and take the flag. There's no bad way to win.

Chevron pipped Lola by a single point to earn the inaugural European 2-Litre Sports Car Championship for Makes but at least Jo could console himself with the drivers' title. For racing car manufacturers and drivers, championships are good for business.

The 1970 Springbok Trophy series
By late 1970 I already had made my decision to retire but decided to finish off my career by doing the Springbok Trophy series in southern Africa. This was an unfortunate move in some ways as it put me in one of the world's loveliest cars at circuits in several of the world's most beautiful areas, placing my retirement resolve at risk.

RIGHT Prior to my short-lived retirement in South Africa, I did the six-round Springbok Trophy series there in late 1970. This is our first race, the Kyalami Nine Hours, where John Hine and I won the 2-litre class.
Brian Redman collection

BELOW At Cape Town, Richard Attwood and I won the second round of the Springbok Trophy series in the Team Gunston Chevron.
Peter Wilson

Worse still, things went so perfectly that I couldn't seem to lose.

The six-race Springbok series was spread over three of this vast continent's southern countries: South Africa, Mozambique and Rhodesia (now Zimbabwe). Other than the nine-hour race at Kyalami, where 5-litre (Group 5) and 3-litre (Group 6) cars also were eligible, the events were each of three hours and exclusively for 2-litre cars. Sharing with a co-driver made a three-hour race more civilised but it was perfectly possible to run solo in a 2-litre Chevron – I did both.

The series began with the Kyalami Nine Hours, where the overall winners were Jacky Ickx and Ignazio Giunti in a Ferrari 512M followed by Jo Siffert and Kurt Ahrens in a Porsche 917K. Aboard our Chevron B16 spyder with sponsorship from Gunston, a local cigarette manufacturer, John Hine and I finished fifth overall and won the 2-litre class.

The hours we spent racing in the Springbok Trophy series seemed miniscule compared with the time we needed to get from circuit to circuit over undeveloped roads in a van with a racing car in tow. To reach our second event at Cape Town, we headed south from Johannesburg for 867 miles, bouncing along for about 13 hours, but the result – a win with Richard Attwood – made the interminable trip worthwhile.

In a fit of whimsical scheduling, the organisers deemed that next we must return to the north, past Johannesburg, on a 1,700-mile, 29-hour jaunt to Lourenço Marques in Mozambique. There I raced single-handed and took my third win.

Turning south again, we clocked an 11-hour drive for the 528 miles to Bulawayo, Rhodesia, where I drove with John Love, an excellent local racer, and together we notched a fourth victory.

Onwards we journeyed to the Roy Hesketh circuit outside Pietermaritzburg (named after a South African soldier lost in the Second World War), a trip of 830 miles and 13 hours, and once more I raced solo and once more I won.

It required only a modest five hours to drive the 304 miles to the final race, held at Goldfields Raceway at Welkom in South Africa's Orange

BELOW At the Roy Hesketh circuit at Pietermaritzburg, I drove the three-hour race single-handedly, and won – only in a Chevron. Six wins out of six races comprehensively nailed the 1970 Springbok Trophy. *LAT*

RIGHT The 1971
Springbok Trophy
campaign made me
long for the previous
year. My best finish
was second with Mike
Hailwood at Cape Town
in our Team Gunston
Chevron B19 spyder.
Brian Redman collection

Free State, and there I was reunited with Richard Attwood for another win, confirming the championship.

Six wins in six races. In snooker, they would say that Team Gunston ran the table.

Return to South Africa, 1971

Derek Bennett went on to create an incredible series of 2-litre cars numbered B19, B21, B23, B26, B31 and B36, improved in each of their six variants.

The 1971 Springbok Trophy series again opened with the Kyalami Nine Hours, where I had my first drive for Ferrari in the 312PB. Clay Regazzoni and I took the overall win, with the Chevron B19 of Mike Hailwood, Howden Ganley and local racer Paddy Driver winning the 2-litre class and finishing a remarkable third overall.

Two weeks later Hailwood and I raced a B19 fitted with the new Chevrolet-based Cosworth Vega engine in a three-hour race in Cape Town. Fuel problems left us second to Helmut Marko

and John Love. In the same car at Lourenço Marques, we were fastest in practice but failed to finish when a piston collapsed. I couldn't race at Bulawayo but Mike and Paddy Driver did, and won. I rejoined the Chevron team at Goldfields and, while we started on pole, problems arose to cause another retirement. So, after almost nothing but wins in 1970, there was almost nothing but problems in 1971. Stop me before I say, '*That's racing.*'

It wasn't until late 1974 that I drove a Chevron sports car again.

My last race with Chevron, 1974

In September 1974 Derek asked if I'd like to race his latest design, the B26, in the Brands Hatch 1,000Kms, a round of the World Championship for Makes. The car was pure magic. Weighing just 580kg and powered by a 290bhp Hart 420R 2-litre engine, it could reach about 160mph and, more importantly, the handling was so willing I could almost wish it around corners. If too much aggression with the throttle caused

the tail to slide, a tiny lift would tame the car's behaviour and bring the rear back into line. Partnering me in 'The Chocolate Drop' – a somewhat rueful description of the car's unglamorous brown colour – was Chevron stalwart Peter Gethin.

Engine builder Brian Hart, there to look after his new baby, assigned us a maximum of 9,200rpm and issued stern warnings about over-revving. After we lost eight minutes changing a broken shock absorber, Hart reconsidered his restriction and allowed that perhaps his engine could tolerate 9,500rpm after all. As we were closing on third place in the late stages of the race, the competitor in Brian Hart – at one time quite a useful driver himself – took over. 'Give it 9,800,' he shouted, and I gratefully did. All in all, Peter and I had a fabulous race, finishing a creditable fourth overall and first in our 2-litre class, even after our unlucky pit-stop.

The best thing about driving in 2-litre sports-car races over the years was that, in any given race, I could count on facing the competitive varsity: Vic Elford, Jo Siffert, Jody Scheckter, Riccardo Patrese, Derek Daly, Jochen Mass, Bob Wollek, Gérard Larrousse, Helmut Marko, Peter Gethin, Ed Swart, Dieter Quester, Keke Rosberg, Alain Prost, Alan Jones, Willie Green, John Watson, Niki Lauda, Derek Bell, Arturo Merzario, Jean-Pierre Jabouille, Vittorio Brambilla, Guy Edwards, Jo Bonnier and Peter Gethin. They, like me, revelled in driving these delightful cars. Any day spent in a 2-litre sports racer, especially a Chevron, was wonderful fun.

Derek Bennett died in a 1978 hang-gliding accident and Chevron, without its inspirational founder, in due course slipped into bankruptcy. The company's bank debts were guaranteed by John Bridges, the youngest of my Bridges family patrons, who lost everything and descended into alcoholism. At the time of Derek's death, Chevron's new Formula 1 car was still in early development, leaving the racing world to wonder if this stillborn project might have been another stroke of Bennett brilliance.

Derek Bennett was 45 years old.

ABOVE Peter Gethin and I drove this B26 in the 1974 Brands Hatch 1,000Kms, managing a win in the 2-litre class and fourth place overall. The race turned out to be my swansong for Chevron Cars Ltd.
Brian Redman collection

CHAPTER 11
Formula 5000

Racing fame has a half-life somewhere between yogurt and sour cream. For every abiding legend, there are hundreds of drivers who were known in their day, and then briskly downgraded to Wikipedia footnotes. All the world loves a winner but sustained winning is hard, especially against the best. A young driver can appear in a blaze of potential and disappear just as quickly when his promise goes unrealised. An up-and-coming racer may achieve his dream of joining an established team and then struggle to compete with last year's technology. Pity the driver signed by an outfit that goes belly-up mid-season, unlikely to be paid and with little chance of finding another ride, maybe ever.

Even a successful driver can find himself silently apprehensive after injuries (like me) or temporarily retired (also like me). If a driver isn't continually in the public eye, he stops existing for teams, media and fans alike. Even the greats can't escape the long shadows of age and declining motivation. Those who are wise stand down before they embarrass themselves.

It isn't just drivers who are permanently temporary. Volatility echoes throughout motor racing, among constructors, categories and championships. Whatever happened to BRM, Cooper, Brabham and Tyrrell? For that matter, where are Formula Junior, the Tasman series and Group C? Sooner or later, most motorsport

enterprises fall prey to unanticipated technologies, or the ennui of enthusiasts, or the vicissitudes of sponsor relationships, at which point they either adapt to a new direction or fade away.

Even the few institutions with seeming longevity are stable in name only: the Grand Prix car has defined open-wheel competition for over 110 years, and IndyCars have exemplified oval racing since the first Indianapolis 500 in 1911, but neither is a model of stability. In fact, the opposite is true. With increasing regularity, the sanctioning bodies for Formula 1 and IndyCar upend their regulations in reaction to technological threats or shifts in public perceptions. As the rules lurch from one specification to another, engineers are obliged to invent new wizardry, team owners must scurry to upgrade sponsorships, and fans habitually moan about cutbacks in horsepower, emasculation of the aural engine delights, or distortions of styling.

Formula 5000 is the poster child for a great series lost.

Abandoned after the 1976 season, Formula 5000 is now remembered largely by a handful of resurrected cars entered in occasional historic races. Yet, in the first half of the 1970s, Formula 5000 was a shop window for motor racing, offering brilliant contests between great drivers competing for handsome purses. While Formula 5000's open-wheeled single-seaters weren't quite as nimble as

OPPOSITE Advice from technical mastermind Jim Hall (left) was always valuable, as proven by three American Formula 5000 championships. Mechanic Davey Evans shares Jim's counsel.
Getty Images/Alvis Upitis

Formula 1 thoroughbreds and not quite as quick in a straight line as IndyCar stallions, they were just as fast around many tracks, and faster on some. Mario Andretti said he could never lap Riverside in his Formula 1 car as fast as he did in his Formula 5000.

Over a career that encompassed Formula 1, the Can-Am, sports prototypes and Formula 5000, it was the latter that I found the most professionally satisfying. It was also the most financially rewarding.

Beginnings

In 1966 the FIA raised Formula 1 engine capacity from 1.5 litres to 3.0. Team Lotus's Colin Chapman – eternally wheeling and dealing – persuaded two brilliant engineers, Mike Costin and Keith Duckworth, to design a lightweight V8 engine that came to be known as the Cosworth DFV (Double Four Valve), and then convinced Ford's Walter Hayes and Harley Copp to fund it. In the Cosworth DFV's initial outing at the 1967 Dutch Grand Prix, Graham Hill put Chapman's

new Lotus 49 on pole and Jim Clark in an identical car took the engine's maiden win. The Ford DFV went on to become the most famous racing engine in motorsport history, with one fortunate unintended consequence.

As Formula 1 constructors increasingly embraced the 3-litre DFV, teams elsewhere began to turn to traditional 5-litre V8s for a more cost-efficient way to go just about as fast. These 5-litre engines were cheap, strong, simple to build and awesomely powerful.

Formula 5000 – for cars with engines of up to 5,000cc – took hold and the category rapidly grew in Britain, mainland Europe, Australia, New Zealand and South Africa. By 1969 it was sufficiently robust to support a European Formula 5000 Championship. Although such series were exclusively for Formula 5000 cars, there were other opportunities to fill out the season and amortise new-car investments, such as free-for-all *Formule Libre* races contested by an array of single-seaters. As the Formula 5000 schedule solidified, occasional drives came my way as helpful fillers

ABOVE After winning
the first heat at Ireland's
Mondello Park in 1971,
a cloud of oily smoke
signalled a holed sump
and my retirement from
the second heat.
LAT

between Formula 1 and serious sports car racing. That soon changed.

In 1968 the Sports Car Club of America (SCCA) allowed its Formula A class to fit 5-litre motors, creating a racing use for the universally available 302 cubic inch small-block Chevy V8 but also similar motors from Ford, Dodge and even AMC (American Motor Company). Thus was Formula 5000 born in the USA, where it grew into a series as American as the throaty rumbles of its signature motors.

Although these iron small-block engines were compact enough for use in single-seaters, they were heavier than the aluminium power plants in Formula 1 and IndyCars, but the extra weight was more than offset by the brawn of 500bhp. Since so many of the mechanical parts were off-the-shelf, finished Formula 5000 chassis were relatively inexpensive to fabricate and their motors were differentiated only by the subtle creativity of each artisan engine builder. In consequence, cars from different constructors with engines from different craftsmen ended up closely matched on track.

For new and experienced teams alike, a season with a fast, reliable Formula 5000 car was considerably more affordable than either Formula 1 or IndyCar. What made the series a roaring success, however, was the prize money, which was at least equal to the purses offered by the elite established series and usually superior. Long before 'Deep Throat' instructed Woodward and Bernstein to 'follow the money', racing teams and drivers had made this their mantra. Some top-level Formula 1 and IndyCar entrants were pulled into Formula 5000 by financial opportunity, while drivers loved its intense competition, with winning owing more to preparation and skill than to factory budgets.

Formula 5000 in Britain

Early in 1971, I returned from my brief South African retirement to learn that I had become professionally invisible. Somehow it seemed inevitable that Sid Taylor, that irrepressible racing entrant, would emerge as my rescuing angel. At the time I fitted Sid's template perfectly: needy,

ABOVE Marion gives her support at our local circuit, Oulton Park, in Cheshire. Her happiness reflects mine, as I loved every moment of my six seasons spent in Formula 5000.

Brian Redman collection

cheap and willing to drive anything. In what became a serial habit, Sid and I moved in and out of each other's lives with disconcerting frequency.

Sid Taylor was nothing if not colourful, ever present in motor racing but not within the inner circle of establishment teams. He made a practice of acquiring the newest racing cars and capitalising on talented drivers in either the formative or opportunistic stages of their careers. His lifetime list of drivers reads like a *Who's Who?* of racing: Denny Hulme, Jody Scheckter, Vern Schuppan, Tony Brise, Frank Gardner, Jack Brabham, Mike Spence, Peter Revson, Trevor Taylor, Alan Jones, Patrick Tambay, Brett Lunger, Howden Ganley, Sam Posey, Eddie Cheever, Keke Rosberg, Johnny Cecotto, Marc Surer, Derek Daly, Geoff Lees, Roberto Guerrero, Jan Lammers, Tommy Byrne and me.

The 1971 Rothmans Formula 5000 Championship was run over 17 rounds, mainly in England but with overseas excursions to Mondello Park (Ireland), Monza (Italy) and Hockenheim (Germany). Sid's McLaren M18

and I did remarkably well in that troubled year, taking two wins, two seconds and one third. This was despite missing three rounds because one clashed with the Targa Florio and two more occurred while I was recovering from the injuries I suffered there. Upon my comeback, the tiring M18 and I endured a quartet of miseries, failing to finish three consecutive races (at Thruxton, Silverstone and Oulton Park) and then crashing in the next (at Snetterton).

That accident involved Frank Gardner, the development driver for Lola. Frank had squeezed a Chevy V8 into a lightweight Formula 2/Formula Atlantic T242 chassis, rendering every other car in the Formula 5000 series out of date. With this weapon, he pipped me for pole by a whole second but, at the start of the first of the two 12-lap heats, I jumped into the lead. I kept him at bay for eight laps but then Frank challenged at the hairpin. We found ourselves side by side heading towards the Esses, him on the outside with two wheels off the track. Neither of us gave way. The crash completely destroyed his lightweight

ABOVE AND LEFT During 1971 my big Formula 5000 rival was Frank Gardner in a Lola. At Snetterton in August I held him off until he attempted what is best described as an extremely brave pass – and took us both out.

Mike Dixon

Lola but only damaged the front suspension of
my McLaren.

From my perspective it was 'a racing incident',
where both competing drivers were equally
at fault, but I wasn't confident that Gardner, a
tough Aussie ex-boxer, would see it the same
way. Tentatively, I joined him for the walk
back to the pits, ready to sprint for my life.
Frank just brooded, staring ahead in stony
silence. Finally, he visibly collected himself,
turned to me and issued his succinct assessment
of the crash. *'That were a hard one.'* I quickly and
thankfully agreed.

My two Formula 5000 wins of 1971 both
came at Brands Hatch, at either end of the
season. In the second event, my main rival again
was Gardner and towards the end of the race
I had a 10-second lead over him. I was
hammering through South Bank, the left-
hander leading onto the back straight, when my
McLaren M18 made a terrible lurch and very
nearly shot off the track. I looked for a cause in
my rear-view mirror and, to my horror, saw that

the top link of the right rear suspension had
come completely adrift. All reason dictated that
I should stop the car immediately but the win
was tantalisingly close and it was impossible
for me not to take the risk. The suspension and
my luck both held and I won by half a second.
Yes, it was a reckless victory, but a win is a win,
and getting away with a calculated risk made it
especially delicious.

For the 1972 Rothmans Formula 5000
Championship, Sid exchanged his McLaren M18
for an earlier M10B model in what seemed to be a
step backwards in theory but proved to be a step
forwards on the track – the M10B was the better
car. I won my first race in it, yet again at Brands
Hatch, and went on to finish third at Snetterton,
second in a return to Brands and another second
at Silverstone. Finally, I achieved one more win
in the Dublin Grand Prix at Mondello Park, my
last race in the M10B.

Little by little, however, my attention began
to turn towards the United States, where the
SCCA-sanctioned Formula 5000 series was

rewarding winners handsomely. The McLaren M10B, however, wasn't going to get the job done against the top American teams, but I had an idea about a car that might. Derek Bennett's success with his 2-litre Chevrons made me confident that whatever he designed and built would be a winner, so I approached him about a car for Formula 5000. Derek, who was in the business of selling his customers replicas of cars in which professionals won races, recognised the opportunity. His answer was, '*Ten weeks and whatever money I've put into it.*' When the Chevron B24 appeared, on time for £3,000, the prototype chassis became mine.

It turned out that canny Sid Taylor had also been eyeing the US Formula 5000 series, and the advertised $20,000 winner's purse at Watkins Glen in June 1972 made him absolutely giddy. I accepted Sid's offer to provide for the Chevron chassis the requisite 302 cubic inch Chevy and gearbox package (from Alan Smith of Derby), arranged for Derek to shoehorn it into my new B24 and took the car to Oulton Park, our local circuit, for testing. As with every Chevron I ever drove, the B24 was quick out of the box, breaking the track record at that Oulton Park test and winning its first event on the same circuit in May, three weeks before Watkins Glen lucratively beckoned.

To America

With a fast car, a hungry driver and an eager owner, Team Taylor was ready to conquer America. Mechanics Ron Bennett and Julian Randles lashed the Chevron onto an open trailer, rolled it aboard a cargo ship in Liverpool and, accompanied by very few spares, sent it to America to avenge George III. In New York City, Sid invested $500 in a suspect station wagon, and we four set off for beautiful upstate New York, our car bouncing along behind.

Watkins Glen is a fast, challenging, enjoyable track set amid spectacular scenery. Nearby, the Finger Lakes wineries flourished, and the Corning Company produced sophisticated commercial glass and mouth-blown Steuben

BELOW In late 1971, after struggling with the difficult McLaren M18 and the older M10B, I asked Derek Bennett to design a Formula 5000 car. He created the splendid Chevron B24.
Bill Warner

ABOVE In my American
Formula 5000 début
at Watkins Glen, I won
the first heat and was
leading the second
when the Chevron's
battery went flat,
leaving Graham McRae
(following in his Leda
GM1) to take the
aggregate win, and
the $20,000 prize.
Bill Oursler

artisanal pieces, including many Watkins Glen
trophies. The Formula 5000 race was to be run
in two heats with the fastest combined times
determining the winner. Problems dogged our
Chevron in practice and qualifying, and for the
first heat I placed a lowly 10th on the grid. Highly
motivated driving abetted by some helpful
attrition allowed me to work my way through the
field and claim a win with a full 40 seconds in the
bank for heat number two. With visions of $20,000
dancing in my head, I had a healthy overall lead
in the second heat until, eight laps from the
chequered flag, my battery went flat and with it
my hopes of victory. Fourth place may have failed
to deliver the anticipated shower of riches, but it
still brought home a decent payday.

On to Elkhart Lake's Road America, a
spectacular Spa-like track in north-western
Wisconsin famous for its elevation changes,
flowing corners, flat-out kink (with no run-off),
up-and-down straights – and delicious Johnson's
bratwurst sandwiches. For we connoisseurs,
cheerful volunteers from the local St John the

Baptist Church served up brats on mustard-
slathered buns heaped with sauerkraut. An
old-fashioned needlepoint sign above the serving
window advised us to 'Always use condiments',
and we always did. Alas, the brats turned out to
be the best part of that particular weekend as
my suspension failed when I was running in
second place.

Next came Road Atlanta, another great circuit,
or at least it used to be before being bowdlerised
in 1996 by the FIA fun police. In 1972 my Chevron
would achieve its 170mph maximum speed on
a long, undulating back straight that ended in a
sweeping downhill curve with a blind apex. My
taking this corner without lifting required a leap
of faith every lap. At the bottom of that short hill
firm braking was required, but not too much
as momentum was needed to climb the steeper
gradient that followed. A bridge over the crest of
the hill left me facing a massive concrete bridge
abutment that necessitated an urgent change
of direction. By snapping the car to the right, I
passed under the bridge and plunged down a

ABOVE Buried in that Lime Rock dust is a Chevron B24 with its unnamed and very embarrassed driver who tried too brave a pass on Brett Lunger's Lola. *Brian Redman collection*

slope steep enough to appear vertical. It levelled off at the bottom in a right-hand bend edged at its exit by an intimidatingly steep earth bank. Nonetheless, a minimum of braking was in order as this corner led to the circuit's second longest straight.

My result at Road Atlanta was better than at Elkhart Lake, but not my luck. While I was lying in second place behind Brett Lunger's Lola, ominously large raindrops splashed onto my visor. I dived into the pits for rain tyres, and was stopped when the monsoon hit. Four cars crashed on the pit straight, causing the officials to declare unsafe conditions and end the race. Instead of waving the proper red flag to stop things immediately, the marshals ended the event with a chequered flag. Since our pit was after the start/finish line and technically we hadn't completed the final lap, Sid shouted, '*Do another, do another!*' Still on slicks, I managed a slow lap that included a spin. We won – or so we thought. After I received the trophy and laurel wreath, Carl Hogan filed a protest on the grounds that the chequer wasn't the correct flag to

end the race and, since a red wasn't waved at the race leader, the finishing order should revert to the previous lap. Hogan's protest was upheld (as it should have been) and Lunger was declared the winner, leaving me demoted to second place.

I finally scored my first US victory at California's great Riverside International Raceway, although Sam Posey disputes this. When he heard that I was writing a memoir, he immediately asked, '*Are you going to admit that you stole Riverside from me in 1972?*' Sam, Sam, Sam – 'stole' is such a harsh word. You might say that the win was a gift. On the last lap, I was in the slipstream of Sam's Surtees TS11, closing fast and lining up to pass before the final turn. Suddenly, the rear of his car loomed large – inexplicable unless he was on his brakes way too early. As I swerved to miss Sam, I failed to realise that he had slowed for a yellow flag signalling that tow trucks were clearing disabled cars ahead, and requiring all cars to slow down and maintain position. Busy as I was saving Sam's life and mine, I missed the waving yellow, passed

ABOVE On the pace lap for 1972's final American round at Riverside, my white pole-position Chevron B24 is followed by David Hobbs' blue Lola T300, Graham McRae's red Leda GM1 and Sam Posey's blue/white Surtees TS11.
Chuck Koske

RIGHT Sam Posey and I chat pre-race at the Riverside finale where the record shows I won but where Sam, undone by a Lancashire steward, was the real and moral winner.
Luke Lundquist

him and took the win. His team immediately launched a protest. The chief steward approached me and, to my surprise, greeted me with a strong Lancashire accident, vowels as flat as his cap. It seemed that he was from Accrington, about 10 miles from my home town of Burnley.

'*Now Brian,*' he began, '*as one Lancashire lad to another, did'st tha see t'yellow flag or not?*'

'*No, I didn't,*' I truthfully replied.

There was no hesitation. '*Right, lad, you're t'winner.*'

Sam is correct in his accusation, of course. Seeing the caution flags is the driver's responsibility and my $100 fine didn't represent a fair adjudication of his protest. Sorry, Sam: even now I blush.

The season over, I arranged to ship the Chevron back to the UK where I entered it in the last two races of the Rothmans Formula 5000 Championship. I was in the lead at Oulton Park when I was forced off the track and out of the race by two crashed cars, but I did win the finale at Brands Hatch.

The great Jim Hall

Some American tracks bear poetic names. Michigan has a circuit called GingerMan Raceway, possibly in tribute to the J.P. Donleavy novel. Connecticut offers little Lime Rock, where your Volvo tow car will feel right at home but you might not without leather-patched elbows. The Monticello Motor Club in New York evokes pillaged Virginian history and drivers at California's Willow Springs celebrate tough races with skinny soy lattes and organic yogurt. Should, however, your beat-up Ford F-150 and faded jeans find their way to Midland, Texas and should you spot a roadside sign (with requisite bullet holes) directing you to Rattlesnake Raceway, be respectful, friend – you're among the men now.

Very few drivers today have ever raced a car without some semblance of aerodynamic downforce. As Ferrari, Porsche and McLaren were spending millions to shape the precise curves of trifling aerofoils, a racer, engineer and oil magnate named Jim Hall was reinventing

ABOVE Although my focus switched to North America in 1972, I still took in occasional British Formula 5000 races, winning here at Brands Hatch in October. *LAT*

motorsport. His $5 slab of plywood perched
above the rear wheels of a white, self-created
Can-Am car changed the racing world forever.
At that moment, years of design conventions,
aerodynamic theories and racing car records
were collectively demolished by Hall's invention
of the now-ubiquitous rear wing. From the
astonishing results produced by this innovative
moment, a series of cars called Chaparrals
proceeded to overturn the world of motor racing.
For the Chaparral 2C of 1966, Hall's rudimentary
plywood wing metamorphosed into a driver-
adjustable metal aerofoil mounted on the rear
struts. The driver could make the wing flat on
the straights to minimise drag and then tilt it
up to create downforce through the corners.
All wing designs since have been just
refinements of this concept.

Jim Hall was a man with a brain as athletic
as his right foot, a respected former Formula 1

competitor as well as the driver, engineer and
developer of brilliant racing cars. As if inventing
winged automotive technology weren't enough
for one man, he went on to conceptualise an even
more revolutionary racing concept.

In 1970 the boxy Chaparral 2J appeared with
its big-block Chevy mated to a shovel-nosed body
that had Lexan plastic side skirts hugging the
ground. Inside this semi-sealed container, a pair
of snowmobile engines drove two huge fans that
inhaled the air beneath the car and whooshed
it out through rear-facing vents. This created
an artificial vacuum that sucked the car to the
track and bestowed previously unknown levels
of cornering grip. It was Hall's complicated and
unlovely Chaparral 2J that ushered in the genesis
of 'ground effects'. Four races and three pole
positions culminated in a McLaren-sponsored
ban, proving that radical technology was
capable of creating havoc in any series.

A very lucky day

Jim Hall and Carl Haas, America's Lola importer, were at Riverside with me in 1972, poised to enter the 1973 Formula 5000 wars but still without a driver. They asked, I accepted: $5,000 per race and 45 per cent of the prize money, equal to what Haas himself received after the mechanics collected their 10 per cent tithe. As the person who had dragged Derek Bennett and Chevron into Formula 5000, it wasn't without guilt that I agreed to drive an Eric Broadley-designed Lola. I felt I was consorting with the devil, but the satanic promises were just too good to pass up.

My major competitors were Graham McRae, David Hobbs, Brett Lunger and a young, wild South African named Jody Scheckter, who became notorious in that 1973 season for causing an 11-car pile-up on the opening lap of the British Grand Prix and regularly reinforced his legitimate right to the title 'most dangerous driver

in the world'. Jody was hired to drive Sid Taylor's Trojan T101, essentially a pseudo-McLaren designed by Ron Tauranac for Peter Agg's Trojan brand. The fact that the Trojan's entrant was the non-sectarian Sid Taylor tells you a great deal about the unorthodox nature of the team.

Formula 5000 in 1973

The first race of 1973 was at Riverside, where I notched a good 13-second win over Scheckter. Unfortunately for the team (though fortunately for me), I then needed to break off from my American campaign and perform Ferrari duties in Europe. While Jacky Ickx and I were suffering a frustrating retirement in our 312PB at Spa, Jody was winning Formula 5000 races at Laguna Seca and the Michigan International Speedway.

I returned for the next race at Mid-Ohio, where engine overheating found me running some 20 seconds behind Jody. As happens sometimes

ABOVE My Haas/Hall Lola T330 heads for another win at Road Atlanta in August 1973, trailed by my strongest rival, Jody Scheckter.
Bill Oursler

in racing, changeable weather also changes outcomes. In this case blessed rain slowed the pace, engine temperature moderated and I drove psychotically, ignoring the warning gauges and carving back precious seconds. On the last lap Jody and I were nose to tail as we accelerated towards the tight right-hander heading into the final straight. Jody's motor – fitted with carburettors rather than the more advanced fuel injection on my engine – hesitated slightly, allowing me to pull level on the favoured inside line at the end of the straight, with an unimpeded right to the corner. Inexplicably, Jody seemed to feel that he was equally entitled to the same line from the outside of the track and turned into me as if I weren't there. As his Trojan touched my Lola we both spun, but now Jody had an unexpected technical advantage. In Jim Hall's maniacal pursuit to save ounces of weight, he had removed first gear from my transmission, so I was slow getting moving again. Jody won the drag race to the chequered flag and we finished mere feet apart.

At Watkins Glen I won the first heat but started the second badly, behind Scheckter and Peter Gethin, both notorious blockers. It took me four laps to get past Peter and by then Jody had pulled out a lead that I couldn't overcome, finishing five seconds in arrears. Soon it stopped mattering. Successive wins at Road America and Road Atlanta pointed our season in the right direction, with Pocono upcoming. The Pocono area of Pennsylvania is forested and charming, favoured then as a honeymoon hideaway and peppered with cottages featuring heart-shaped bathtubs and beds; discrete enquiries about lodging were required to avoid embarrassment. It turned out to be a fabulous weekend for the Haas Lola: I qualified on pole, won my heat and blitzed the main event – triply rewarding.

The final race in Seattle continued the duel with my South African rival, and once more we found ourselves side by side, this time on the opening lap, going into the chicane. I knew Scheckter wouldn't give way and I'd be damned if I'd accommodate his intimidation. Inevitably we touched but this time luck kept me pointing down the track while Jody disappeared in a cloud of scattering earth. I won the race, Mark Donohue finished second in his AMC-powered Lola and Jody came home a dusty third.

Still, although I had won five races to Jody's four, Jody won the 1973 L&M Formula 5000 Championship with 144 points to my 130. My absence from two of the season's nine races had cost our team dearly.

Formula 5000 *versus* Formula 1 – 1974

Shadow owner Don Nichols offered me a Formula 1 drive for 1974 but I so loved working with Jim Hall and Carl Haas that I declined. As the American Formula 5000 season wasn't due to start until June, I spent the early part of the year at home in Britain racing Sid Taylor's Lola T332 in the Rothmans Formula 5000 Championship.

My third place at Brands Hatch and a retirement at Mallory Park preceded a real punch-up with David Hobbs and Peter Gethin at Silverstone, where I finally managed a win

with just 1.7 seconds covering our three cars. In the fourth round at Oulton Park, I was pursued relentlessly by Gethin and his teammate Teddy Pilette in their Chevron B28s, they in turn pushed by David Hobbs in his Lola T330. Conveniently, Pilette ran wide at Knickerbrook, knocking Peter out of the race, but this somehow so energised the Belgian driver that he caught and passed me. Hobbs was in third and under control but to beat Pilette I needed a break, which materialised quite literally as a crack in his rear suspension. That left me cruising towards a comfortable victory with 27 seconds in hand when my Lola's rear wing support snapped, causing a violent 160mph swerve. After I gathered up the car and had a chance to check my mirrors, I was horrified to see the wing tilted at a distressing angle. David Hobbs saw it too and, as we started the final lap, he put his car's nose practically against my gearbox. Staring at the dangling wing – potentially an aluminium guillotine – must have made David as apprehensive about its potential collapse

BELOW Sid Taylor's Lola T332 shows some opposite lock at Silverstone, where I narrowly edged out Peter Gethin and David Hobbs for the win. *LAT*

as it did me, but I couldn't quit so close to the chequered flag. Somehow the one remaining support held for the last few hundred yards and I came home the winner by just two tenths of a second.

A geo-political nightmare nearly put paid to the entire 1974 season. In 1973 the middle-eastern Organization of Petroleum Exporting Countries (OPEC) raised prices by 70 per cent and punished America – and the UK – with an oil embargo for its support of Israel in the *Yom Kippur* war. As we were preparing for our US racing season, OPEC doubled the price again and cut production by 25 per cent. In towns and cities across America, cars circled gas stations in hopes of meagre allocations while industry ground to a halt. With a looming national disaster and the loss of title sponsor L&M cigarettes, the SCCA faced reality and cancelled its Formula 5000 season.

Upon learning this, Don Nichols rang to renew his invitation for me to drive his Formula 1 Shadow for the rest of the season, as Peter Revson – the man he'd hired after I'd turned down his

previous offer – had been killed practising for the South African Grand Prix. As has been often repeated in my career, the death of a fellow driver prompted a new opportunity. Apprehensive, but with no other drive available, I took it. On the Sunday morning of the Monaco Grand Prix, my third race with Shadow, Carl Haas phoned to say that the Formula 5000 series was back on. The SCCA had a new partner, the United States Automobile Club (USAC), and this bolstered the series with additional teams, star drivers and new sponsors. For me, the decision was easy: the lure of rejoining Jim Hall and Carl Haas was irresistible. Moreover, the American series promised to be the most competitive open-wheel racing in the world. Before the Monaco race, I told Don it was my last outing in Formula 1 and I was returning to America for Formula 5000. Don was gracious, and we parted friends.

The seven-round Formula 5000 season of 1974 shaped up to be one of tough racing, with nine different manufacturers and 29 competent drivers including 15 international stars: Bobby Unser,

Al Unser, Gordon Johncock, James Hunt, David Hobbs, Graham McRae, Johnny Rutherford, Tony Adamowicz, Eppie Wietzes, Evan Noyes, Sam Posey, Warwick Brown, Horst Kroll, Jerry Grant and Lella Lombardi. There was also another team from the USAC stable, fielded by racing legend Parnelli Jones and Southern California car dealer Vel Miletich. Their car was a Lola T332 to be driven by one Mario Gabriele Andretti, possibly the toughest competitor I ever faced. Not only would Mario have the same type of Lola as me but he would enjoy the additional advantages of my former chief mechanic, Jim Chapman, and an exclusive contract with Firestone tyres. We suspected that the Firestones were generally superior to my Goodyears, as they repeatedly proved to be.

The season opener at Mid-Ohio was run as two heats and a finale. I won my heat but Mario absolutely clobbered his with a 40-second margin over Brett Lunger. In the finale, Andretti jumped into the lead with me trailing in second place. Reeling in a spirited Mario is not the job of a

moment and passing him is even harder. After my strenuous efforts to accomplish both, Mario's Lola suffered a cracked exhaust, putting him out of the race and me comfortably into the winner's circle.

At Mosport, in Canada, I chose the wrong qualifying tyres and ended up third in the finale behind the flying Mario and the relentless David Hobbs. David defended his second place vigorously and, by the time I got by, Mario had walked off into the distance. No matter: I came together with a backmarker and my race ended with the Turn Two catch fence wrapped around the car and me, leaving us trussed up like a chicken. At Watkins Glen Mario's Firestones showed their superior grip, worth about two seconds a lap in qualifying. We both won our respective heats but, frustratingly, he again led me home in the main event, this time by 13 seconds. Eerily, a similar scenario played out at Elkhart Lake, where we repeated our respective heat wins with Mario again taking the finale by 0.8 seconds after I couldn't quite pull off a last-turn pass.

BELOW In 1974, Formula 5000 in North America was a contest between Mario Andretti and me. At Watkins Glen, Mario lines up on the left in his Vel's Parnelli Jones Lola T332 whilst I get ready on the right in Jim Hall's identical car.
Getty Images/ Bob Harmeyer

RIGHT It was an honour and a pleasure to drive against the great Mario Andretti for two seasons in Formula 5000. It was the toughest and best racing of my career.
Getty Images/Alvis Upitis

OPPOSITE Brett Lunger (right) and I lead the parade lap at fabulous Road America.
Getty Images/Alvis Upitis

BELOW After winning the sixth of 1974's seven rounds, I stand proudly on the top step at Laguna Seca, with James Hunt second and Mario third.
Brian Redman collection

The next stop for the Formula 5000 circus was Ontario Motor Speedway, a road course that merged with part of its sweeping banked oval and was home to the Vel's Parnelli Jones racing team. Ontario is not a great circuit but the record entry of 39 cars proved that professionals will race anywhere that offers healthy rewards. I won my heat and, for once, Mario failed to finish his, forcing him to start the finale in 17th – and last – place. Being Mario, he worked his way up to fourth and, being lucky, inherited second when the two cars ahead dropped out. By this time, thankfully, my 25-second lead was too much even for him to overcome.

The 1974 championship would come down to which of us prevailed in the last two races in California, at Laguna Seca and Riverside International Raceway. I led on points, but not by enough mathematically to exclude Mario.

At Laguna Seca Andretti cooperatively punctured a tyre, his lengthy pit-stop allowing me to cruise to a 29-second win, with James Hunt second in Dan Gurney's Eagle.

At Riverside, the last race of the season, the pressure was on. Whilst I didn't have to win, I did need to finish with enough points to top Mario for the championship, something he never made easy. In the end Mario won at Riverside by five seconds but my second place was good enough for a season tally of 105 against his 95, and I took home my first Formula 5000 Championship title.

In an odd but much-appreciated congratulatory gesture, Carl Haas shipped a John Deere ride-on mower to Gargrave to help me tend our two acres of walled gardens. Upon seeing this splendid machine, a neighbour sniffed that the former owner of Taira House had done the Lord's work caring for the churchyard and cemetery grass, as now should I on the John Deere. The Lord and families of the deceased might have thought this a mixed blessing as I careened from gravestone to gravestone with my mower blades chewing grass and granite with equal satisfaction.

ABOVE In the 1974 finale at Riverside I finished behind Mario, but that second place added enough points for me to win the championship.
Bob Tronolone

OPPOSITE Andretti and Bobby Unser (on the wider trajectory) lead me on the opening lap at Riverside.
Getty Images/The Enthusiast Network

LEFT It's hard to know the significance of Carl Haas's gift to his new champion but I used it enthusiastically at home.
Brian Redman collection

Star drivers, tough series – 1975

Mario Andretti and I pretty much had our way with the 1974 season but 1975 shaped up to be much more competitive. Lola had introduced a new model, the T400 with rising-rate suspension*, and in practice for the first race at Pocono the car was bewilderingly slow. I qualified in 11th place and Jim Hall asked me what needed to be done with the car. I replied, '*Nothing, it feels fine. It's just slow.*' Fortunately, a torrent of unrelenting rain caused Pocono to become a pool of standing water and, therefore, unsafe. The race was postponed for a month.

Jim Hall, Carl Haas and I shared a hunch that Eric Broadley's new T400 had taken a design step backwards. This led Carl to make an unusual decision that demonstrated why his discernment was so respected. He located a wrecked T332 –

In cars with rising-rate suspension, the spring resistance increases as the wheels are pushed up into the chassis by road surface bumps or the compression induced by a steep hill or a banked corner.

the model I had driven the previous season – and shipped it to Rattlesnake Raceway to benefit from Hall's immaculate repair and chassis tuning. Since Carl was the Lola importer, this was dangerous business; he had already sold six of the new T400s to our competitors and wasn't looking to take them back. When the weekend of the delayed Pocono final arrived, we rolled the T332 out of the Hall/Haas trailer to the perplexed looks of Haas's T400 customers. Their shock was exceeded only by ours when the Vel's Parnelli Jones crew unloaded an identical T332 for Mario. It seemed that they, too, had figured it out.

For Pocono's Purolator 500, I was at the back half of the grid in my 11th place from the original qualifying session, but now I had a real racing car under me. I drove hard, leapfrogged everybody and pulled out a win, followed by Al Unser and Jackie Oliver. Bobby Unser complained that I passed him on the inside rather than the outside as was *de rigueur* in USAC racing. '*Redman*,' he said confronting me after the race, '*what the hell you doin' passin' me like that?*' When I replied that

there was a gap, he said, '*Is that the way you road racers do it? Right, now I know.*' Bobby finished a pissed-off sixth but a wiser racing driver. Mario limped home in 17th place.

Andretti came back strongly at Mosport, as expected, strategically flattening his rear wing for better straight-line speed. I considered following his example but decided that I'd prefer the better grip a tipped wing yields in the corners. It was a big mistake. Although I could close up within inches, Mario romped away from me on the straights and I never could gain the necessary momentum to set up a pass. So intense was our battle that we lapped every other car in the field, finishing 1–2 with Mario nosing over the line 0.62 seconds ahead. A hard-fought second place can be as satisfying as a win – well almost.

At Watkins Glen, both Mario and I lapped under the Formula 1 and Can-Am records, and we both won our respective heats. In the finale, Mario lost valuable time when his car refused to start but, by driving superbly, he managed to finish sixth. Jackie Oliver led for 15 laps in the

ABOVE The flooded Pocono race was postponed for a month, by which time we had reverted to the faster Lola T332. It could still deliver, and did, for a win.
Bill Oursler

LEFT After winning Pocono from 11th on the grid, I celebrate a perfect start to the season in time-honoured fashion, with an interview and appropriate refreshment.
Bill Oursler

Shadow before suffering a head-gasket failure, conceding me the win, 33 seconds ahead of Al Unser. At Road America I had a troubled weekend. First an unusual rear hub failure in the heat race and then a flat tyre in the finale dropped me to eighth overall. Andretti, Oliver and Wietzes claimed the first three places.

I went on to Mid-Ohio for what proved to be a heart-rending weekend. In 1975 the promising B.J. Swanson was on the threshold of his dream to be a professional racer. B.J. had been making such impressive progress in Formula 5000 that Dan Gurney had signed him for the following year's Indy 500, but first invited him to Mid-Ohio as a private Gurney entry. Having qualified the Bay Racing Lola T332 a solid fourth in his heat, B.J. was in a good position to do well in the finale. As the flag dropped for the start, the throttle on his Lola jammed wide open and the car turned sharply left into the guardrail. The wooden support post broke and B.J. hit his head on the top of the barrier, damaging his spine. The car bounced off the railing and continued backwards

up the track before stopping under the bridge, on fire and with the engine still screaming. B.J. never regained consciousness, and his life support was removed two days later. The rest of us continued. I won the race.

B.J. Swanson was 26 years old.

A rain-soaked race at Road Atlanta came next. I led until very near the end when my tyres gave up, allowing Al Unser to get around me. I finished runner-up, just 0.1 second behind.

The street race in Long Beach, California attracted a star-studded cast. Formula 1 contributed Jody Scheckter, David Hobbs, Tony Brise, Vern Schuppan, Chris Amon, George Follmer, Brett Lunger and Tom Pryce. Adding to the strength of the field were the Aussie sports-car driver Warwick Brown and Formula 5000 Champion Graham McRae – plus, of course, Mario.

The Long Beach street circuit had a challenging first corner where the road fell away so sharply it was almost a jump, taken with the front wheels in full droop while the car was still

BELOW The streets of Long Beach echo with thousands of horsepower, my Lola T332 (wearing white Boraxo livery for those with good eyes) in third place here but ultimately finishing first.

Jutta Fausel

turning. There was just time for a brief shot of acceleration before braking for the next corner, a tight left-hander. Towards the end of qualifying, I approached Turn One at full throttle and threw the car into the corner. The combination of this rough transition and the twisted landing snapped the T332C sideways and broke the limited-slip differential. The drawback of limited-slip is that it takes a lot of mechanical complexity to make this trick happen, increasing the transmission's vulnerability. Jim Hall and his crew fitted a new Weismann differential for the race but it was clear that either I'd have to accommodate Turn One or the same would happen again.

In the race I took pains to be gentle but obviously wasn't gentle enough. Whilst I was in fourth place, my limited-slip became damaged again and, without its help, I rapidly lost ground to the trio ahead – Andretti, Brise and Al Unser. As I nursed my car along, trying to maintain fourth, the race unexpectedly came to me. First, Al stuck his car into the wall, then Mario's transmission failed, and finally Tony broke a

half shaft. It's just possible that the troublesome Turn One suddenly became my friend. At driving school, every novice learns that, '*To finish first, first you have to finish.*' This eternal principle also applies to professionals.

The penultimate Formula 5000 race at Laguna Seca yielded a third-place finish and I arrived at Riverside for the season's finale leading the championship, but not by enough that Mario couldn't snatch it away. That weekend I was scheduled to run in two races, the Formula 5000 headliner and the popular supporting event, a marketing spectacle known as the International Race of Champions (IROC) in which well-paid professionals from Formula 1, NASCAR, IndyCar and sports prototypes raced against each other in identical semi-race-prepared Chevy Camaros.

The IROC schedule featured four races over three weekends. In the Michigan opener Jody Scheckter spun on the first lap and divided the field, relegating me to seventh behind NASCAR legend Richard Petty and ahead of Al Unser. The second and third races were to be held at

ABOVE My Long Beach winner's celebration was a Queen-Palooza. The trophy, including a model of the nearby *Queen Mary*, was presented by Patti Queen (wife of sponsor Boraxo's president Jack Queen), standing in after the race queen had prematurely repaired to a bar.
Bob Tronolone

Riverside the same weekend as the Formula 5000 decider. By the time I arrived at the track, I was completely focused on Formula 5000, such that the two IROC races, one on Saturday and the second on Sunday, became unwelcome diversions. Little did I anticipate the trauma that lay ahead.

In Formula 5000 practice on Friday morning my Lola T332 blew a tyre in the fast Turn Nine bowl, throwing me across the track and into the concrete wall at over 100mph. This bounced my head from side to side with such violence that my helmet smashed the Plexiglas screens on both sides of the cockpit. With my neck quite sore, I wasn't looking forward to two IROC races.

In Saturday's IROC heat Richard Petty couldn't quite pass me so, being from NASCAR, he nudged my rear bumper, edging me into a gentle spin and the roadside gravel. Later he told me he did it considerately, in a place he knew I couldn't get hurt. On the next lap a stone jammed my throttle wide open at my nemesis, the banked Turn Nine, and I was thrown against

its outside wall once again, but this time head-on at 150mph. I was fortunate that no bones were broken but, in my battered state, I didn't feel very lucky. The second IROC race on Sunday was held immediately before the final Formula 5000 event. Somehow, I struggled around unable to hold up my head, finishing seventh again, this time behind Formula 1's James Hunt and ahead of NASCAR's David Pearson.

By the time I started the Formula 5000 main event, my blue race suit was dark with perspiration and matched the colour of the bruises on my neck and chest muscles. It took my full effort to get the spare T400 around the course, but racing produces adrenalin – and adrenalin blocks out pain. In spite of my never having raced the spare Lola, I managed to finish third. Mario won the race but, with points to spare, I secured my second Formula 5000 title, made all the sweeter by the duels with my brilliant rival. Later that day Mario told me he was going back to Formula 1 the following year, a decision that left me dumbfounded.

OPPOSITE The Corkscrew at Laguna Seca is dramatic but not very difficult. Tony Brise is on my tail in the penultimate 1975 round, which Mario won with me placed third.
Jutta Fausel

BELOW In the first 1975 IROC race at Riverside, Richard Petty edged me off the track – but kindly so, in a place I couldn't get into trouble.
Bob Tronolone

ABOVE A burst tyre
and heavy crash during
practice at Riverside in
1975 badly damaged
my Lola T332, requiring
us to dust off our
unloved T400 for the
race. My third place
was good enough to
make me champion
for the second time.
Jutta Fausel

'Mario,' I said, '*those young guys are going to eat you alive!*'

History proved me a poor prophet. Two years later Andretti became Formula 1 World Champion in Colin Chapman's glorious Lotus 79.

Once more unto the breach – 1976

Lola replaced the lethargic T400 with a new model called the T430. It was smaller than the T332 and nearly as quick, but we still judged the older car to be marginally better.

Our initial outing at Pocono was challenging, with the hard-charging Danny Ongais ('On-The-Gas') hounding me in the two heats as well as the finale. Ultimately I won all three races but only by six seconds in the one that counted most. Mosport came and went with second place in my heat but only eighth in the finale owing to a misfire and a pitstop. At Watkins Glen, Al Unser was on pole with me in second. When rain poured down at the start, I was quite happy that my outside line into Turn 1 would have better grip than Al's oily inside position. Unfortunately, Al decided

he would out-brake me anyway and, as was predictable, slid into my car and forced us both off the track. Later, a four-minute pit-stop to fix a puncture left me trailing the winner, Alan Jones (another future Formula 1 World Champion), by two laps. Going into Elkhart Lake's Road America, I was second in the championship with 44 points to Jones's 76. Things weren't looking good.

Somehow the Road America management talked the SCCA/USAC sanctioning body into two races that season – not unwelcome to the drivers as it's the best track in North America. The first was 20 laps in late July, the second a 20-lapper in late August. After picking off and pulling away from Ongais, Bobby Unser and Jones in the July event, my magneto failed and I was forced to drop out. Jackie Oliver's win in the Dodge-powered Shadow DN6B was the first in five years for a car without a Chevrolet engine. My retirement pushed me down to fourth place in the championship behind Jones, who led with 84 points, leaving Oliver in second with 60 and Unser in third with 48. My miserable season's total was a discouraging 44. Things

ABOVE My 1976 Formula 5000 campaign brought three wins from seven rounds – Pocono, Mid-Ohio and Road America.

Brian Redman collection

BELOW During practice at Road America, a suspension breakage put me into the barrier. It was the only preparation shortcoming I experienced in four years with Haas/Hall.

Harry Kennison

weren't looking good and it was time to get on with the campaign.

In between the two Elkhart Lake events came Mid-Ohio, where the Lola and I were perfectly suited to the twisty course and we won by a full 28 seconds. This left Oliver and Jones tied at the top of the championship table with 84 points each, and me in striking distance with 80. At the second Road America event, a front tyre began to chunk and Ongais quickly closed the gap, but I held on for the win by a slim four seconds. Now I entered the season's finale at Riverside with 116 points, up 32 on Jones and Oliver. With the championship very much in mind, I drove conservatively to finish third behind Al Unser and Jackie Oliver's Shadow.

The 1976 season's final points score put me on 132 points followed by Unser on 112, Oliver 108, Jones 96, Ongais 78 and Schuppan 45. I became Formula 5000's only three-time champion.

Four years of fantastic Formula 5000 racing produced three championship titles and one year as runner-up. Credit must go to the best team in racing: Jim Hall for his cerebral engineering and for leading from the front; Jim's super-capable wife Sandy who not only ran the office but helped style the cars; Carl Haas and wife Berni who tended to all the unglamorous management duties; Franz Weis, the ultra-competent Texas engine builder and fast test driver; and our three superb mechanics, Troy Rogers, Tony Connor and Davey Evans, who prepped the car at Rattlesnake and worked on it at the races. I thanked them profusely then, and I thank them again now.

I would like to conclude with some gracious words from Jim Hall: *'Brian Redman… did the best job that I could imagine. I've got a lot of respect for Brian. He can drive the car. If it isn't right he can do a good job with it and if it's right he'll really do a job with it. We finished so many races and won so many races during those four years and it's hard for me to imagine that we were able to do that. We had good reliability and Brian took care of the equipment and was quick enough to win. I'll guarantee you the last ten laps of the race I wouldn't have traded anybody for him. He might not have put it on the pole, but it wasn't because he didn't want to. He didn't have to.'*

ABOVE Missing from this particular photograph is artwork added by my crew, a helper with a brush and a shovel standing behind the team of 20 mules.
Brian Redman collection

BELOW I went to Riverside with a decent lead in the championship and my 'safe' third-place finish secured my third consecutive Formula 5000 title.
Jutta Fausel

CHAPTER 12
Stories from the 1970s

In January 1970 the sleet whistled across the barren Lancashire moors and lashed the windows of our sitting room. Surprisingly, a call came from the Porsche racing department at Weissach.

'*Herr Redman, please come to test the new Porsche 908/03.*' Certain that the 908/03 would be selected for the next Targa Florio, I flew to Stuttgart where I found that it was snowing as well. Engineer Helmut Flegel picked me up at the airport and, on the way to the Porsche's private track at Weissach, I asked politely how we expected to test in the snow.

'*Herr Redman, don't vorry. Herr Director has some special material from ze airport.*'

Ferdinand Piëch, the august director of Porsche motorsport and grandson of Ferdinand Porsche, the company's founder, was not a man to be dissuaded from his decisions. In fact, when I arrived at the Weissach track, it had been neatly ploughed and its surface indeed was black.

I did three slow laps to feel out the track and warm up the car before accelerating to race pace on the fourth. Whistling down the straight at a mighty clip, the car suddenly rotated 360 degrees and slid off into a snow bank, fortunately without damage. As I walked back onto the track to understand what made me spin, I instantly found myself seated on the asphalt. A few minutes later, Herr Piëch and his coterie arrived to investigate.

'*Vat is ze problem, Herr Redman?*' he asked. '*This is the problem,*' I replied, taking a few quick steps and sliding for yards on a layer of black ice. That revelation proved to be sufficient for everyone to call it a day.

'*This iss the last time vee ever test at Weissach in ze vinter,*' declared a frustrated Piëch. I flew home to England the same afternoon.

The vicissitudes of racing fortunes

Friends, teammates and even team owners have suggested that I was too reserved in public and with the press, a proxy way of saying that I was terrible at self-promotion. So ingrained is my reputation for unproductive modesty that it has become a cornerstone of my humble mythology. Sam Posey delights in emphasising this embarrassing fact in his Afterword to this memoir, an eloquent tribute originally written when I was the honoree at the Road Racing Drivers Club's 2013 Legends banquet. (This and other driver salutes are in his latest book, *When the Writer Meets the Road*.)

In truth, Sam's characterisation isn't wrong. I was shy in many ways, particularly when it came to self-promotion. Yet, attendees at the Kyalami Nine Hours in 1967 might have concluded I was an extrovert. Name one other driver with the temerity to serenade his peers with *On Ilkla Moor Baht 'at (On Ilkley Moor Without*

OPPOSITE In the 1970s my career evolved towards maturity and contentment with racing success in America, above all in Formula 5000. *Porsche-Werkfoto*

ABOVE Following Piers
Courage's death in 1970,
Frank Williams asked
me to drive his Formula
1 team's De Tomaso:
the car was withdrawn
during practice for the
British Grand Prix at
Brands Hatch and
I failed to qualify for
the German Grand
Prix at Hockenheim.
Sutton Images

a Hat) in an incomprehensible Yorkshire accent
while expecting them to like it? Yes, copious
amounts of alcohol were involved, the signature
conclusion of every racing weekend. It would be
a cop-out to say that I always let my driving do
the talking because there were racers around me
who drove brilliantly and marketed themselves
with equal skill; Sir Stirling Moss, Sir Jackie
Stewart, Mario Andretti, Derek Bell and David
Hobbs come to mind. I don't deny that I could
have done better in managing my opportunities,
some of which were simply foolish but others
tragic. With Frank Williams, I experienced both.

Piers Courage, heir to the Courage brewing
fortune, was not only Frank Williams' driver
but also Frank's close friend. Williams had
purchased a De Tomaso Formula 1 car that
proved to be heavy and slow, and Piers
struggled in the early 1970 races. At the
Zandvoort circuit in Holland, something broke
in the front of the car at the high-speed *Tunnel
Oost* corner, launching it into an embankment
where it came to pieces and caught fire.

This inferno was especially vicious, fuelled
by the magnesium that Gian Paolo Dallara
the car's designer, had employed in the chassis
and suspension.

Piers Courage was 28 years old.

When drivers died, teams carried on and one
family's tragedy became another's good fortune.
Shortly after the accident, I received a call from
Frank. Would I like to take over Piers' seat for
the British Grand Prix at Brands Hatch? We came
to a quick agreement. Early in practice, Frank
and the race crew had an intense conversation
and suddenly withdrew the car with no further
discussion. I never knew what the mechanics
found but was always unsettled that they may
have discovered a flaw that led to Piers' death,
and might have injured me.

Frank, who remained a believer in my
abilities, put me in the car again for the German
Grand Prix at Hockenheim and hinted at a
continuing relationship. Nowhere were my poor
PR skills demonstrated to worse effect than in
a conversation with Frank at that time.

'Brian, you are going to be World Champion, aren't you?' Frank inquired. Instead of responding with a casual, 'Yes, of course I am', I reacted in typical Redman fashion. 'Good Lord, Frank, I shouldn't think so.'

Frank Williams went on to build a series of Grand Prix cars that made him one of the most successful Formula 1 entrants. Williams Grand Prix Engineering won no fewer than seven World Championships, four after a road accident that rendered Frank a quadriplegic. The Williams list of World Champions is distinguished: Alan Jones, Keke Rosberg, Nelson Piquet, Nigel Mansell, Alain Prost, Damon Hill and Jacques Villeneuve – with no Redman among them. Damn!

A leg up from Big Lou

When fans asked Peter Gethin about the symbolism of the two circling sharks on his helmet, he would shrug it off as 'just a design' but insiders knew better. One shark represented Sid Taylor and the other Louis Stanley. The rather unpopular Gethin was, ironically, Sid's most successful driver as they won the 1969 European Formula 5000 Championship together with a McLaren M10A, but Peter was also Sid's most caustic critic. Whilst one can only surmise why Peter viewed his relationship with Sid as predatory, the story behind his disdain for Louis Stanley was legend.

Following Bruce McLaren's death in 1970, Peter was drafted into that sombre team as Denny Hulme's partner in Formula 1. When Gethin's relationship with McLaren team principal Teddy Mayer turned sour, he left mid-season in 1971 and was hired by Stanley to drive the BRM P160 for the rest of the year. During the Italian Grand Prix at Monza, only Peter's second race with the team, Stanley spent the entire weekend openly soliciting Frenchman François Cevert to replace his existing driver for the following season. Peter's ultimate indignity came at Saturday night's pre-race dinner when he was directed by Stanley to move to the foot of the table so that negotiations with Cevert could be conducted at the head. A delicious twist of circumstances

BELOW Sid Taylor orchestrated three races for me – two Interserie, one Can-Am – with this BRM P167 in the autumn of 1971.
Bob Tronolone

unfolded the following day. Exiting the final
corner on the last racing lap, third-placed Peter's
BRM unceremoniously shoved second-placed
Cevert's Tyrrell out of his way and stormed on
to pip Ronnie Peterson's March at the line. It
was the unappreciated Peter Gethin who gave
the unappreciative Louis Stanley a fine BRM
Formula 1 win at the Italian Grand Prix, by a
slim one-hundredth of a second.

Louis Stanley – 'Big Lou' as Dan Gurney
had nicknamed him in 1960 – may have been
imperious, bombastic, vain and intransigent, but
he was a true lover of racing. After marrying the
sister of Sir Alfred Owen, industrial magnate
and saviour of British Racing Motors, Stanley
assumed BRM's chairmanship and engaged
the sport at large. In 1967, as Jackie Stewart
was facing uphill odds in the battle for racing
safety, Stanley founded the Grand Prix Medical
Service. Later he served as a trustee of the Jim
Clark Foundation, originated the Jo Siffert
Advisory Council (honouring the only driver
ever killed in a BRM), and worked to improve

fire safety in motor racing. Stanley even tested
early forms of fire-retardant racing suits
himself, walking through flames in them.

His obituary in *The Independent* ended in
this salute. '*With terrifying frequency, like many
of his contemporaries, [Stanley] was obliged to pay
dues in the currency of lost friends. But he was not
prepared simply to don a sad but tolerant face while
mourning each tragedy. Instead, he did everything
he could to bring about the changes that are taken for
granted today.*'

Around the time of Gethin's famous victory
at Monza, Stanley agreed to a suggestion put
to him by Sid Taylor. In preparation for the
1972 Can-Am season, BRM upgraded its P154
(commissioned in 1970 by Canadian stores
millionaire George Eaton) to P167 configuration,
and Sid borrowed it for the last two Interserie
races of 1971. Interserie racing rules were
similar to those of the North American Can-Am
series, and attracted the same sort of 'big-
banger' sports cars. The costs were reasonable,
the racing was exciting, entrants were plentiful

and the level of driver competence quite good. For BRM, it was a great way to put an undeveloped Can-Am car to a real-life test without attracting much attention. Castrol provided the sponsorship and I was hired to drive.

In early September we took the BRM to Imola, Italy for our first event. It poured with rain from start to finish, favouring drivers and cars comfortable in wet conditions. The P167, typical of every car designed by Tony Southgate, was excellent in the rain and I was able to fly. Not only did I win, my advantage was so commanding that I lapped the entire field. As recounted in Chapter 6, Ferrari's Mauro Forghieri, there to run the *Scuderia*'s new 312PB, was among the embarrassed entrants. After the race *Ingegnere* Forghieri invited me to visit the factory to discuss a possible drive in one of the 312PB sports racers for the 1972 World Championship for Makes.

He met me at Maranello and immediately the Ferrari politics began. It seemed that my Formula 2/Formula 1 demurral had not been forgotten and I was reminded of Ferrari's habitual shortage

ABOVE Back in the Ferrari fold, here in 1973 at Dijon where Jacky Ickx and I followed the Pescarolo/Larrousse Matra-Simca home.

Getty Images/Rainer Schlegelmilch

BELOW Jacky Ickx and I, with the entire Ferrari team, savour our triumph in the 1973 Monza 1,000Kms. Winning for Ferrari in Italy is an indescribable feeling.

Brian Redman collection

of forgiveness. When Italian posturing had run its course, we worked out a contract with little difficulty and I signed. Drivers in that era received no share of the prize money but my salary was something of a breakthrough at the time – the princely sum of £20,000 a year – and the first time Ferrari ever paid its sports car drivers.

Three weeks after Imola I won again with the BRM P167 at Hockenheim. Encouraged by these successes, Sid arranged to have the car shipped to California for the last two Can-Am races of the season, at Laguna Seca and Riverside. I qualified sixth at Laguna Seca and finished fourth. At Riverside Howden Ganley replaced me so I could attend Jo Siffert's funeral in Switzerland and he finished a very creditable third.

More Formula 1

The 'Heritage' section of the McLaren website says this of me. '*[Redman] had a handful of races for McLaren in 1972 during which period he convinced those he worked with on the team that he had the talent for F1 if not, perhaps, the inclination.*' For the record,

the 'handful' comprised four races: I finished second in the non-championship Rothmans 50,000 at Brands Hatch, fifth at Monaco and the Nürburgring, and ninth at the French Grand Prix. McLaren's historian is only part right in the opinion expressed about me. I was a driver for hire and, as a matter of timing as much as preference, more financially attractive offers came through sports car racing and Formula 5000 than Formula 1.

In 1973 Don Nichols asked me to drive a third Tony Southgate-designed Formula 1 Shadow in the end-of-season United States Grand Prix at Watkins Glen. The race itself wasn't particularly noteworthy – dirt in the Shadow's throttle slides stopped the engine and the restart push resulted in disqualification – but the weekend will always be remembered for a different reason.

I had pitted during Saturday morning practice when the activities suddenly were red-flagged and the track was closed. Jacky Ickx rolled into the pits to tell us why; an appalling accident had just taken the life of François Cevert. Handsome, charming François drove the second Formula 1

Tyrrell as Jackie Stewart's understudy and, considering the ground he had made up on his mentor, was destined to be his racing heir. There was much speculation on what caused the accident but Jackie later provided a careful analysis of the situation.

'Cevert crashed violently in the uphill Esses heading onto the back of the circuit. Fighting the car... he brushed the curb on the left, whipped across the track and hit the guardrail on the right. The car began to spin, and he swerved back across the track at 150mph and hit the outside guardrail almost head-on.'

François Cevert was 29 years old.

Stewart, who secretly was planning to retire immediately after Watkins Glen, chose to quit on the spot, foregoing the completion of his 100th Grand Prix but still claiming that season's World Championship title. The rest of us raced, as we always did.

My abbreviated drive in the Shadow at Watkins Glen impressed Don Nichols sufficiently for him to ask me to join his Formula 1 team full-time for 1974. I turned him down, not out of fear

for my safety but because I thought I'd be better off staying in the USA with the Carl Haas/Jim Hall Chaparral Formula 5000 team with which I'd just had a successful season. In my place, Don hired Peter Revson.

Peter was the nephew of Charles Revson, the Revlon cosmetics magnate, and exemplified every gossip column's concept of a wealthy, handsome, daring driver. Peter was casually at home with everyone in the paddock, especially the beautiful women. His racing motto, 'Speed with Style', summarised perfectly his approach to life. In practice for the South African Grand Prix, a poorly machined titanium ball joint caused a suspension failure that resulted in a crash and Peter's death. In tribute, Bob Akin, his friend and mine, adopted Peter's 'Speed with Style', perfectly expressing the standards by which Akin ran many immaculate and successful race teams.

Peter Revson was 35 years old.

Before the next race, Nichols called to ask me to take Peter's place for the rest of the season. Since his invitation came just after I'd learned that the

ABOVE I close on Tim Schenken's Surtees TS14 in the 1972 United States Grand Prix, but this one-off outing in a BRM P180 ended with engine failure.
Bill Oursler

ABOVE In 1974, I did three early-season races in Don Nichols' Shadow DN3, my final foray in Formula 1, before returning to the more congenial – and better paying – world of Formula 5000 in North America.
Getty Images/
Rainer Schlegelmilch

1974 US Formula 5000 Championship had been abandoned because of the oil crisis, I signed up immediately. Our results were mixed.

For the Spanish Grand Prix at Jarama, our first race together, Tony Southgate had replaced all of the Shadow's titanium ball joints with steel, adding a bit of unsprung weight but eliminating our mutual concerns about safety. During practice I flattened the rear wing for more overtaking speed and in the race I dragged the Shadow and myself from 21st to seventh place, a decent finish but not without controversy. At the airport, Denny 'The Bear' Hulme accosted me, ranting that he couldn't pass me on the straight, and I held him up in the corners. I found this confusing as Denny finished ahead of me in sixth. Still, Hulme's tirade made me long for the friendly, respectful atmosphere of Formula 5000 in America.

The Shadow failed to finish the Belgian Grand Prix at Zolder but Monaco was next and I hoped for a better result on the principality's anachronistic circuit. During Saturday's practice I received a call from Carl Haas, who told me that

the 1974 Formula 5000 season in America was back on. The lure of driving for Hall and Haas again was irresistible. Moreover, the American series promised to be the most competitive open-wheel racing in the world. Nichols was gracious and we parted friends, but not before sharing an unfortunate racing drama.

On the opening lap of the Monaco Grand Prix, Hulme's McLaren caused a cascade of smash-ups by tangling with Jean-Pierre Beltoise in his BRM, taking them both out and leading to crashes by Arturo Merzario (ISO Marlboro), Carlos Pace (Surtees) and me, while Vittorio Brambilla (March), Vern Schuppan (Ensign) and Tim Schenken (Trojan) also sustained damage and had their races ruined by lengthy pit-stops. As far as I know, not one of we seven abused drivers lectured Hulme on racing etiquette as he had me.

Don Nichols' Shadows were good cars run by professionals, but the team was snakebitten by bad luck. On my return to Formula 5000, my Shadow Formula 1 seat was filled by Tom Pryce. During the 1977 South African Grand Prix, the talented Welshman was in a string of cars dicing for position. Directly ahead, Hans Stuck's March-Cosworth swerved to avoid two marshals running across the track to put out a small fire in the Shadow of Renzo Zorzi, Tom's teammate. Only one marshal made it. Pryce, foot to the floor with his view blocked by Stuck's car, hit the second, killing him instantly. Tom, struck on the head by the marshal's fire extinguisher, sadly died too.

Tom Pryce was 28 years old. Frederik Jensen van Vuuren was 19.

Vasek Polak

I first met Vasek (*Vah-shek*) Polak in 1969 at Daytona, where I was driving a factory Porsche 908. By that time, Vasek, a Czech emigré who fled his native land in 1948, had built his independent Porsche and Volkswagen repair business into such a phenomenon that Porsche allowed him to open its first single-marque dealership in America. That entrepreneurial success fuelled a growing stable of increasingly sophisticated racing cars, all Porsches of course. When it came time for Vasek to name his driver for the 1973 Can-Am season, he spoke with me but ultimately selected Jody Scheckter. Many years later, Vasek spent a long evening drinking and sharing stories with historic racer Joe Hish.

'Why Jody and not Brian,' Hish asked?

'Brian was a more experienced driver but more laid back,' Polak admitted, 'while Scheckter was more aggressive and the better talker.'

Better talker? I now feel doubly insulted! Vasek then went on to make an extraordinary admission.

'Not giving that ride to Brian was the biggest mistake of my racing career.'

While I appreciate the retrospective compliment, Jody was a hot property at that time and, while he was often quicker over a single lap, I was better at finishing races. If only I had sold myself harder and helped Vasek not make that mistake!

Vasek and I would meet once or twice a year at races scattered around the USA but nothing happened between us. In the autumn

of 1973, perhaps he was feeling some regret. My phone rang.

'*Brian, this is Vasko!*' he shrieked, using his preferred nickname. '*You know I run Jody Scheckter in Can-Am in Porsche 917/10? Now, I have second car for you to drive at Laguna Seca and Riverside. Come to Willow Springs and test your car, and also you drive Jody's.*'

Willow Springs is a fast and somewhat remote circuit about an hour north of Los Angeles, private enough to be the destination track for car testing. I arrived there one blustery day in September to find Vasek's two identical 917/10s sitting in pitlane. I met with crew chief Alwin Springer to go over the idiosyncrasies I would encounter in testing these fearsome 1,100bhp turbocharged monsters. Alwin was one of the few people in the world who could build a 917 engine from scratch and later became head of Porsche Motorsports North America. My trust and confidence were high.

After I drove both cars, Vasek impatiently waited for my comparative assessments.

'*What they like, what they like?*' he asked. I replied that my car was a bit loose and difficult to drive quickly, but that Jody's car had a much more solid feel and could be driven harder, with more confidence.

'*They same, they same,*' Vasek insisted. Well, I thought, my car probably just needs a bit of development. Quite happily, I signed on to drive Vasek's second Porsche 917/10 in the last two races of the 1973 Can-Am.

Following a rather miserable experience at Laguna Seca where engine problems cut short our day, the team went on to the Riverside International Raceway. A long-legged track nestled beneath the San Bernardino Mountains just 55 miles east of Los Angeles, Riverside was the preferred location for most important west coast racing and the outdoor set for many Hollywood films. Racers knew Riverside as a fast, dangerous and wonderful circuit. In 1973 the track hosted the grandly titled *Los Angeles Times Grand Prix*, the last round of the Can-Am series. The Porsche 917/10 field was strong – George Follmer and Charlie Kemp racing for Bobby

Rinzler, Hurley Haywood in a single Brumos-sponsored car, Jody and me in Vasek's twin entries – but we were all resigned to racing for second place.

Mark Donohue dominated that year's Can-Am driving the ultimate iteration of the Porsche 917, the Penske-owned and Sunoco-sponsored 917/30, winner of all but two races. Not only had the Porsche 917/30 made obsolete the once-dominant 11-car McLaren juggernaut, but also it was a full generation more advanced than our five 917/10s. And, of course, Mark's car was beautifully developed and perfectly prepared, signatures of every Roger Penske entry, then and now. In practice, Donohue quickly proved to be in a class of his own, turning laps that were an astounding three seconds faster than the best of the rest.

Late Friday afternoon, I felt something wasn't quite right in the rear of my car while pressing on at 190mph through the fast kink, the absolute worst place for a problem to happen. The kink was near the end of Riverside's drag strip that doubled as the back straight for the road course. This fast left-hander had been created artificially by a line of temporary cement barriers that directed our cars away from the drag racers' finish line and linked the kink to a short chute leading to a banked bowl at the track's southern end. It wasn't hard for any good driver in a well-prepared car to stay flat through the kink, but the barriers left no run-off area when something went wrong, as it did for me. After getting the car under control, I returned the car to pitlane where the mechanics and I conducted an inspection. To our surprise, we found a broken right rear suspension support tube, a major structural component of the chassis. It is always serious when the integrity of the chassis is compromised as the reduced stiffness sets off a cascade of handling problems.

Vasek's mechanics competently welded the broken tube but again, on Saturday afternoon, I felt something in the car suddenly go amiss. One more pitlane inspection exposed one more fractured structural tube. For a driver, a single break in the chassis would have been rare

and worrisome, but two were deeply alarming. Curiously, Friday's repair held perfectly and this was a new break in a different part of the same right rear suspension. By now, I was becoming extremely concerned. Following my usual sleepless Saturday night, I told Vasek on Sunday morning that I didn't think the car was safe and that I didn't want to race it.

'Brian, the guys work all night,' he said. 'The car is perfect, perfect, but – you don't wanna drive, it's okay. I understand.'

Vasek's sincerity was convincing. He had a solid reputation as a very good mechanic and a savvy team manager. Besides, he left the choice to me, without conditions. I softened. Vasek was probably right, the car would be perfect, perfect.

'OK, Vasek, I'll drive.'

In Sunday's qualifying heat race, I outran

the other four 917/10s, finishing second behind Donohue. In the Cup Final, the car's demons returned; something significant broke at close to 200mph in the same high-speed kink that earlier had twice fractured a chassis tube. The car swerved sideways, pointing to the outside of the track. When I caught the slide, it demonically switched back and headed towards the cement drag-strip barriers. Sawing vigorously at the wheel, I eventually managed to get the car to face in the right direction, although the rear wheels continued to slew side to side in a frightening series of violent fishtails.

Gingerly, I crept back to the pits, to be confronted by a screaming Vasek.

'What the matter, what the matter?' he roared.

'What's the matter?' I shouted back. 'Something big let go in the rear of the car.'

ABOVE The first lap of my Can-Am qualifying heat at Riverside International Raceway, Mark Donohue leading in his all-conquering Porsche 917/30, me close behind in Vasek Polak's older Porsche. We finished in this order.
Getty Images/ Rainer Schlegelmilch

ABOVE In the Can-Am
Cup Final at Riverside,
my Porsche suffered
an unusual suspension
failure – and eventually
a disquieting truth
emerged about the car.
McKlein

The mechanics lifted the tail, disclosing
a broken Heim joint, one of the articulated
bearings connected to the rod that controlled
the directional stability of the right rear wheel.
Heim joints are so critical that they are routinely
over-engineered and so strong that failure is
very rare. As I peered closely at the suspension
with suspicious intensity, I became chilled to
the core, suddenly aware of the distressing truth
behind the car's difficult handling and terrifying
sequence of structural problems.

My car was not equipped with the twin
parallel-linked suspension characteristic of a
true 917/10, which meant that I had trusted my
life to a car that was not a 917/10 at all. Now that
I looked at the suspension carefully, I realised
that Vasek's second car was the 1969 ex-Siffert
Porsche 917PA disguised as a 1973 factory-built
910/10. It was the same car I had driven during
John Wyer's pre-1970 testing, recently purchased
by Vasek, inexpensively no doubt. What made
the realisation so disquieting was that the four-
year-old 917PA chassis had been designed for a

relatively modest 580bhp engine, almost exactly
half the power of the behemoth that, moments
earlier, propelled me around Riverside. When the
combination of the engine's huge torque and the
kink's heavy cornering forces twisted the car's
chassis, the lighter tubing couldn't handle the
stresses and broke, three times. Then and only
then, did the confronted Vasek and his mechanics
admit their deceit. Cunning Vasek had cloned
the bodywork of Scheckter's real 917/10, fitted it
to the well-used 917PA, and inserted his 'spare'
1,100bhp turbocharged engine. Vasek had made
no upgrades to the original frame nor had he
prepared the suspension for the immense torque
of his turbo motor. Unsurprisingly, my weekend
was over. Surprisingly, my relationship with
Vasek Polak was not.

Vasek became very wealthy catering to
Southern California's insatiable appetite for
new Porsches while quietly and economically
acquiring wonderful racing cars rendered
obsolete by newer models. He also bought all
the NOS (new-old-stock) parts that dealers,

disbanded teams and the factory itself decided to dump. Thirty years later, Vasek's vintage 917s, 908s, 906s and RSRs became extremely valuable. The affluent collectors who purchased them at eye-watering prices also required Vasek's stream of replacement components to restore the cars and keep them running in historic racing. Vasek had cornered the historic Porsche market.

Despite the fact that Vasek almost killed me, he and I became personally very close. He died in 1997, in textbook manner, following an accident when driving his recently collected Porsche Turbo S on an *autobahn* near Regensburg, Germany. Something made Vasek lose control and the officials estimated that he left the road at over 100mph. Badly injured, he was flown back to America in a private jet air ambulance. Whilst it was stopped for fuel in Great Falls, Montana, Vasek's heart said 'enough', and he succumbed. His collection manager, Carl Thompson, and I were appointed as the estate trustee advisors on the disposal of his vast number of Porsche racing cars and his huge inventory of equally

rare spare parts. All proceeds funded the Vasek and Anna Maria Polak Charitable Foundation, his philanthropic beneficiary.

Unhappily, Riverside's demise preceded Vasek's. California's frenetic late 20th-century development was omnivorous and, in 1989, Riverside became another example of 'Where the hand of man hath trod'. To the regret of every driver who flicked a car through turns two and three or chased a competitor across the up-and-down terrain between eight and 13, or flew down the 1.1-mile back straight and through the kink with his right foot planted, Riverside International Raceway succumbed to the tender mercies of 7mph bulldozers. When the developers had completed their work, 'The House that Dan Gurney Built' had mutated into yet another boring Golden State residential tract where life centred on a requisite perky mall, with 'shoppes'.

My Can-Am drives continued to be difficult even before my near-fatal accident at St Jovite, Canada in 1977. Two were memorable for opposite reasons.

Can-Am in a Ferrari

In July 1974, for the Formula 5000 race at Watkins Glen, a Can-Am race was added to the weekend's schedule. On the Saturday afternoon, just before the Can-Am heat race, Luigi 'Coco' Chinetti Jr, son of the Ferrari distributor and organiser of many racing programmes, asked if I would like to drive the NART (North American Racing Team) Ferrari 712 in the race because its regular driver, Sam Posey, was feeling unwell. Since I hadn't practised in the car, I was concerned that I wouldn't be allowed to take part, but Luigi said he had it all arranged. I was to start at the back of the grid and do my best, and he thoughtfully added that I could retire if I were uncomfortable driving the car. For $1,000, I agreed.

The five-minute warning horn had just sounded when a journalist ran up and asked what I was doing climbing into Posey's Ferrari. When I replied that Posey wasn't feeling well, he warned me that Sam had strained muscles and ligaments when the 712's brake pedal suddenly

went to the floor. This didn't fit my definition of 'feeling unwell'.

'Yes, that's true,' Luigi conceded, 'but Sam got hurt because we tried an experimental brake fluid. Now everything is in order.' With hard driving and some inherited positions, I overcame my back-of-the-grid handicap and finished second to George Follmer in the UOP Shadow. Before Sunday's Cup final, my Formula 5000 mechanic Franz Weis looked over the 712 and offered his opinion.

'Brian, what are you doing driving that piece of shit?'

In the race, attrition was my friend until, abruptly, it wasn't. Having worked the car up to second place, I was feeling quite good about myself when a suspension link broke on the main straight at 170mph, sending me down the track in a series of violent swerves. Fortunately, I hit nothing and the car eventually stopped in perfectly fine condition – this time. I should have listened to Franz Weis.

Can-Am in the ultimate Porsche

In October 1973 OPEC took control of the world's oil and pushed up fuel prices by limiting supplies. By March 1974 oil prices had quadrupled. This gave Can-Am's SCCA sanctioning body the perfect excuse to kill off the all-conquering Porsches, particularly the 917/30, by mandating that every entrant had to average more than 3mpg. Those 917/10 owners desperate to hang on retro-fitted their cars' normally aspirated engines with carburettors or fuel injection. Many others simply dropped out and the series was cut to just five races.

In July I received a call from Roger Penske asking if I'd like to drive his fire-breathing Porsche 917/30 in the following month's Mid-Ohio Can-Am race. Surprised, I said that I thought the 917s were unable to meet the new fuel regulations.

'Come and see me,' Roger simply replied. Obediently (and hopefully), I went to Reading, Pennsylvania and found myself sitting across from Roger at his perfectly polished mahogany desk.

'The car can run,' he explained. 'How much do you want?'

Bravely, I asked for $5,000. Roger smiled, and made a comment I now realise was dubious praise.

'Brian, you're the most reasonable racing driver I ever met.'

The 917/30 and I were united at Mid-Ohio for its one-and-only 1974 contest, the fourth meeting of the season and the last hurrah for the fastest road-racing car of that era, possibly all time. It promised to be a triumphant weekend. Mark Donohue had retired from driving (temporarily, as things turned out) to become Penske's Can-Am team manager but was looking particularly uncomfortable in this new role. Mark acted like a man assigned to help me steal his girlfriend, and beautiful the 917/30 certainly was. With exquisite handling and 1,100bhp available at the driver's whim, the 917/30 could reach 200mph from zero in a little more than 10 seconds, and not be breathing hard when it got there. Given a long

RIGHT Mark Donohue and I flank Miss Mid-Ohio in 1974. Mark dominated Can-Am in 1973 but the fuel consumption of his Porsche 917/30 ruled it out for the 1974 series, apart from its single outing at Mid-Ohio, with me at wheel.
Rob Neuzel

BELOW Strong competition in the Cup Final at Mid-Ohio came from the two Shadow DN4 cars. Jackie Oliver makes a wild pass on teammate George Follmer, who later returned the favour but put himself out of the race.
Brian Redman collection

enough straight, it was capable of speeds in the range of 240mph. Mark once called it '*The perfect racing car*' but others damned it as '*The car that killed Can-Am*' – it was that dominant.

As fuel allocations for racing were slim that season, the SCCA officials decided to run the event in two sections: a sprint qualifier that set the grid (since lightly fuelled cars consume less

over more laps) and a Cup Final. My only real on-track competition would come from George Follmer and Jackie Oliver, both in Shadow DN4s, but another challenger showed up that I hadn't expected – wet weather.

I handily won the sprint heat in steady drizzle using Firestone's excellent rain tyres but the skies definitely were brightening as the main event approached. If I started the race on full wets and the racing line began to dry, the soft rain tyres would degrade rapidly, necessitating a stop for replacement. If I started on slicks and conditions remained wet, every car with tyres designed to siphon away the water would roar past. I asked Mark, a superb race engineer, what he thought about manually grooving a set of slicks, essentially creating intermediates, something halfway between wet and dry tyres. The hand-cut channels would throw off the lesser amount of water while the tyre's harder compound would be tough enough to last the race.

'*Let's do it,*' said Mark, inferring that he had tried this previously.

When the track did dry, as expected during the Cup Final, our grooved slicks turned out to be an unmitigated disaster. The 'perfect car' went from brilliant to painful, ploughing through corners with what drivers call 'terminal understeer'.

Jackie Oliver won in dramatic fashion after his teammate George Follmer attempted an impossible pass and took himself out of the race. I finished a disappointed second driving the world's fastest racing machine, 14 seconds behind Oliver. It turned out that the Porsche 917/30 was a racing car that could only be beaten by itself.

With OPEC woes continuing, entrants' cars becoming obsolete and spectator interest flagging, the 1974 Can-Am series limped through just one more race and into the dustbin of history.

Facing reality

Racing in my era was like a game of deadly musical chairs. We competed driver-on-driver and marque-on-marque but, on a global scale, our real adversary was mortality and history left its cumulative scars. This wonderful, terrible ten-year span claimed many distinguished drivers with vital lives outside of their racing cars, some my teammates and companions, a few my friends. To bring things full circle, there is one little-known driver who deserves to be noted, despite the fact we never met.

As recounted in the chapter on my early years, John Taylor drove David Bridges' 2-litre Brabham-BRM BT11 at the Nürburgring in the 1966 German Grand Prix where he suffered a fiery collision on the first lap, succumbing to infections a few weeks later. David asked me to succeed him in a replacement car, the opportunity that impelled me into a career in racing.

John Taylor was 33 years old.

Each time Marion and I parted, we both knew the potential consequences; the children, thankfully, were oblivious. Without driving, I was unemployable and without employment all the pleasures of seeing my family thrive would have been lost.

So, I drove.

ABOVE A misjudgement resulting in the wrong tyres when the damp track dried, meant that I had to settle for second place at Mid-Ohio, behind Jackie Oliver's winning Shadow.
Brian Redman collection

CHAPTER 13
My brief encounter with death

Racing is an up-and-down sport, and not just for its drivers. Teams surge into a season with optimism and bravado only to learn that costs were higher than anticipated and that a sponsor's funding can wax and wane like phases of the moon. Even sanctioning bodies and major series are vulnerable, subject to team participation and fan fickleness.

The Formula 5000 series had a stout run from 1968 to 1976 and was the hottest schedule in racing for five of its last six years. During the 1976 season, crowds began to thin and the organisers were going through troubled financial times. The SCCA (Sports Car Club of America) sanctioning body became nostalgic for the big crowds that had followed the old Can-Am series, with its closed-wheel brutes powered by big-block engines that made Armageddon noises. As a result, the SCCA changed the rules to eliminate Formula 5000 and introduced what it hoped would be a return to the popularity of the Can-Am era.

If the Formula 5000 series suffered, so, too, the racing teams that made up the grids. Few could afford to abandon their current cars and build proper big-block Can-Am entries. The answer was obvious: camouflage the existing Formula 5000 cars with fibreglass bodywork, change their designations, and declare each a new Can-Am competitor. This compromise suited our Lola T332C, Jim Hall and me just fine. We had been

the dominant team over the previous three years of Formula 5000 and there was every reason to believe we could continue as such in 1977. When First National City Travelers Checks signed on as Hall's principal sponsor, we were back in racing.

The first 'new-age' Can-Am race was run in June at Quebec's challenging 2.65-mile St Jovite circuit, south of the skiing town Mont-Tremblant. The track was built in 1964 with an additional mile tacked on the following year to provide a long and wickedly fast straight. Unfortunately, the terrain chosen for the new straight included a complicating rise known as The Hump that created mischief with the faster cars. While The Hump wasn't a full tyres-off-the-ground jump for us, the transition did make our cars very light on their wheels and momentarily unstable; in 1966 two cars were launched into the air and flipped. Canadian winters didn't do the track surface any favours and the resulting lumpy asphalt added to our cars' erratic landings. Still, Canadians are enthusiastic race fans and, as a French speaker, I enjoyed the atmosphere. For me, St Jovite was like being back at Le Mans.

Death gets personal

In practice at St Jovite, our Lola was running well although it seemed to me that we could improve the balance and perhaps gain a little more top-end speed. I asked Jim Hall to trim out the car

OPPOSITE Poignancy and pensiveness seem appropriate before my disastrous race in 1977 at St Jovite, Canada.
Getty Images/ Bob Harmeyer

ABOVE The Haas/Hall
Lola T333 creates
rolling thunder in
practice for the 1977
St Jovite race, the first
in the new-era Can-Am
series designed to link
the best of Formula 5000
with the earlier big-
banger Can-Am ethos.
Getty Images/
Bob Harmeyer

by lowering the front wing a quarter of an inch,
swapping a few pounds of front-end downforce
to reduce its tendency to oversteer. Lowering
the wing was a relatively minor tweak and Jim
thought it worth a try. I returned to the circuit
and, after a warm-up lap, entered St Jovite's long
straight at maximum speed.

As I crested The Hump, the car's nose lifted
slightly to present a sliver of its underside to
the wind, causing a cascade of unfortunate
consequences. As the underbody of the car
became exposed incrementally to the airstream,
the front end was lifted completely off the ground
and the car performed a languid backwards
somersault. To me, it seemed forever before it
and I violently landed upside-down on the track,
crushing the air box, bending the roll bar and
leaving my head dragging along the surface. The
Lola may have been thoroughly broken but it was
still travelling forwards at considerable speed
and it's probably fortunate that I was completely
knocked out as the car slid (and slid, and slid), so I
didn't hear the asphalt grinding away my helmet.

Had the fibreglass worn completely through, my
head would have been next.

The wrecked T333 finally came to rest,
mercifully the right way up. By the time the
medics arrived, my heart had stopped but (as is
self-evident) they got it running again. Removing
me from the car required some rough handling,
none of which I remember as I remained
mercifully unconscious. They placed me in
an ambulance that raced to a nearby hospital,
although not without many minutes lost with its
own drama. A tyre blow-out required the medics
to perform an emergency wheel change while I
remained strapped to the stretcher. By afternoon,
the presses were rolling and the headlines
in Montréal's papers read, '*Redman Est Mort*',
Redman Is Dead, and I suppose that briefly I was.

Recovery

After three days in an induced coma, I woke up in
the Montréal Neurological Institute and learned
that I had sustained a broken neck, a shattered
shoulder, a split sternum and an assortment of

fractured ribs. I was very lucky that my spine turned out to be just slightly scratched; had it been damaged more, I would be a quadriplegic today. The first person I saw when I opened my eyes was Jim Hall.

'*How are you?*' he asked.

'*I think I might have to miss the next race,*' I quipped, certain that I was very funny.

Marion immediately flew to Montréal accompanied by David Hobbs, who came along to have a look at his old pal – or perhaps he just enjoyed being with his old pal's wife. Marion decided there was no point in her staying as we believed the hospital competent and I'd be unable to move for some time. After several days, she returned to England to take care of the children while I remained among the seven other patients at the Institute, all with injuries similar to mine. One had hit a tree while skiing, another was a victim of a motorcycle accident, a third had been badly hurt in a car crash, and so on. It was instructive for me to learn that I didn't have to go racing to break my neck. All of the ward

ABOVE Not much remained of my Lola T332C, or me, after we somersaulted off The Hump and became racing wreckage.
Getty Images/Bob Harmeyer

BELOW The racing car and I were flattened, and my recovery was slow and troublesome. Still, I was fortunate that the crash didn't leave me with permanent physical and mental damage.
Getty Images/Bob Harmeyer

residents appeared to be sedated most of the time, and possibly over-sedated. While my earlier two accidents required drugs to control the pain, none had effects like those prescribed for this recovery. At first I thought these opiates were wonderful, causing me to pass weeks of tranquil immobility in a pleasant haze. Later, I came to believe they warped my judgement, deadened my emotions and encouraged me to attempt foolish things.

Two weeks after the accident, the doctors removed the 'halo' that immobilised my broken neck, a space age-looking device attached by self-tapping screws to each side of my head, and braced against my shoulders. Finally, with just a collar I could move my neck, if only slightly. In my confused state, this now meant I was fully mobile. I woke at 1.00am, worked my way down the bed, climbed over the bottom rail, pushed the table out of the way, and dropped my legs onto the floor. Triumphantly, I stumbled into the nurses' room having no idea why I thought this might be prudent. The medical staff went totally berserk and decided I was self-destructive. To

prevent further break-outs, they strapped me to the bed with knotted cloths around my legs and waist as if I were a disruptive mental patient. Once again, I had rendered myself helpless until, lesson learned, I became the model patient and the restraints were loosened.

Companionship in this bizarre setting was equally surreal. There was another patient who had sustained spinal injuries and the staff decided that he should be my hospital buddy. Every morning they'd push him to the foot of my bed in a wheelchair so he and I could silently commune. The fact that neither of us ever spoke makes me suspicious that he was as heavily drugged as I was, but stare at each other we did, uncomplainingly for long hours. Out of frustration one day, my new best friend got a gleam in his eye and, with a conspiratorial glance at me, laboured strenuously to free his urine bottle. In what I can only imagine was a statement of befuddled defiance, he hurled it onto the floor. I mention this distasteful prank only to note that it was the single most entertaining thing that happened during my entire hospital convalescence. Life on the ward had come to that.

I recall being quite happy over these weeks but now realise that I was probably just stoned. After more than a month in a narcotic-induced reverie, I was released from the hospital and flew home to England by myself, thankfully in first class. I was oblivious to the fact that there were almost eight months of rehabilitation ahead of me and no visible means of income. In my mentally decoupled way, I really didn't care.

Retrospective considerations about those days suggest that, even though I was off the drugs, they continued to exercise a negative influence on my mood. All I could do, or chose to do, was lie around Taira House in an uncommunicative silence, expecting to be served by Marion while oblivious to her needs. I couldn't think clearly, had a hard time paying attention to conversations, and exhibited no interest in anything, including getting well.

It's also possible that I was suffering a head trauma from being dragged upside-down on the road. There was evidence that I did bruise my brain – giving Marion every opportunity since to

insist it was an injury from which I have never recovered. More likely I had received serious concussion, the effects of which were unknown in those days. Slowly my physical health began to return, as did the feeling I had lost between my chest and toes. By November, I was able to take walks in the village of Gargrave, sort of shambling along until, finally, I could even jog a little. The curious thing was that I didn't feel capable of any sort of driving, even our family car. As a result, Marion was required to add the role of chauffeuse to her multiple obligations. Bless her, she ferried this morose passenger through the countryside daily, hoping the simple therapy of sunlight and beautiful byways might encourage my return to normality. Astonishingly, Marion's wish came precisely true, in a most unexpected way.

Alive again

One day, she and I were on a country lane when we came across a 200-acre farm called Eshton Grange, offered in four parcels and due to be auctioned a few weeks later. The main lot consisted of 20 acres that sloped down a hill towards a stream and included the original, historic farmhouse as well as equally ancient outbuildings. Even though Gargrave was only two miles away, the contours of the land created a lovely sense of isolation and the nearest neighbours were completely unseen. When I came upon Eshton Grange, something clicked in me and the possibility of owning and operating a farm became the focus of my life.

With neither warning nor explanation, I became obsessed by the impending auction and suddenly felt very much alive. I simply had to have Eshton Grange. Seeing stirrings of hope, Marion put aside her love for Taira House and offered every encouragement. Reality snapped back into place and I began to think and act as if my St Jovite accident never happened. Concluding that our current home was worth about the same as the expected auction price of Eshton Grange, I dashed to Skipton to meet the manager of Barclays Bank, one Mr Bainbridge.

ABOVE Eshton Grange, the Yorkshire farm that Marion and I bought in late 1977, had a profound therapeutic influence on my physical recovery and mental initiative after the worst crash of my racing career.
Playaway Centre (Mark Hughes)

Redman: '*Mr Bainbridge, I need a bridging loan until I can sell my current home.*'

Bainbridge: '*What cash can you raise as protection for a loan?*'

Redman: '*I own a Porsche 917.*'

Bainbridge: '*What's a 917?*'

Redman: '*It's a race car, and an historic one.*' This didn't impress Mr Bainbridge at all.

Bainbridge: '*Bring me £20,000 and I'll lend you the rest.*' I knew exactly how to raise the £20,000.

In 1975 I'd got wind from Jerry Entin that a Porsche 917 was going to be sold under a mechanic's lien. The competent German restorer, Bernd Booch, had just overhauled the car, so I knew it would be in excellent shape. It didn't hurt that the 917 really *was* the car Steve McQueen had driven during the filming of *Le Mans*. In theory, owner/driver provenance adds importantly to a car's retail value so I acted quickly and put in a bid at the favourable price of £8,500 (about $13,500), enough to secure the purchase.

My Porsche 917

The idea that such a rare historic car could sell for so little at that time will pain contemporary collectors, as it does me even today. Then, in desperate need of the £20,000 to secure the loan that made my farming ambitions possible, I needed a cash buyer with some relationship to an exotic racing car. The perfect person was Richard Attwood, my friend and occasional co-driver who, of course, won the 1970 Le Mans 24 Hours in a 917.

'*How much?*' Richard asked.

'*£30,000,*' I responded bravely, hoping for a sweet 350 per cent profit. The deal was done.

As Richard and I were friends, I thought it prudent to deliver a running car. I had fired up the engine from time to time, lubricating its critical moving parts, but, as luck would have it that day, the clutch was seized to the flywheel.

I hooked a rope to the Porsche and, with me in the driver's seat, asked my friend Ian Green to tow the car backwards to the top of a nearby hill. After Ian untied the rope, I started the engine and allowed gravity to drop the car down towards our village. As it gathered speed, I shoved the transmission into first gear and stood on the clutch, brake and throttle, all at the same time and all as hard as possible. The 917 hurtled forward until suddenly, with a bang and a roar, the clutch freed.

It was a lovely Sunday afternoon in sleepy Gargrave, and people were no doubt meditating after a hearty roast-beef lunch or sleeping off the effects of their mid-day visit to the pub. That all changed as I enthusiastically revved the unsilenced 12-cylinder engine all the way to my home. Ian, following behind, described the stir I caused. Dozing villagers were roused and gardeners frightened. '*It's that daft racing driver,*' one citizen exclaimed to Ian.

Much later, acting on Richard's behalf, I sold 'our' 917 at an RM Auction in Monterey, California for $1.2 million; so much for my 'sweet' £21,500 profit. Still, Richard's auction envy surely surpassed mine when a 917 purporting to be the same car was offered at Gooding's 2014 Pebble Beach auction at the eye-watering anticipated price of $20 million. Richard's jealousy was premature. The Gooding's car turned out not to be the 917 he and I had owned but one with a doubtful history, and it was withdrawn from the sale. Save your pennies; the real McQueen 917 is still out there.

With funds secured by the car's sale, Marion and I were the high bidders at £75,000 for the main portion of Eshton Grange. We'd already put Taira House on the market and thankfully it sold quickly. Now, in addition to repairing a late 18th century farmhouse and making my family comfortable, there was a great deal of work ahead to bring back the rest of the property. I embraced farm life with new-found enthusiasm. Within a year, the house renovations were completed, the garden planted, and the outbuildings newly housed a proper assemblage of farm animals – Hereford cattle, a giant Shire workhorse, and a flock of Dales sheep. Additionally, we shared our home with a cat and a Labrador retriever.

Eshton Grange, with its complement of birds and beasts, became my psychiatrist. It refreshed my marriage with Marion, warmed my relationships with James and Charlotte and, probably, saved my life. Somehow, it took the after-effects of a horrendous accident for me to rediscover racing happiness.

In the meantime, over the second half of the 1970s, the sport made substantial progress in safety. I had survived the consequences of a terrible, wonderful period and 15 more years of good teams, good times and winning days lay ahead.

In a bizarre postscript to my St Jovite accident, it turns out that Marion herself was injured on the very same day of my crash. She had just finished a riding lesson and was trotting back to the stables when a wasp stung her horse's nose. Zebedee reared and Marion was thrown. Typical of her intrepidness, she ignored the pain and flew to Canada to help with my recovery. Some 40 years later, Marion was feeling some discomfort above her shoulders and had an X-ray. After viewing the film, the doctor asked a question.

'When did you break your neck?'

ABOVE My very own Porsche 917 – which I bought for £8,500, sold to my good friend Richard Attwood for £30,000, and he sold for $1.2 million – is now worth tens of millions, to his and my envy.
Bill Warner

BELOW My best friend Ian Green was my partner in crime when we caused my Porsche 917 to rattle the quietude of our fellow Gargrave residents one Sunday.
Brian Redman collection

CHAPTER 14
Closure

By the late 1970s, the early stirrings for driver safety had grown rapidly into an international cause. Jackie Stewart and the Grand Prix Drivers' Association (GPDA) spearheaded the drive in Europe while Mark Donohue and the Road Racing Drivers Club (RRDC) led the way in America.

The improvements in technologies, racing car designs and track modifications were nothing short of revolutionary. Helmets had to meet Snell test standards and racing suits were created in three layers of fire-resistant Nomex. Six-point safety harnesses bound drivers to their seats while stronger monocoques and stout roll-over bars protected them in crashes. Pedals were placed behind the centre-line of the front axle, fuel bladders made of high-tensile elastomeric materials virtually eliminated the risk of fire, and head-and-neck devices reduced spinal injuries.

As each new driver-safety development unfolded, tracks were also undergoing transitions. Protective barriers were installed, hazardous corners were modified with run-off areas, and additional fire and medical stations became standard.

For me, these improvements in safety were gifts, allowing me to pursue my profession in good conscience without jeopardising my health and exposing my loved ones to potential hardship. For the first time in my professional life, I enjoyed my pre-race nights in the sleep of deep peace.

Danger may make the profession glamorous to spectators but not for drivers and their families. Still, all drivers know that danger is part of the spectacle. Dan Gurney put it well to journalist Brock Yates during the 1971 Cannonball, Yates's illegal race across America. '*Of course, they want to see crashes,*' Dan observed, '*They want to be where the action is. That's a natural thing.*' When asked about death, Dan said, '*Very few people at races want to see anyone killed. Wild crashes are all right, but they don't ask for blood.*' After the 1970s, my chances of injury never went away completely but the risks became reasonable and tolerable, as in other adventurous occupations.

Lean times

My near-fatal crash at St Jovite in June 1977 ruled out any more racing that year. In 1978 I managed just six races, and then only 10 in 1979.

As a favour, Porsche/Audi/Volkswagen competition manager Joe Hoppen fixed me up with my first 'comeback' drive. This was in March 1978 in the Sebring 12 Hours with Dick Barbour's second Porsche 935, partnered with Bob Garretson (who prepared Dick's cars) and Charlie Mendez (the Sebring promoter). We surprised everyone, including ourselves, by winning, vanquishing all the favourites and even our own team's number one car.

OPPOSITE I wasted a lot of champagne in 1981. As well as winning the 24 Hours of Daytona with Bobby Rahal and Bob Garretson in the Cooke-Woods 935, there were five more IMSA victories driving the Lola T600.
Bryan Watson

ABOVE Our result in the 1978 12 Hours of Sebring, the first race after my horrendous crash at St Jovite, astonished everyone, me included, when Bob Garretson, Charlie Mendez and I won overall in Dick Barbour's number two Porsche 935.
Porsche-werkfoto

RIGHT The night was dark and chilly as I geared up for my final stint at Sebring in 1979, when Charlie Mendez, Paul Miller and I took second in a Porsche 935.
Getty Images/ Bob Harmeyer

My big adventures in 1979 resulted in a very used Porsche 936. Jochen Mass crashed the car heavily at the Silverstone Six Hours and I survived a damaging spin at Le Mans, neither of us at fault – well, maybe me a little bit, in both.

Later that year, it was clear that I needed a regular job. No racing meant no income, and my finances were becoming desperate. I approached Carl Haas, the US importer of Lola racing cars and Hewland gearboxes for whom I'd raced in Formula 5000. Thinking that I might have dual value as a salesman and a racing driver, Carl suggested I join him in selling Lolas but continue racing when opportunities arose. Marion, the kids and I loved our country life in England but without wholesome racing contracts like those with Porsche and Ferrari, there was no way to sustain it. At the beginning of 1980 I once again uprooted my family and dragged them to Highland Park, Illinois (outside Chicago) where I joined the Haas operation for the princely (and vitally necessary) salary of $30,000 a year.

My racing picked up, with 12 events that year,

all bar one in Porsche 935s. I took an IMSA class win (and fifth overall) at Le Mans with John Fitzpatrick and Dick Barbour in Dick's Kremer K3 Porsche 935, leading for a while until Sunday morning when the car went onto five cylinders. I was also teamed with Fitzpatrick in the Barbour 935 for the six-hour races at Watkins Glen and Mosport, where we finished third and first respectively. My single non-935 outing was in Roy Woods' Lola T333 with David Hobbs in the Lumberman's 500 at Mid-Ohio – and we won it.

By now, concern about Porsche's domination with its all-conquering 935 was growing throughout sports-car racing. To encourage new entries able to compete against the 935s, John Bishop's International Motor Sport Association (IMSA) introduced a new category, Grand Touring Prototype (GTP), and I saw an opportunity to create a V8-powered car capable of winning. Carl Haas agreed and dispatched me to England to consult with Eric Broadley, Lola's founder and chief designer. Eric jumped at the chance to develop a 200mph prototype

ABOVE Mostly I drove Porsches, mainly 935s, in 1979. In this one exception, Bobby Rahal, Tony Cicale and I won the Mid-Ohio 500 Miles in Tony's Ralt RT1.
Bill Oursler

LEFT My only non-Porsche race of 1980 was a good one, winning the Mid-Ohio 500 Miles for a second time, this time with David Hobbs in a Lola T333 run by Roy Woods Racing.
Michael Botsko

with ground effects* but firmly stated that, to
begin, he needed an order for two chassis at
$75,000 each. The additional costs of an engine,
transmission and spares would take the price
to well over $100,000, which was too rich for
Haas. If I wanted to further my driving career,
I needed to find buyers, preferably *aficionado*
racing drivers equipped with inheritances.

Ralph Kent Cooke, son of media mogul Jack
Kent Cooke, was one candidate; Roy Woods,
from Oklahoma and in oil, was the second. I
persuaded them to form Cooke-Woods Racing,
for which I was to be driver and manager. I
roped in the appropriately named John Bright to
build, test and prepare the two new Lola T600s
– 'an heir and a spare' as only one would race

*Ground effect is the term used to describe the downforce
achieved in racing cars by managing underbody airflow.
The Lola T600 obtained its favourable ground-hugging
cornering from an undertray shaped like an upside-down
aircraft wing that accelerated the air to create a bubble of
negative pressure – the Bernoulli effect.*

at any time. John was a superb mechanic and, to
the embarrassment of many gentlemen entrants
for whom he wielded spanners, a very fast driver.
The plan was that John would stay at Lola Cars to
help build the T600s and then come over to run
them from Bob Garretson's shop in Mountain
View, California. As the cars weren't going to
be ready until the late spring of 1981, Ralph and
Roy purchased a Porsche 935 so that we could
participate in the early races of the season.

Winning at Daytona

The 24 Hours of Daytona was the 1981 season
opener for the Cooke-Woods 935, which I drove
with a youthful Bobby Rahal and Bob Garretson.
I had qualified 15th but Bobby insisted he could
move us higher. '*Leave it*,' I said, knowing how
unimportant qualifying was in that era of car
fragility. If we simply circulated successfully for
24 hours, a top-ten finish was assured and, given
the strength of our car, drivers and mechanics,
much better could be expected.

In the race Bobby finished one of his stints

LEFT Prudently, I check the tyres in this early-morning pit-stop at Daytona in 1981. The pounding meted out by the banking meant that tyres were always a particular concern in the 24 Hours.
LAT

BELOW Our Daytona-winning car still looks pretty good here, but by the end of 24 hours of high-speed running the nose is shot-blasted, duct tape holds bodywork together and paint is scarred by grit, rubber and scuffs.
Porsche-Werkfoto

DAYTONA, U.S.A.

and appeared in our motorhome at 2.00am.

'*We're leading,*' he gleefully reported. Seeing the dark look on my face and anticipating my consummate displeasure, he quickly pleaded his case. '*I swear I didn't pass a single car in our class all night. Everyone else just broke down.*'

Our team went on to take the overall win, thanks in large part to mechanic Greg Elliff, who slid underneath the car and managed to change a red-hot exhaust header under truly hellish circumstances.

Unfortunately, Bob Garretson flipped the 935 at Sebring in March and we were lucky to finish, in 17th place. Rahal and I then drove the car to third place at the Riverside Six Hours.

My 1981 Lola campaign

I had asked John Bright to make sure the new Lola T600 was in America by March 1981, no matter what Eric Broadley said or did. John delivered, as always. We tested throughout the spring but decided to skip a few races in order to perfect our new weapon. Laguna Seca

was selected to be the T600's maiden event and Broadley joined us there for the launch of his newest design. The night before the race, Carl Haas took me aside.

'*Brian, if this car doesn't win tomorrow,*' Carl said, '*Lola Cars will go bankrupt.*' John Bright confirmed this grim assessment, reporting that activity at the factory had become sparse. Lose the race and lose the company – no pressure there!

The T600 was designed with enclosed rear wheels in order to enhance the ground effects. Later these wheel coverings were found to be of limited value, but in our first race they probably saved the day. Shortly after the start, the car began to weave inexplicably, scaring me in the fast corners. I dropped to tenth place, all the while remembering Carl's urgent request that I win. Inexplicably the handling then improved and the Lola once again felt normal. I began to catch cars in rapid succession, passing John Paul Jr's leading Porsche 935 seven laps from the chequered flag.

'*I just saved Lola,*' I thought – and maybe it was even true.

When we returned the car to Garretson's California shop, we noticed strange things about the left rear wheel and I suggested that Broadley take a look.

'Well, Brian,' he said after thoughtfully wiping his glasses, '*that's what it's supposed to do, but I've never seen it happen.*'

Our inspection had revealed that the hub was missing its sprung steel safety pin on the outside of the wheel nut and the nut itself was quite chewed up. By design, the threading on the left and right wheels of racing cars are mirror images, so that the wheel nuts tighten with forward motion. If the rear wheels hadn't been enclosed and I'd slowed down, the nut would have fallen off. Instead, as I pressed on quickly, the rapid rotation of the wheels screwed the nut back on its thread. Luck? Good engineering? Both – and a good win for Eric Broadley. More Lola T600s began appearing immediately and ultimately grew to a fleet of 11. Eric's salesmen got commissions, but not the driver who saved the company.

Lime Rock Park in Connecticut's scenic north-western corner is a wonderful track for small racing cars but not for larger, faster machinery – a lap in our Lola T600 took just over 50 seconds. After testing on Tuesday, an innocuous bystander approached and asked what I thought of the track.

'Bumpy,' I replied, '*It's a little dangerous in a heavily sprung car like ours.*'

At signing-on, the redoubtable Peg Bishop, John's wife and IMSA's co-owner, was incensed.

'*What are you doing registering?*' she demanded. '*We don't need people like you around here.*'

Apparently the quiet little man with whom I'd chatted was a track safety inspector.

From third on the grid, I won the Lime Rock race, thanks to lots of hard work and some fortunate race attrition.

Next came Mid-Ohio, where I found myself chasing John Fitzpatrick's Porsche 935. An inadvertent tap from me under braking – I swear my foot slipped off the brake – sent John sliding sideways and me into the lead. In three races we

ABOVE New for 1981, the Cooke-Woods Racing Lola T600 was a fabulous car and I won my first three races with it. One element of the car's ground-effects design was enclosure of the rear wheels – a concept later disproven but not before helping me win the first race.
Al Moore

ABOVE The future literally overtakes the past as Eric Broadley's radical Lola T600 lines up IMSA's staple racer, the Porsche 935, paving the way for the great GTP races of the 1980s.
Bill Oursler

RIGHT The Cooke-Woods entry looked good at Le Mans but the unproven, Porsche turbo-powered Lola T600 rarely left the pits and failed to qualify. With several mechanics, I investigate some predictable disaster whilst team owner Ralph Kent Cooke looks on (far right, blue racing suit).
Bruce Anderson

had taken three wins. That was very satisfying, until I was confronted by an unintended consequence.

While in London to attend the Memorial Service for Mike Hailwood, I called John Bright and learned some disturbing news. Ralph Kent Cooke, swelled by the success he undoubtedly attributed to his inspiring leadership, had decided to install a turbocharged Porsche engine in the team's second Lola T600 and take it to Le Mans. Without time to develop and test the new configuration, this was folly in the making. Undaunted, Ralph super-sized his Le Mans team to 25 employees, most of them pretty useless hangers-on. I was certain that it would end in embarrassment, in front of a large audience 5,500 miles from California and reality, and indeed it did. Nothing about the car worked, especially the turbocharged engine. The T600 barely ran during practice and Bobby Rahal and I failed to qualify. Pleas to the Gallic race management were sympathetically heard but firmly dismissed. Ralph dealt with this disappointment by calling a team meeting at which he fired everyone except John and me – another example of brilliant leadership.

There were more Ralph-initiated distractions – including a one-off Trans-Am race at Lime Rock in a beast of a Camaro that ended in a crash – before I resumed in IMSA with the original car, having missed a couple of rounds of the series.

At the Napa Valley's Sears Point circuit, I cleanly passed Klaus Ludwig's Ford Mustang-based car to head the race, only to be rewarded by an intentional hit from him that sent me off into the bushes. I set a new lap record trying to catch Ludwig and return the favour but was unable to make up the difference. He won and then apologised, saying that it was necessary for his Ford to win as Mr Ford was in attendance with his chief executive. Right!

Then came a win at Portland, a pair of second places at Mosport and Road America, another win at Road Atlanta and one more second at Pocono, where the race was red-flagged because of monsoon weather. That sequence of results left

BELOW This angle at Daytona reveals some of the void at the back of the Lola T600, part of the ground-effects concept. The fairings over the rear wheels proved to have little effect, so we usually raced without them.
Fred Lewis

us firmly in charge of the championship, with just one race to go. As life turned out, the last lap of the finale at Daytona brought back memories of earlier, dangerous times.

I led most of the three-hour race pretty handily but, as we approached the tri-oval finish on the final lap, the engine in George Alderman's Datsun 240Z exploded, issuing an impenetrable cloud of smoke and covering the track with debris. A lapped car immediately behind the Datsun had no chance to slow down and disappeared into the gloom. Now there was the possibility that two crashed cars with helpless drivers were blocking the smoke-obscured track. I lifted off – but 21-year-old John Paul Jr didn't. He flew past me into the smoke and, by chance, emerged unscathed and in the lead of the race. I offered no apologies then for my decision and I have no regrets now. Memories of the pointless deaths during the 1960s and 1970s informed that moment of caution. John Paul Jr may have won the race, but I hadn't risked my life – and I was still the season's champion.

At the end of 1981 the prospects for Cooke-Woods Racing were in decline so, once again, I decided to retire. Ford's Mike Kranefuss asked me to come to Detroit to work on a new racing programme, a turbocharged, front-engine design, one sadly that was out of step with the era's newest technologies. It took just a few meetings, in which departments with no connection to racing attempted to get a piece of the action, to make me realise that corporate life wasn't for me. Nonetheless, Kranefuss hired me to report on the 1982 24 Hours of Daytona and there I had the good fortune to meet the imposing Bob Snodgrass, managing director of the Brumos Porsche dealership in Jacksonville, Florida owned by Deborah Gregg, Peter Gregg's widow. As well as being a major retailer of Porsches, Brumos was also a regular IMSA contender, represented for many years by the talented Hurley Haywood. In Porsches run by Brumos, the Porsche factory and private entrants, Hurley won the 24 Hours of Daytona five times, the Le Mans 24 Hours three times and the 12 Hours of Sebring twice, plus

BELOW As we set up for the end of the 250-mile Daytona Finale, the last IMSA race of 1981, I am leading John Paul Jr's blue Porsche 935 before the incautious bravery of youth snatched a chancy win from a more prudent survivor of 1960s and 1970s racing.
Fred Lewis

ABOUT The Jaguar XJR-5 looks swift on its 1984 début in the 24 Hours of Daytona, where I set fastest lap, but wins were elusive in my three interesting but relatively fruitless 1984–86 seasons with Bob Tullius's Group 44 team.
Bill Warner

many other professional races. He was, is and perhaps always will be America's finest long-distance driver.

Brumos hired me to work in a succession of sales positions, but I was no more suited to being a salesman in Florida than I had been in South Africa. I was miserable and so were my employers. Occasional races softened our mutual displeasure and I hoped that better days were on the horizon as my family now was anchored in the seductive south where the sun warms the land and life moves at a pleasant pace. Florida must have a special attraction for elderly British racing drivers: my family and I have lived here for over 30 years, joined by Derek Bell, Vic Elford and (recently) David Hobbs. Sir Stirling Moss also has a home here.

The jungle cat

At the end of 1983 Bob Tullius called, asking me to join his Group 44 racing team for the following season. Long associated with Jaguar as an entrant and driver, Bob had secured major funding

from the British car manufacturer to build three prototypes powered by its 5.3-litre V12 engine. Lee Dykstra was commissioned to design the new XJR-5s, which would be finished in brilliant white highlighted by stripes of Jaguar green. Dykstra's goal was to create a car with sufficient downforce when cornering to offset the 100bhp deficit of its normally aspirated engine given up to rival turbocharged prototypes. He almost did it.

Tullius ran the team like an autocratic drill sergeant. Everything matched the livery of the cars – the uniforms of every team member and even the toolboxes – and all had to remain spotless. The same exacting attitude transferred to team management. When I first drove the XJR-5 in practice at Daytona in 1984, I told Bob the car was good but I'd really like rear-view mirrors I actually could use. *'Who the hell uses rear-view mirrors?'* he asked.

In the race, the Redman/Bill Adam/Pat Bedard car broke while the Tullius/David Hobbs/Doc Bundy entry finished third. Bob's only post-race comment was directed at me. *'Redman, what the*

RIGHT The elation of winning experienced at Miami in 1984, my second race with Group 44, was repeated in 1985 only at Road Atlanta, as we struggled to remain competitive with the Lowenbrau Porsche 962.
Bill Warner

BELOW On a city circuit, horsepower means less and driving accuracy more, allowing me to lead the Al Holbert/ Derek Bell Porsche 962 in the 1985 Miami Grand Prix before retiring with a transmission problem.
Bill Warner

hell you doing setting fastest lap?' I thought that was what I was supposed to do.

Before the Miami Grand Prix, Ford's racing director, my friend Mike Kranefuss, came up to wish me luck. Three years earlier, Klaus Ludwig had punted me out of the lead at Sears Point to secure a smile from the attending Henry Ford II. Now I was in the Group 44 Jaguar XJR-5 directly behind Ludwig on the grid.

'Do you remember Sears Point in 1981?' I asked Kranefuss. Clearly he did.

'Brian, you wouldn't,' he replied. *'I might.'*

As it happened, Ludwig caught his Mustang's left rear wheel rim on a piece of concrete barrier and ripped off the car's suspension. Oh, hard luck, Klaus!

In the three-hour race, Doc Bundy and I finished first with Tullius and Pat Bedard behind us, causing joy at Jaguar and leading the company's Mike Dale to make an unwise decision – that the team should go to Le Mans, in spite of the fact that we had never run more than 12 hours without problems. Not surprisingly, both cars

went out of the 1984 race, and did so again the following year.

For the 1985 season, I was paired with Hurley Haywood, taking one win and four thirds, but by 1986 the best the Jaguar team could manage was three thirds.

When Tullius reduced his operation to just one car for 1987, I accepted a drive with Chris Kneifel in a Porsche 962 run in the name of Primus Motorsport. No wins came our way and, for that matter, no money either. When our flamboyant sponsor's cheques didn't show, I continued to race by paying my own expenses while Kevin Jeannette, who prepared the car, faithfully put it on the track. We both lost significant sums, Kevin much more than me. The sponsor turned out to be a fantasist and a fraudster.

Privateer Jim Busby hired me early in 1988 to drive his Porsche 962 with Bob Wollek and Mauro Baldi in the 24 Hours of Daytona, known by this time as the Rolex 24. We swapped the lead eight times with Tom Walkinshaw's

fierce Jaguar XJR-9, which ultimately prevailed, leaving us to make do with second place. A Le Mans drive in a 962 run by Aussie racer Vern Schuppan and sponsored by Takefuji proved troublesome, but Jean-Pierre Jarier, Eje Elgh and I did at least finish, in 10th place. For the rest of the year I only did one other race, the Fuji 1,000Kms, Japan's late-season round of the FIA World Sports-Prototype Championship. The clock and I seemed to be winding down.

The last Hurrah

My last season of professional racing was 1989. It yielded little in the way of glory but it was a glorious racing experience.

The owners of Aston Martin, Peter Livanos and Victor Gauntlett, commissioned Canadian designer Max Boxstrom to create a new Group C prototype called the Aston Martin AMR1. Richard Williams ran the team under the banner of Hugh McCaig's famous *Ecurie Ecosse*, Ray Mallock was chief engineer, Reeves Callaway developed the Aston Martin V8 engine, and David Leslie was my driving partner. Testing in England on the smooth Silverstone and Donington circuits went well, but when we arrived at Dijon for our first race the car proved to be skittery over the French track's many bumps. Because the suspension was designed with zero droop (the amount the chassis is able to rise before the wheels leave the ground), it

had no travel and the car bounced from bump to bump. By Brands Hatch, our third race, Mallock had engineered half an inch of droop into the chassis and the handling improved enough for us to finish fourth, our best result of the year.

The AMR1 was handicapped by a deficit in both horsepower and aerodynamics. At Le Mans the Jaguars, Mercedes and Porsches topped out at 240mph on the *Mulsanne* while we poked along at 215. It proved enough for us to complete the race in 11th place – and we concluded it in great style. The AMR1 was one of those rare prototypes that a driver could power-slide and ours did so readily at *Arnage*, the 90-degree right-hander taken at around 80mph. Peter Livanos asked if I'd like to drive the final hour so, after getting the car a little sideways a few times, I settled down to a normal line. Immediately, a hand-written sign popped up from a small group of British enthusiasts.

'*Give us some oppo*,' they requested, meaning 'opposite lock', the counter-steering technique where sliding rear tyres require the driver to point his fronts away from the corner to keep the car from rotating. After I complied, they signalled again.

'*Now, fastest lap.*' Again, I tried my best, and my effort must have pleased them judging by their final sign.

'*Crumpets and tea with the Queen!*'

I tactfully would avoid mentioning our experience at the modern Nürburgring, where we finished an unexceptional eighth, were it not for one amusing pre-race incident. In practice, I was learning the track by following a veteran racer in a Porsche 962 when, inexplicably, he braked at the fast kink. I had no choice but to lift and my Aston spun instantly, sending me backwards at 150mph in the direction of a solid barrier. Steering in reverse whilst going backwards, I edged away from the barrier and then spun the steering wheel to point the car in the right direction, still moving at an impressive rate. Richard Williams came on the radio and, with just a hint of sarcasm, offered his congratulations.

'*Well done, Brian,*' he said. '*Bet you can't do it again!*'

Although the Aston Martin AMR1 was uncompetitive, it was a good car to drive and the team was composed of true racers. All in all, this was a nice way to end my career – no victories but lots of sweet memories.

Recent times

Before and after my professional retirement in 1989, I have enjoyed steady (and necessary) employment consulting with race circuits, advising car manufacturers and entertaining automotive gatherings as an after-dinner speaker. My involvement with historic racing has gradually become stronger. My son James and I have organised three Porsche Rennsport events, the Jefferson 500, and, for over 25 years, my own annual Targa Sixty Six club meeting in Palm Beach, Florida. Invitations from generous owners at these and many other events have allowed me to drive quite often, mostly a Chevron B19 but also many other cars, including a Lola T70 MkIII, a Lola T330 Formula 5000 car and, occasionally, a Porsche 908/03 and a 917.

Although there are wonderful historic meetings all over America (including 'The Hawk at Road America, with Brian Redman'), none compares with Lord March's two events on his magnificent Sussex estate: the Goodwood Festival of Speed and the Goodwood Revival. It has been an honour to be invited to each and every one – 35 events at the time of writing. In 1964 *Car & Driver* editor David E. Davis mounted a 'Dan Gurney for President' campaign. May I be the first to suggest 'Charles March for Prime Minister?'

It has been well over a half century since I began to race and I still enjoy attending all kinds of motorsport events, meeting young and older racers, talking with racing fans, and reminiscing with peers. Those who are familiar with racing in the 1960s and 1970s know that we veterans are the fortunate survivors of that era's terrible odds. Yet, I am here today, blessed with a lovely family and many memories from an enviable life. In the increasingly frequent moments that I reflect on my years in racing cars, I realise that I am a lucky old driver, and am grateful to be so.

BELOW The 1989 season – my last of professional racing – was a pleasure in every way. The Aston Martin AMR1 was a good, if somewhat underpowered, car and the team spirit was unmatched. We had lots of fun.
Brian Redman collection

EPILOGUE
Marion Redman

For years I joked that if Brian ever got around to writing about his racing career, I'd have to do a companion book that told the truth. I never thought he'd actually do it, and secretly hoped he might just let it go.

Life with Brian was always interesting and exciting. In the early days of our relationship I occasionally went to races but only when I had nothing better to do. We married on 8 September 1962 when Brian was 25 and I was 21, and by then I had accepted that racing and Brian Redman were synonymous. I learned that he drove for two very simple reasons: he was very good at it and it made him happy. This contentment rubbed off on me and, as the years passed, on our whole family. Even with racing's ups and downs, we led very satisfying and rewarding lives. Mostly, I remember the great fun we had travelling to races together.

We also had good times with many wonderful racing people, especially Jo Siffert and Pedro Rodriguez. These two drivers were among the few racing companions with whom Brian allowed himself to develop friendship, and their deaths devastated both of us. Ultimately, the era's casual acceptance of fate became ingrained in all of us, and I took Brian's cue and adopted the habit of avoiding close relationships.

In his descriptions of the dark days following each of his terrible crashes, note how unfailingly appreciative he is of my take-charge attitude but then has little or nothing to say about our conversations during his convalescence.

There was never a time when I didn't support Brian's racing ambitions – not in his early days as a young star and not through the sometimes difficult periods that followed.

In part, this is because I knew from the outset that he was always going to race, even after his terrible injuries. I knew that if Brian stopped he wouldn't be the same person, the man I loved and chose to marry. Brian's frequent absences, his three accidents and the deaths of many friends weren't easy for either of us to rationalise, but they were part of racing and the life that we, together, chose to live.

There's nothing casual about a driver being killed. Brian says he tried not to form friendships with other drivers, but that wasn't humanly possible for someone as outgoing and friendly as he is. I can assure you that he was saddened by each and every death, and so was I. You'd have to be stupid not to be affected. From the beginning, I learned early on how cruel racing can be. In 1969 we were with our friend Paul Hawkins at Oulton Park chatting with him just before the start of a race. An hour later he was dead. Brian and I talked about Paul's death, of course, but there was no mention of Brian quitting. We both knew he never would.

My personal *bête noir* was Le Mans. Just as Brian was always happy when the Spa 1,000Kms was over, so it was with the Le Mans 24 Hours and me. In one sense I felt very comfortable in France as my language fluency had been honed by schooling in Paris and youthful travels throughout the country. What made me uneasy was the annual expectation of driver deaths.

Brian first raced at Le Mans in 1967, when he and Mike Salmon were hired to drive Viscount Downe's Ford GT40. I went along with two-year-old James in tow. Brian has told the story of the poorly secured petrol cap, the resulting fire, and Mike's terrible burns. In a way this and other near

misses helped me to appreciate the important things in life and do so in real time.

Brian kept on racing, of course, and went back to Le Mans 13 more times in spite of its dangers, because it's the only major sports car race he never won. This imperfection in his record so bothered him that he would tell me, 'If I win Le Mans, I'll retire', but I never took it seriously. I knew that there was no way he was going to stop racing. Even his two attempts to retire, by taking jobs away from motor racing, proved to be temporary. As our friend Bob Akin put it, 'You know, racing isn't tennis.' Sadly, Bob himself validated this observation when he was killed practising for a historic race in 2002.

Please savour the poignant recollections about a special racing era. Brian brings passion, thoughtfulness, honesty and integrity to every story he tells. The only way you could know more about racers, racing and the racing life in this era was to have been there.

Marion Redman.

AFTERWORD
Sam Posey

You always read that he's underrated – The Underrated Brian Redman. It is used so frequently you'd think Underrated was his given name and Brian his middle name.

Where did this idea come from? Who does the rating? What system is used? We'd like to know.

Ferrari asked him to drive for them and he turned them down. 'You'll never get a second chance with Ferrari,' people told him. But four years later Ferrari asked again. Brian accepted and proved to be as fast as the team's stars: Ronnie Peterson, Jacky Ickx and Clay Regazzoni. In two years, he

BELOW Night-time celebration with Sam Posey after a very satisfying win for BMW in the 12 Hours of Sebring in 1975. *BMW*

won seven races in the Ferrari 312... yet they say he was underrated. Apparently not by Ferrari.

He drove Porsche's fearsome 917, won five of 10 races in 1969 and more the following year driving for John Wyer. Paired with the highly touted 'Seppi' Siffert, Brian matched his times.

He drove a Chevron in South Africa's Springbok Series and won six of six.

He drove for Jim Hall and won three consecutive Formula 5000 championships, beating the likes of Mario Andretti and Al Unser.

He won Sebring for BMW in 1975 and three years later he won it again in a Porsche.

He drove a Lola T600 for Cooke-Woods, winning five races and the 1981 IMSA Championship.

But they say he was underrated. Obviously, 'they' never had to race him.

Brian's many wins speak for themselves. He is one of the great drivers of his generation. Period. What's more, he achieved it against a backdrop of fear, self-doubt and frightful pain.

First the fear: he will tell you in all candor that the Porsche 917 terrified him... 235mph on the Mulsanne, the car changing lanes without warning, the frames cracking, John Woolfe killed in one... but it should be added that Brian eventually came to grips with the 917 and was the fastest of all at the notorious Spa.

He also comes from an era where a third of all top-line racing drivers were killed – and Brian feared he could be one of them.

ABOVE Sam Posey and Hans Stuck laugh after Hans
has given one of his famous yodelling demonstrations.
BMW

Self doubt: Brian never doubted his ability but he was constantly asking himself whether he should be racing at all – and in fact, right in mid-career, he retired and took his family to South Africa to run a dealership. It didn't work out. As sort of a farewell to racing, he entered a 2-litre race and won it. Then he won five more, in a row.

Pain: few drivers have suffered like Brian, who had three major accidents. His face was burned in a Porsche at the Targa Florio, his arm crushed in a terrifying crash in a Formula 1 Cooper at Spa and his neck broken at St Jovite when his car got airborne. Each crash put him in the hospital for weeks: endless stretches of pain and boredom; plenty of time to think about quitting. But as it happens, each crash only worked to strengthen his belief in persistence, his conviction that things will come around if you persevere.

He has persevered, and his exploits in vintage car racing have made him deeply respected by everyone. At age 76, he wins virtually every race he starts.

On the whole, luck has been with him. He has been married all of these years to the fabulous Marion, and he has an irrepressible sense of humor. He can regale you with his impersonations – and then there is the spoon trick.

As we have seen, there are several words that apply to Brian, but there is one that encompasses his raw speed, his qualities as a gentleman, his character-defining persistence and love of the sport. One word, summing up the man and his career. One word to replace 'underrated' once and for all.

One word – Champion!

Sam Posey

Acknowledgements

My objective in writing this memoir was to make readers feel what it was like to be a professional racer in a particularly dangerous era, using the experiences of my life in racing to provide personal insights into a wonderful, terrible decade. The book, therefore, is less about me than that consequential era when giants like Mario Andretti, Bobby Unser, Jo Siffert, Jim Hall, Pedro Rodriguez, John Wyer, Jackie Stewart, Enzo Ferrari and Jacky Ickx walked the earth. My gratitude begins with them, my valued peers, colleagues, competitors and friends.

As I didn't feel comfortable attempting this task alone, 'my' memoir is a true collaboration among a small band of mutually supportive (if occasionally fractious) racing enthusiasts who, considering the spare financial realities of today's motorsport publishing, contributed their skills as a labour of love. Jim Mullen, a racer himself, gave me the initial shove to tell my stories and managed the memoir's direction throughout. He and I agree that editor Mark Hughes made our writing clearer, stronger and more evocative, and that Mark's splendid photo selections themselves form a powerful storytelling narrative that breathes life into our words. My friend Michael Keyser provided much of the background information that allowed me to attack the work with efficiency, and was first among those who freely donated their superb photographs.

Other generous contributors of their imagery to this memoir are Bill Oursler, Bill Warner, Bob Tronolone, Jutta Fausel, David Pearson, Peter McFadyen, Mike Hayward, Mike Dixon, Chris Beach, Fred Lewis, Al Moore, Larry Peterson, Bruce Anderson, Michael Botsko, Chuck Koske, Luke Lundquist, Harry Kennison, Rob Neuzel, Bryan Watson, Udo Klinkel, John Holroyd, Peter Wilson, Peter Doran and Jay Gilloti.

The world's best motorsport photo libraries have played their part in this book: LAT (thanks to Kathy Ager and Tim Wright for supplying the work of numerous photographers, including Peter Burn), Getty Images (thanks to Darrell Ingham and Chevy Palmer for supplying the work of, among others, Rainer Schlegelmilch and Bob Harmeyer), Grand Prix Library (thanks to Doug Nye and Paul Vestey), Sutton Images (thanks to Annie Lydon and Keith Sutton for supplying the work of David Phipps), McKlein (thanks to Reinhard Klein) and the UK's National Motor Museum (thanks to Jon Day).

Manufacturers have been involved, above all Porsche (thanks to Jens Torner), with further images from BMW and Ford.

A few photos have been kindly provided from the personal collections of John Horsman, Alan Hearn, Mark Koense, Michael Brown, Thomas Horat, Peter Davies, Hal Crocker and Stephanie Anderson. Nicholas Watts allowed his marvellous painting of me on the 1970 Targa Florio to be reproduced.

To these friends and colleagues, I am deeply grateful.

Sam Posey permitted the reprinting of his funny, poignant description of my wobbly relationship with the sport, taken from his own book, *When the Writer Meets the Road*. Thank you, Sam, you are my racer/writer role model. Many people read and made valuable improvements: Jeremy Shaw was an early and critical reader, and Tom Davey gave unstintingly of his time and abilities.

Many other habitués of that era checked my facts and shared their memories. Alain de Cadenet, Gérard Larrousse, Gijs van Lennep and Arturo Merzario permitted me to include their recollections verbatim and improved my memory. John Horsman, Willi Kauhsen, Vic Elford, Serge Dubois and Paul Owens jogged and refreshed my memory.

Mario Andretti was extremely considerate in his expressive Foreword. Considering the many opportunities I had to displease him during our Formula 5000 dust-ups, I am both relieved by his agreeability and honoured by his graciousness.

Eric Verdon-Roe, the redoubtable founder and chairman of Evro Publishing, and his partners Jeremy Vaughan and Mark Hughes (him again), deserve medals for believing in this book and I'm proud to have it listed among their seminal works by Sir Stirling Moss and John Surtees. My satisfaction with the book is all the greater for its eye-catching and elegant appearance, the work of Evro's talented designer, Richard Parsons.

I have saved my deepest gratitude for my wife Marion, for her patience and support. My debt to her is immeasurable, as is my love.

Our son James, his wife Dawn and our daughter Charlotte have provided their steady support, with grand-daughter Victoria supplying joyful inspiration.

Finally, dear readers, I thank you. Ours is an inclusive sport and without you at its heart, my life would have been much less interesting and enjoyable.

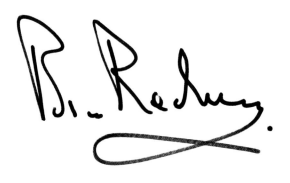

Index